Why We Vote

Why We Vote

HOW SCHOOLS AND COMMUNITIES
SHAPE OUR CIVIC LIFE

David E. Campbell

PRINCETON UNIVERSITY PRESS   PRINCETON AND OXFORD

Copyright © 2006 by Princeton University Press

Published by Princeton University Press, 41 William Street, Princeton, New Jersey 08540

In the United Kingdom: Princeton University Press, 3 Market Place, Woodstock, Oxfordshire OX20 1SY

All Rights Reserved

Library of Congress Cataloging-in-Publication Data

Campbell, David E., 1971–
  Why we vote : how schools and communities shape our civic life / David E. Campbell.
    p. cm.
  Includes bibliographical references and index.
  ISBN-13: 978-0-691-12525-1 (hardcover : alk. paper)
  ISBN-10: 0-691-12525-2 (hardcover : alk. paper)
  1. Political participation. 2. Community development. 3. Social exchange.
  4. Voluntarism. I. Title.
  JF799.C35 2006
  323'.042—dc22   2005032902

British Library Cataloging-in-Publication Data is available

This book has been composed in Sabon

Printed on acid-free paper. ∞

pup.princeton.edu

Printed in the United States of America

10 9 8 7 6 5 4 3 2 1

To Kirsten, Katie, and Soren
Who form my most important community

Contents

Figures

Tables

Acknowledgments

IT IS APPROPRIATE that in writing a book about how communities affect us, I have been supported by many people in different, but often overlapping, communities. This book began as a doctoral dissertation, which was guided by the members of my dissertation committee: Andrea Campbell, Paul Peterson, Bob Putnam, Kay Schlozman, and Sid Verba. They saw this project grow from a half-baked idea to the book you now hold in your hands. I am grateful for their insights along the way. In particular, I have benefited from the wisdom of Bob Putnam. His formal title is chair of my dissertation committee, but that hardly captures the many ways he has shaped my scholarship. Bob's fingerprints are all over this book, sometimes in places where I initially did not even recognize his influence.

At various stages of this project, I have benefited from the generous financial support of a number of organizations. The genesis of this project came during the time I spent, at Paul Peterson's invitation, as a research fellow with Harvard University's Program on Education Policy and Governance (PEPG). In ways both obvious and not, my fellowship at PEPG served to hone my research skills and catalyze my thinking about the relationships among communities, schools, and civic engagement. I have learned much from working with Paul, as he taught me that good scholarship can have a public face. After PEPG, I was fortunate to spend a year as a visiting fellow at Princeton University's Center for the Study of Democratic Politics. Nowhere else were my ideas challenged more rigorously, leading me to sharpen my arguments and evidence. Larry Bartels, Chris Achen, and Marc Hetherington were especially helpful during my year at Princeton. Finally, I completed the book during a postdoctoral fellowship with the National Academy of Education, funded by the Spencer Foundation. Thanks are also due to the University of Notre Dame's political science department, which has been a welcoming and supportive environment for a young scholar. Other financial support has been provided by the Center for American Political Studies (CAPS) and the Saguaro Seminar: Civic Engagement in America (both at Harvard), as well as Notre Dame's Institute for Scholarship in the Liberal Arts. Excellent research assistance was provided by Jacqueline Wilson and Jacqueline Genesio.

I have also received the intellectual support of friends and colleagues as they have offered their feedback, criticisms, and suggestions. These include Peri Arnold, Ben Deufel, Bill Galston, Jim Gimpel, Kristin Goss, John Griffin, Rodney Hero, Bert Johnson, Andy Karch, Scott McClurg, Wendy Rahn, John Roos, Theda Skocpol, Rob Van Houweling, Marty West, and Christina Wolbrecht. Although I did not always take their advice, their input was invaluable. Of course, they are not to be held responsible for any oversights on my part.

Portions of this book have been presented at annual meetings of the American Political Science Association and the Midwest Political Science Association, as well as at Notre Dame's Program in American Democracy, the University of Minnesota, Harvard University, and Princeton University.

While there is no doubt that I have benefited from all of the above, the greatest support of all has come from within the walls of my home. My children, Katie and Soren, consistently teach me what it really means to be a good citizen, as does my wife, Kirsten. In fact, you could say that this book was inspired by her. She joins, she votes, and she volunteers (in fact, she was once even in a bowling league!). But more important, her unwavering faith in me has been an inspiration at every step of the way—even in the face of all my threats to just give up and go to law school.

Why We Vote

CHAPTER ONE

Introduction: Voting Alone

ON SEPTEMBER 26, 1989, Traci Hodgson cast her ballot in Boston's City Council election. It was the only vote cast in her precinct. For a number of reasons, the political science literature predicts that Traci should have been like the other 275 registrants in her precinct and not turned out to vote. She was only twenty-one, she had lived in Boston for less than two months, and she admitted that she was "not very familiar with the candidates running." So why did she vote? When asked she replied, "I just think it's important to vote. If you have the right, you ought to exercise it—whether you are going to make a difference or not" (Mooney 1989).

This book is about why Traci voted, and why she voted alone.

MADISON AND TOCQUEVILLE: A TALE OF TWO MOTIVATIONS

Our starting point in answering this question is not what *did* motivate Traci, but rather what did *not*. Clearly she did not vote to protect or advance her interests, as she admitted that she did not know enough about the candidates to select them on the basis of who best represented her. To someone with only a cursory familiarity with the study of American politics this may seem difficult to explain, as politics is typically described as a forum for the "clash of interests." Equating politics with conflict underpins much of the political science literature and is an assumption shared by scholars working within many theoretical frameworks. I recall an introductory political science course in which a professor defined politics as the "scarcity of consensus." In 1960, E. E. Schattschneider wrote simply, "At the root of all politics is the universal language of conflict" (2). Forty years later, Morris Fiorina and Paul Peterson note matter-of-factly in their introductory textbook on American politics that "politics is fundamentally about conflict" (1998, xvi). For all the ink spilled by contemporary political scientists, however, no one has ever expressed this way of understanding politics better than James Madison in *Federalist 10*. Madison writes compellingly of how "the latent causes of faction are thus sown in the nature of man," and that "the most frivolous and fanciful distinctions have been sufficient to kindle their unfriendly passions and excite their most violent conflicts" (1961, 79).

It does not seem, however, that Traci had her passions kindled as Madison describes. Instead, by her own account she was motivated by the glowing embers of obligation. She felt that she ought to vote, that it was her duty.

In invoking a sense of duty as a motivation to vote, Traci highlights a second, if more subtle, theme in both contemporary and classic writings on political engagement. If, in *Federalist 10*, Madison has written the quintessential statement on political participation as "protecting one's interests," then perhaps Tocqueville has written an equally quintessential description of political participation as driven by "fulfilling one's duty." In *Democracy in America*, Tocqueville observes that American political institutions lead citizens to see that "it is the duty as well as the interest of men to be useful to their fellows. . . . What had been calculation becomes instinct. By dint of working for the good of his fellow citizens, he in the end acquires a habit and taste for serving them" (1988, 512–13).

These two opposing views of politics are not merely the abstract statements of theoreticians, the political science rendition of how many angels can dance on the head of a pin. They also inform the writings and doings of political practitioners, with some of America's founders as notable examples. Of course, Madison was one of the founders and, as noted, in his words we find a cogent description of how politics is inevitably defined by conflict. However, George Washington's vision was of a republic free from strife among its citizens, in which citizens were involved in public affairs out of duty (Schudson 1998). Ironically, given their disagreements on so many other matters, Thomas Jefferson's vision for the new republic mirrored Washington's. Jefferson idealized a nation of small Tocquevillian communities, mentioning his ideal in almost every speech he gave (Morone 1990).

The ongoing debate between civic republican and liberal political philosophers over the nature of political life at the time of America's founding underscores the two competing visions of democracy's nature. In summarizing this extensive literature, James Morone writes,

> [T]he dominant interpretation of liberal America focuses on the pursuit of self-interest. . . . In the republican view, the colonial and Revolutionary ideal lay, not in the pursuit of private matters, but in the shared public life of civic duty, in the subordination of individual interests to the *res publica*. Citizens were defined and fulfilled by participation in political community. (1990, 16, emphasis added)

The distinction between engagement driven by interests versus duty need not be seen as either/or. The very fact that evidence can be mustered to support both interpretations of the founders' ideals suggests that neither one dominated to the exclusion of the other. Nor should we assume that the essential difference between engagement spurred by a threat to one's interests and engagement motivated by a sense of civic obligation has faded over time. Indeed, the distinction between interest-driven and duty-driven engagement is at the core of this book, which is about contemporary patterns of public engagement in the United States.

TRACI AND TOCQUEVILLE

While articulating that engagement in the public square is driven by Tocquevillian as well as Madisonian impulses underscores that there are two fundamentally different motivations for political activity, this observation alone does not provide much theoretical traction for empirical analysis. On its own, "fulfilling one's duty" remains at best a tautological explanation for political participation. It is far more interesting to ask *why* Traci felt that voting was her duty.

A potential answer to that question was intuitively included in the newspaper article that told of Traci's lonely ballot. Traci, the reader learns, had just moved to Boston from Kansas. She was born and raised in the town of Little River, population 693—a community that advertises itself as a "town with a lot of civic pride."[1] Significantly, in 1992 voter turnout in Little River was 67 percent, 12 percentage points higher than turnout nationwide, and 27 *points higher* than in Boston.[2] Armed with this information about Traci's hometown it seems plausible, even probable, that Traci voted because she hails from a community where voting is common. One might say that you can take the girl out of Kansas, but you can't take the Kansas out of the girl.

There has long been a strain of research in political science that examines the role of place in understanding political behavior, although with the dominance of survey research in this literature, far more attention has been paid to individuals' characteristics (King 1997). Loosely grouped together in a literature often labeled "contextual effects," a small but growing set of studies have examined how the characteristics of the communities in which people live affect their political activity. Decades ago, Paul Lazarsfeld and his Columbia School colleagues took voters' social environments seriously (Lazarsfeld, Berelson, and Gaudet 1948; Berelson, Lazarsfeld, and McPhee 1954), as have authors like Robert Huckfeldt and John Sprague (1995), Eric Oliver (2001), and James Gimpel, J. Celeste Lay, and Jason Schuknecht (2003) more recently.

The burgeoning literature on social capital has redirected political scientists' attention to important differences among geographic units, whether they be Italian regions, U.S. states, or nation-states. As Putnam explains in *Making Democracy Work*, social capital consists of "trust, norms, and networks" (1993, 167) that foster collective action. Putnam demonstrates that Italian states have deep, longstanding historical differences in the extent to which their residents engage in various forms of collective action. In *Bowling Alone*, he employs a multi-item index of social capital for each of the fifty states, which includes voter turnout (2000).

Viewed through the lens offered by the social capital literature, then, we might be tempted to attribute Traci's vote to her having lived in a place with a lot of social capital. The problem with this explanation is that it still provides little analytical leverage. Rather than "people vote because they feel they should," now the explanation is "people vote because they live in a place where voting is the norm." And how do we know that voting is the norm? Because many people vote there. This might be a small theoretical step forward, but not much more. The challenge is to find an explanation for *why* those norms are stronger in some places than in others.

The first section of this book deals precisely with just such an explanation. Presaging an argument that will be detailed further in chapters to come, I suggest that people vote out of both Madisonian and Tocquevillian motivations. In some communities more voters come to the polls in order to protect their interests, whereas in other places more of them cast a ballot because they feel it is their duty to do so. In these latter communities, civic norms are strong. Those norms are strong, in turn, because of consensus over values—what political scientists are more likely to call interests, and what economists call preferences. Where many people share the same values social norms are more easily enforced, specifically a norm encouraging civic participation. Diverse interests breed conflict, while uniformity fosters consensus; voter turnout can spring from both, but for different reasons. Furthermore, some forms of engagement in the community are more common in consensual communities, other forms in places better characterized as conflictual.

Assuming that I convince the reader that communities vary in the degree to which they can be characterized by their consensus over values, and thus in the extent to which their residents act in accordance with civic norms, Traci's vote will nonetheless remain unexplained. Remember that when she cast her ballot, Traci was not actually living in homogeneous Little River, Kansas, but heterogeneous Boston, Massachusetts. Why would Traci vote out of a sense of duty once she had moved away from a place with strong civic norms? Tocqueville hints at the answer when in the quotation above he refers to people acting out of duty because it had become their "instinct," having acquired a "habit and taste" for it. Traci had internalized the norm that voting is a duty and continued her duty-driven behavior even when she moved to a place where those norms would not be enforced. Critically, she spent her adolescence enmeshed in a community where civic norms were strong. During this particularly formative period of our lives, we are prone to developing habits that stay with us throughout our lives. In short, one can be socialized into acting out of a sense of duty, and an important (probably the most important) period of our lives for that socialization to occur is adolescence.

Again foreshadowing a more thorough discussion later, socialization is an important, if often implied, component of social capital theory. For example, while Putnam does not specifically raise the importance of childhood socialization in his discussion of civic traditions in Italy, it is certainly implied. How else would civic traditions perpetuate across time if the norms that constitute social capital were not transmitted across generations? Likewise, Putnam's more recent stress on differences in civic engagement among generational cohorts implies that members of different generations have, collectively, undergone distinctive socialization experiences.

Why did Traci vote? Because she was raised in a community where she internalized the norm that voting is her civic duty. The simplicity of this statement, however, belies the complexity of the theoretical foundation upon which it rests. Implicit within it are a number of claims, none of which is necessarily conventional wisdom within political science. To make the case that the communities in which we spend our adolescence affect whether we vote in adulthood first requires establishing that

    a. communities shape the civic and political engagement of the people who live within them, or *what you do now depends on where you are now*

    b. the engagement of adolescents in particular is shaped by where they live, or *what you did then depends on where you were then*

    c. adolescents' engagement links to their engagement as adults, or *what you do now depends on what you did then*

Together these claims lay the foundation for the book's central argument: the civic norms within one's adolescent social environment have an effect on civic participation well beyond adolescence: *what you do now depends on where you were then*. These points all require theoretical justification and empirical evaluation, and so a section of the book is devoted to each.

What You Do Now Depends on Where You Are Now

Chapters 2–4 demonstrate that the communities in which we live shape the nature of what I will refer to as our *public engagement*. I use this particular term to describe what other authors generally call, inter-changeably, civic or political engagement. I do this because I draw a distinction between engagement which is civic and that which is political. We will get into more formal definitions in chapter 2, but for now an intuitive example provides a sense of what I see as the critical difference between the two. Imagine that someone wanted to help the homeless population in her community. One way would be to volunteer at a soup kitchen that serves the homeless, an example of what I mean by civic, or civically motivated, engagement. Another way would be to volunteer for a candidate who has promised to enact policies to assist the homeless, or to march at the state capitol in support of a bill designed to address their needs. This second type of activity is what I define as engagement with a political motivation. Both types of engagement are public, in the sense that they have an effect beyond oneself and the people in one's immediate sphere of influence. The fundamental distinction between them is not their ends—in both cases, the intention is to assist the homeless—but rather their means. Political participation has as its immediate objective to affect public policy, while its civic counterpart does not.

In places characterized by conflict, politically motivated public engagement is more common. Conversely, communities where there is relative consensus are more likely to host civic engagement, because these communities have strong civic norms encouraging engagement in publicly spirited activities. This, in a nutshell, is what I have labeled the *dual motivations theory* of public engagement. Chapter 2 applies the theory to voter turnout, one form of engagement that shares both motivations. Contrary to a strictly Madisonian perspective on politics, voter turnout rises where there is a relative absence of political conflict—where elections are blowouts—because voting has civic, as well as political, underpinnings. Madison, however, is redeemed by the observation that turnout also rises in communities where there is a high degree of political conflict. Chapter 3 then turns its attention to other evidence in support of the dual motivations theory. First, we see that voters are more likely to report voting out of a sense of duty in politically consensual communities, and more likely to vote to accomplish policy objectives in places with a high degree of conflict. Similarly, engagement on the civic side of the spectrum is more likely in consensual than conflictual communities, while politically motivated activity is more common in places known for conflict. Chapter 4 continues to test implications of the dual motivations theory, in this case by changing the focus of the inquiry from large-scale communities like cities and counties to personal social networks. Living in a homogeneous community makes it more likely that someone will have a homogeneous social network, which in turn spurs civically motivated public engagement.

WHAT YOU DID THEN DEPENDS ON WHERE YOU WERE THEN

Having established that place matters for adults, the next step is to examine whether it matters for adolescents. Is the collective action of youth affected by their social environment in the same manner as for adults? This is by no means assured, as we might think that adolescents are concerned only with the norms of their immediate peers. Chapter 5 demonstrates, however, that the political complexion of adolescents' social environments does affect their degree of public engagement. As go the parents, so go the children. Young people in consensual communities are more likely to engage in civically motivated behavior, reflecting the strong civic norms in such places. However, the homogeneity one observes in such environments also has consequences that are normatively troubling, including lower levels of political tolerance among youth.

WHAT YOU DO NOW DEPENDS ON WHAT YOU DID THEN

The reader might be willing to accept that place matters for both adults and adolescents, but might be skeptical that participation among adolescents has an impact on what they do as adults. Speculation that activity in one's youth affects activity as one ages is common; evidence on the matter is less so. The data demands for such evidence are high, as respondents need to be interviewed and then re-interviewed years later, during and just following what is probably the most disruptive period in the average person's life. Fortunately, a new archive of data that, to my knowledge, has previously been unexamined by political scientists is now available to explore this subject. These data track a representative sample of high school seniors over a ten-year period, with follow-up surveys administered every two years. With these data, it is possible to test for links between civic participation, namely community service, in one's youth and both civic and politically tinged public engagement in early adulthood. Chapter 6 details the results of this analysis. In this chapter, we shall see that volunteering in one's adolescence leads to voting later in life.

WHAT YOU DO NOW DEPENDS ON WHERE YOU WERE THEN

To this point, the reader will have seen evidence for separate strands of the explanation for why Traci voted. While each is necessary, however, in seriatim they are not sufficient. Chapter 7 weaves them together, with evidence that one's social environment in adolescence has far-reaching influence on public engagement in adulthood. Testing such a claim requires data that combine both a longitudinal component—interviewing the same respondents first in adolescence and then as adults—as well as a contextual element—information about the communities in which respondents live. In particular, the analysis focuses on the social environment of what is arguably the greatest importance to adolescents: their schools. Specifically, chapter 7 demonstrates that strong civic norms in an adolescent's high school lead to a greater likelihood of voting well over a decade following high school.

This book has as its primary objective understanding the motivations underlying voter turnout for the purpose of adding to the theoretical literature on voting. In particular, I hope to make the case that we should not ignore the civic dimension of turnout. When previous research has acknowledged that civic duty is a factor explaining why people vote, it is usually done grudgingly. Somewhat oddly, a factor that almost everyone agrees is important in explaining the vote has been virtually ignored in the political science literature. By shining more light on the simple question of why some people consider voting a duty of citizenship while others do not, we can advance our understanding of why some people turn out to vote while others do not.

The book concludes by proposing how theory might be put into practice. Understanding the forces that shape who votes is an intrinsically important endeavor, given voting's central role in a democracy. It is especially imperative, however, given that we live in an age of low voter turnout among all Americans and declining turnout among young people especially. In the past, various reforms have been enacted in an attempt to reverse that decline, with varying degrees of success. At worst such reforms have had no effect. At best they have made a modest difference. I suggest that their underwhelming impact is because they have focused on relatively minor impediments to voting, like the rules governing registration. Since theory suggests that a sense of civic duty is a major influence on whether people vote, perhaps efforts to strengthen civic norms will have a greater participatory payoff. To that end, the evidence I have gathered suggests that schools are a lever to enhance young people's sense of civic commitment. An investment made in enhancing the sense of civic responsibility taught in our schools has the potential to pay big dividends over the long haul in enhancing voter turnout and other forms of civically oriented public engagement. The final chapter, therefore, discusses some ways that this might be accomplished.

DATA SOURCES

A theory is only convincing insofar as data exist to test it. Over the remaining chapters, a wide range of data will be employed. Since the basic research strategy is to see how living in a certain type of community affects individuals, I needed to combine data on individuals with data on the communities in which they live. Constructing these data sets has required me to compile data describing particular communities (usually counties but also metropolitan areas) and then merge them with data describing the individuals who participated in the survey. For example, I know whether an individual is an African American, as well as the percentage of African Americans within that individual's community. To combine data in this manner requires identifying the geographic location of survey respondents, in some cases for surveys that are decades old, and then the relevant information about their communities. The specific sources of data[3] I draw upon throughout the course of the book include (in order of their appearance):

1. A data set combining information on U.S. counties from multiple sources, including the *County and City Data Book*, the U.S Census Bureau, and *America Votes*.
2. Current Population Surveys in 1989, 1992, 1996, 2000, and 2002 with county and metropolitan area–level data merged with individual-level data.
3. Citizen Participation Study, again with individual and aggregate data merged.
4. Social Capital Community Benchmark Survey. Individual-level respondents were matched with the aggregate characteristics of their communities.
5. The 1987 General Social Survey, combining individual-level and community-level data.
6. Civic Education Study (U.S. component), conducted under the auspices of the International Association for the Evaluation of Educational Achievement. Individual-level responses were combined with data about each community included in the study.
7. The 1996 National Household Education Survey (both parent and youth surveys). First, data from parental interviews were merged with data from their children. That file was then combined with county-level data.
8. *Monitoring the Future: A Continuing Study of American Youth*. This study draws on longitudinal data collected as part of the Monitoring the Future series.
9. Youth-Parent Socialization Study. This includes both the longitudinal component of the study, as well as the cohort data collected in the student panel members' high schools. For both the 1965 and 1982 waves, community-level data were combined with the data on individuals.

PART ONE

What You Do Now Depends on Where You Are Now

Putting Madison and Tocqueville to the Test: The Dual Motivations Theory of Public Engagement

In the first chapter, I argued that there are two fundamental motivations for public engagement. One is Madisonian—people engage to protect their interests. The other is Tocquevillian—people engage to fulfill a sense of duty. This chapter puts Madison and Tocqueville to the test and in so doing develops the dual motivations theory of voter turnout. We see that communities—literally, the collective attributes of the places in which we live—can facilitate one motivation over another. In politically heterogeneous communities, there is conflict. In homogeneous communities, there is consensus. Both conflict and consensus facilitate voter participation, and so turnout should rise in heterogeneous and homogeneous communities, and fall in the communities that lie between. It does.

IN THE PREVIOUS CHAPTER, we were introduced to the Madisonian and Tocquevillian perspectives on participation—that engagement in politics is driven by either *protecting your interests* or *fulfilling your duty*. The objectives of this chapter are, first, to demonstrate that this tension between Madison and Tocqueville echoes across a vast literature. I thus develop the dual motivations theory, which proposes that public engagement—voter turnout in particular—can have either Madisonian or Tocquevillian overtones. Second, this chapter makes the case that the places in which we live can foster one motivation over another. Together these two claims constitute the foundation of the theoretical framework under construction, namely that *whether you vote* depends on *where you are*.

LEARNING FROM RATIONAL CHOICE

In reading through the research that seeks to explain why people turn out to vote, it is striking how often one finds the footprints of Madison and Tocqueville. Virtually every major piece of scholarship on the subject of voter turnout acknowledges what I call the *fundamental motivations* for participation, although the language they use to describe them differs. Take, for example, an article in the flagship economics journal, the *American Economic Review*, which contrasts the two approaches to studying voter turnout in these terms:

> One approach assumes that voters engage in a *strategic cost-benefit calculation*—people vote because their vote might decide the election. . . . An alternative explanation . . . is that people vote because it is a *consumption activity*—they vote because they enjoy it, not because they are concerned with affecting the outcome. (Shachar and Nalebuff 1999, 525, emphasis added)

Writing decades ago, Lester Milbrath drew the same distinction using only slightly different language: "Casting a vote . . . may be primarily *expressive* in one situation for one person but primarily *instrumental* for another situation or person" (1971, 29; see also Butler and Stokes 1974; Wolfinger and Rosenstone 1980; Teixeira 1992). Even though Stephen Rosenstone and Mark Hansen focus on how voters are instrumentally mobilized by political elites, they also note that "some people believe it is their responsibility to participate in politics—and in particular to vote—regardless of whether their participation has any effect on the outcome" (1993, 19). Sidney Verba, Kay Schlozman, and Henry Brady (1995) make a similar distinction in their discussion of why people get involved in political and civic participation. Still other authors have contrasted the two motivations as "self-interested" versus "altruistic" (Berry, Portney, and Thomson 1993) or have spoken of "adversary" and "unitary" democracy, which also bear a strong resemblance to the Madisonian and Tocquevillian impulses, respectively (Mansbridge 1980). In short, this distinction between an interest- and duty-driven motivation for public engagement is common across scholarship in different genres of research, from the psychologically oriented work of political behavioralists to the economically rooted rational choice school.

Ironically, one of the clearest discussions of the two motivations can be found in the literature least amenable to attributing any activity to a noninstrumental motivation like adherence to a norm, namely scholarship within the rational choice tradition. In the world according to rational choice, politics is very Madisonian. People participate in politics, rational choice models assume, because they wish to advance (or protect) their preferences. Putting such a conflictual cast on political activity, however, makes explaining why people participate difficult. Few topics have occupied, and stumped, rational choice scholars more than the simple question of why ostensibly rational people turn out to vote or participate in any other form of public engagement. In a paradox long noted in the rational choice literature, the infinitesimal chance that any individual voter could cast a deciding vote means that a cost-benefit analysis of voter turnout should always result in greater costs than benefits (Downs

1957; Tullock 1967). In an oft-cited discussion of this problem, William Riker and Peter Ordeshook (1968) theorize that voting is only rational in light of the gratification that results from civic involvement. They have developed a formula to explain the decision to turn out to vote, which they refer to as the *calculus of voting*:

$$\text{Vote} = pB + D > C$$

where p is the probability of casting a decisive ballot in a given election, B represents the benefits that come with the election of one's preferred candidate, C represents the costs of voting, and D is the voter's civic gratification derived from voting, or what is commonly referred to as a sense of civic duty. While numerous articles have attempted to refine this basic model using variations of what constitutes rational behavior, "[r]ational choice scholars have continually retreated to the fallback position articulated by Riker and Ordeshook" (Green and Shapiro 1994, 59). Morris Fiorina, addressing his comments to his fellow rational choice theorists as much as anyone else, puts it thus:

> [The] voting decision has both instrumental and expressive components. The Downsian formulation is purely instrumental: the citizen's vote has value only insofar as it helps push his preferred candidate over the top. In contrast mainstream political science, at least the older tradition, has made us aware of the expressive component of the voting decision. One may vote to . . . enjoy the satisfaction of having performed one's civic duty. (1976, 393)

If one wishes to predict who is going to vote, there is a problem in introducing what Fiorina calls the expressive component of voting. It borders on tautology, by leaving us with the prediction that the people who will vote are those who feel they should vote. The problem is that civic duty is a "taste," and rational choice theory is "silent about the process by which people develop tastes" (Green and Shapiro 1994, 68). As Fiorina suggests, even at the time that they proposed it Riker and Ordeshook's model was not really a theoretical advance, as Angus Campbell and his colleagues had already empirically demonstrated that many people vote out of a sense of duty (Campbell, Gurin, and Miller 1954; A. Campbell et al. 1960).

Notwithstanding the criticism their model has faced both inside and outside rational choice circles, there is actually much value in the very starkness of Riker and Ordeshook's simple equation. Unlike the litany of literature cited above, they have attempted to integrate the Madisonian and Tocquevillian motivations underpinning public engagement. To a rational choice scholar, having to include "sense of duty" in the calculus of voting may be a theoretical annoyance, even a mark of analytical failure.

Outside the confines of the rational choice literature, though, it serves to enrich our understanding of the motivations for political activity. It forces us to confront the question of why it is that civic duty varies across individuals. In other words, why are some people more likely to vote out of a sense of duty than others? In a nutshell, that is the central question this chapter and the next seek to answer.

A TALE OF TWO MOTIVATIONS

While the literature is peppered with different labels for what I have called the fundamental motivations, it is important that I ensure consistency and clarity with a single pair of terms. To do so I borrow from a classic work in political science, Robert Dahl's *Who Governs* (1961). Dahl has given the abstract notions of interest versus duty a human face by observing that human beings come in two varieties—*homo civicus* and *homo politicus*—that parallel the Tocquevillian and Madisonian perspectives on why people engage in public matters. Simply put, the former are not engaged by politics while the latter are. While Dahl has obviously oversimplified to create two ideal types, the distinction has an intuitive feel to it. But where he distinguishes between types of people, I draw a distinction between types of participation: political or civic. In choosing these labels for the fundamental motivations I must stress that, notwithstanding the terms' etymological legacies, their use in this study is restricted to how I have defined them. No more, no less.

Therefore, what I have thus far loosely referred to as public engagement motivated by instrumental or Madisonian considerations I will define explicitly as *political participation*. Specifically, I borrow my definition from Sidney Verba and Norman Nie's Seminal book *Participation in America*:

> Political participation refers to those activities by private citizens that are more or less directly aimed at influencing the selection of governmental personnel and/or the actions they take. (1972, 2)

The key to the definition is the *end* to which the activity is directed—actions taken or policies enacted by public officials.[1]

What other authors have characterized as activity driven by expressive, Tocquevillian, or duty-driven motivations, I will refer to as *civic participation*. It, too, is defined by its end.

> Civic participation refers to public-spirited collective action that is not motivated by the desire to affect public policy.

These definitions necessitate that I make three things clear.

First, the motivations described in these definitions are at the end points of a continuum, as many activities are driven by a mixture of both impulses. Dahl's distinction between *homo politicus* and *homo civicus* is instructive, as he has clearly constructed two ideal types. Just as some— probably most—people have a mix of these characteristics, so are various activities driven by more than one motivation. But just as some people more closely resemble *homo politicus* than *civicus* (and vice versa), there are clearly activities that tilt more to the political than civic side (and vice versa). For example, we would expect writing a letter to one's member of Congress to have a predominantly political motivation, while volunteering to tutor a child is likely to be civically motivated. In chapter 3, we will see some empirical evidence justifying the distinction between civic and political participation.

Second, these two motivations are not exhaustive. I recognize that the activities I discuss, like all human behavior, really have multiple motivations. The key for the discussion at hand, however, is that civic and political motivations are both systematically related to the nature of the social environments in which we live. And it is people's social environments that will occupy our attention.

Third, I do not mean to attach any normative weight to one motivation or another. This is the point on which I might most fairly be accused of asking to both eat and have my cake, since I have consciously adopted language from normative theory. Furthermore, I readily acknowledge that in common discourse, the terms "political" and "civic" have a normative flavor. "Political," of course, is generally a pejorative term. To accuse someone of being political is to label him as self-serving and manipulative. To be civic, or civic-minded, though, connotes selflessness and virtue. I question, however, whether these terms deserve their common connotations, at least as I have defined them. Essentially, I have defined political as the desire to influence public policy. By this definition, being political does not seem so deserving of opprobrium. Is it really so bad that people vote or otherwise participate in public affairs because they have an interest in a policy outcome? In the United States generally, and within the discipline of political science particularly, there is a common lament that voters are woefully uninformed. Why else should voters be informed but to determine where they stand on the issues? To flip the question around, is it really such a good thing for individuals to participate in politics without an interest in the outcome? The example of Traci Hodgson from the previous chapter drives this point home. Recall that Traci voted because she felt that it was her duty, not because she knew anything about the candidates. Having voters drawn to the polls out of obligation, only to cast totally uninformed ballots, seems far from the democratic ideal.

I am under no illusions that these definitions are novel. Indeed, I hope to have convinced the reader that they are decidedly not innovative, but merely empirically tractable formulations of concepts with deep roots. By incorporating the two motivations into a single study, I hope to resolve the nagging concerns that plague two broad streams of research into public engagement (although that term is indigenous to the study at hand and thus not to be found within this body of research). The first is the political behavior literature. Heavy on empirical evidence and light on theory, there is a large and venerable literature using survey research to explore the factors influencing individuals' propensity to participate in various political activities. The models—laden with individual demographic characteristics—usually seem to be disturbingly removed from "politics," as it is commonly understood (Brady 1999).

The second stream of participation research is that of formal theorists. As mentioned above, many researchers working in this literature have tried to tackle the question of why presumably rational people turn out to vote, which is thought to be a most irrational act. Like the behavioral models, rational choice models fall short of capturing the essentials of political activity. Formal theory has a difficult time predicting turnout rates that are anywhere near what we actually observe. Furthermore, the formal literature on participation has a problem that is the inverse of what we find in behaviorally oriented scholarship. Rational choice scholars have a high theory-to-data ratio. Often no empirical test of the theory is attempted at all.

Taking both the civic and political motivations seriously would enrich the behavioral and rational choice schools. Behavioral research would incorporate a conventional understanding of politics as a clash of interests. And by integrating rather than dismissing the role individuals' sense of duty plays in facilitating turnout, formal theorists might develop models that come closer to explaining empirical reality.

PLACE MATTERS

Thus far, I have made the case that public engagement has two faces and thus can be driven by two motivations, civic and political. This is step one in the theory I am building. If we recall Traci Hodgson, the lonely voter introduced in the previous chapter, this distinction illuminates how her vote could be motivated by fulfilling her duty rather than protecting her interests. Step two is to link these two motivations to the communities in which we live, to show why place matters. Recall that the explanation for Traci's solitary trip to the polls is that she had internalized the norm of voting out of duty while growing up in Little River, Kansas. This chapter will thus construct a theoretical apparatus to explain why some communities foster the development of such norms and thus have high rates of voter turnout. In doing so, we will also see how some communities spark engagement motivated by political conflict and thus also have high voter turnout, but for the very different reason that voters are acting to protect their interests.

To do this, I draw upon two disparate literatures. The first is a venerable body of research that has examined the simple hypothesis that competitive elections spur voter turnout. The second is a newer literature that links the composition of one's social context to the presence of civic norms. While these are two streams of research that generally do not speak to one another, a close look at both reveals that they are actually two sides of the same coin.

ELECTORAL COMPETITION

Political participation, as I have defined it, is rooted in conflict. To the extent, therefore, that voter turnout is politically motivated, we should expect it to rise as conflict heats up. As indicated in the calculus of voting, the closer an election, the greater the value for "p"—the probability that a single vote will decide the election. Expressed in operational terms, this leads to the prediction that close elections lead to high voter turnout.

Presumably because rational choice scholars have the greatest theoretical investment in finding this relationship, they are most likely to have looked for it. Others have too, though, and so an extensive literature has accumulated that largely—but by no means entirely—confirms that voter turnout rises with electoral competition. The competition-turnout connection has been observed in a variety of political jurisdictions, including states in presidential elections (Patterson and Caldeira 1984; Caldeira, Clausen, and Patterson 1990; Cebula and Murphy 1980; Nagler and Leighley 1992; Milbrath 1971; Cox 1988; Cox and Munger 1989; Filer and Kenny 1980; Gray 1976; Kau and Rubin 1976; Chambers and Davis 1978; Settle and Abrams 1976; Kim, Petrocik, and Enokson 1975; Leighley and Nagler 1992; Shachar and Nalebuff 1999), counties in presidential elections (Hoffstetter 1973), congressional districts (Crain, Leavens, and Abbott 1987; Caldeira, Patterson, and Markko 1985; Silberman and Durden 1975), states in gubernatorial elections (Patterson and Caldeira 1983; Barzel and Silberberg 1973), and state legislative districts (Caldeira and Patterson 1982). A few studies have found the closeness of the election at the national level to spur political participation (Filer, Kenny, and Morton 1993; Rosenstone and Hansen 1993). Tellingly in light of the discussion to come, however, most research has found that the significant relationship is between localized electoral competition and voter turnout, even in elections for national or statewide offices. In a similar vein, a recent book has argued that political heterogeneity triggers political involvement not only among adults but also among adolescents. James Gimpel and his collaborators have shown that high school students have a higher level of political efficacy where there is greater partisan diversity (Gimpel, Lay, and Schuknecht 2003).[2] This is broadly consistent with the literature on electoral competition, demonstrating again that political heterogeneity triggers politically motivated participation (or, in the case of these adolescents, the belief that political participation is effectual). In summing up the large literature on the effects of political competition, one scholar has written, "The close relationship of electoral competition and voter turnout at the individual level and at the system level is a frequently verified proposition, bordering upon the status of a law" (Gray 1976).

Political scientists and economists are not the only people who expect close elections to produce high turnout; journalists do, too. The experience of the 2000 presidential contest is instructive. The 2000 election was as close as they come, and in the aftermath of election day many newspapers ran stories on how the tight margin led to record turnout, sometimes in prose with a distinctly purple hue. For example, the day after the election the *Atlanta Constitution* wrote, "Georgians packed the polls in heavy numbers Tuesday—fired out of their ballot box apathy of the past eight years by a tight presidential contest" (Stepp 2000). *The Independent* of London was equally colorful: "Energised by a nail-bitingly close race, voters across the United States flocked to the polls in strikingly large numbers yesterday" (Gumbel 2000). In less colorful language, the *Los Angeles Times* reported record voter participation in counties around L.A., attributing it to "the possibility that, in a race so tight, every vote might actually count" (Fiore 2000). In the immediate wake of the photo-finish, anecdotal reports circulated of individual precincts overwhelmed with voters. To many observers it seemed that turnout must have gone up, and by a lot.

It did go up, but only by a little. According to Michael McDonald and Samuel Popkin (2001), turnout in the 2000 election was 55.6 percent, three points higher than in 1996.[3] Three percentage points *is* an increase, but a turnout of 55.6 percent hardly suggests voters flocking to packed polls.

Should we have been surprised by the paltry increase in turnout from 1996 to 2000? Perhaps not. While the bulk of the research on electoral competition and turnout argues that close elections boost turnout, there are also a few dissenting voices. There has long been a crosscurrent in the literature suggesting that perhaps, as John Ferejohn and Morris Fiorina (1975) memorably put it, closeness counts only in horseshoes and dancing—not in voter turnout. Here and there various authors have presented evidence to question the conventional wisdom linking electoral competition and turnout. Ferejohn and Fiorina find little evidence that the perceived closeness of an election affects turnout. Similarly, James Robinson and William Standing (1960) report that in Indiana there has historically not been a correlation between the closeness of an election and voter turnout. Margaret Conway (1981) finds inconsistent results when testing for a relationship between electoral margin and turnout in congressional elections; in some years, turnout has actually been higher in less-competitive districts. Carroll Foster (1984) also reports that when turnout is measured at the state level there is a weak, unstable, or nonexistent relationship between closeness and turnout. Likewise, while Gary Cox and Michael Munger (1989) find a closeness-turnout relationship in congressional elections, they also stress that it is quite modest. John Matsusaka (1993) finds no relationship between the closeness of the electoral margin and turnout for ballot propositions in California. Based on this array of studies it would appear, therefore, that the "law" linking competitive elections and turnout is far from immutable.

Fast forward to 2004. Again, there was every reason to expect a close vote as election day approached and thus a high level of voter turnout. This time, turnout was relatively high by the (pretty low) standard of contemporary presidential elections: 60 percent, according to Michael McDonald.[4] Given that the elections of 2000 and 2004 were equally close, why was turnout so much higher in 2004 than 2000? The answer lies in the fact that the literature on competitive elections and voter turnout proposes two complementary explanations for why the former enhances the latter. The first explanation is that voters feel they are more likely to affect the outcome of an election when it is perceived to be close (Barzel and Silberberg 1973; Crain, Leavens, and Abbott 1987; Filer and Kenny 1980). The second explanation is simply that political elites, particularly parties, strategically concentrate their resources in electorally competitive places (Chambers and Davis 1978; Copeland 1983; Cox and Munger 1989; Key 1949; Patterson and Caldeira 1983; Settle and Abrams 1976). Furthermore, party mobilization is a major factor affecting voter turnout (Gosnell 1927; Green and Gerber 2004; Kramer 1970; Rosenstone and Hansen 1993; Wielhouwer and Lockerbie 1994). These explanations are not mutually exclusive of one another, as the two processes clearly work in tandem. Political professionals mobilize voters where the electoral margin is narrow, but their appeals are only effective if they can successfully convince voters that in a close contest, every vote matters.

How was 2004 different from 2000? The greater scale and sophistication of voter mobilization efforts in 2004. The 2004 campaign saw a massive effort to get out the vote by supporters of both George W. Bush and John Kerry, dwarfing what was done in 2000. The contrast between the two elections provides strong evidence that both explanations work in tandem. High turnout results from an intensive get-out-the-vote effort, which in turn is most likely to be effective when and where an election goes down to the wire.

Voter mobilization, spurred by a close election, may be sufficient for high turnout, but is it necessary? I wish to advance the provocative claim that it is not necessary to have a close election in order to observe high voter turnout. Rather, we have reason to believe that turnout *increases* as electoral competition *decreases*. When stated in these terms, this claim seems to be sharply at odds with the conventional wisdom in contemporary political science. Even the provocateurs who have questioned the link between electoral competition and voter turnout have simply pointed out the absence of a relationship between them. My argument— that competition and turnout are negatively related—has its roots in the burgeoning literature on community heterogeneity, a topic in which both economists and political scientists are taking an increasing interest.

COMMUNITY HETEROGENEITY

It is probably not immediately obvious how the findings of the literature on community heterogeneity and civic engagement lead to the hypothesis that noncompetitive elections produce high turnout. The claim rests on two propositions, both of which will be elaborated upon. First, community homogeneity *in general* lifts rates of civically oriented participation *in general*. Second, by the logic of the existing literature on community heterogeneity, we should expect that political homogeneity—another way of saying "noncompetitive elections"—should produce high voter turnout.

In an article reviewing the literature on heterogeneity and participation, economists Dora L. Costa and Matthew E. Kahn note that "at least fifteen different empirical economic papers have studied the consequences of community heterogeneity, and all of these studies have the same punch line: heterogeneity reduces civic engagement" (2003a, 104). This conclusion holds across different measures of heterogeneity, whether ethnic, racial, or economic, and different measures of civic engagement: group membership, response rates to the 2000 census, and interpersonal trust (Costa and Kahn 2003b; Glaeser et al. 2000; Vigdor 2001). If voter turnout has civic underpinnings, we should therefore expect it to fall as ethnic, racial, and economic heterogeneity rise.

Figures 2.1, 2.2, and 2.3 constitute simple tests of the relationship between three different types of heterogeneity and voter turnout in the

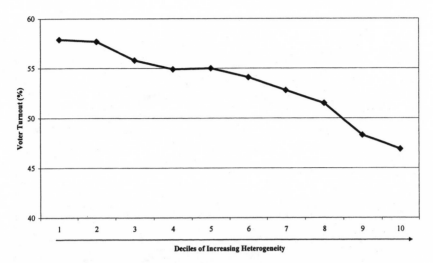

Figure 2.1. Ethnic heterogeneity and voter turnout in the 2000 presidential election, counties

2000 presidential election.[5] Both heterogeneity and turnout have been measured at the level of the county, an approximation of an individual's "mid-range" social context—smaller than the state or metropolitan area but larger than the neighborhood. The measures of heterogeneity have been taken directly from the existing literature. The first is *ethnic*

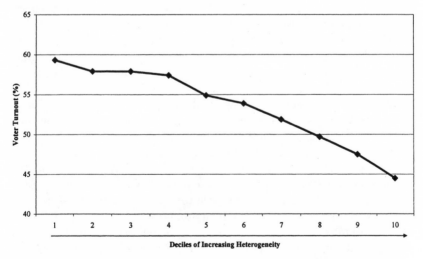

Figure 2.2. Racial heterogeneity and voter turnout in the 2000 presidential election, counties

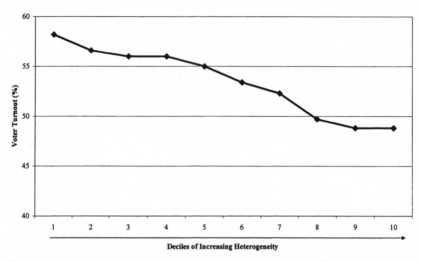

Figure 2.3. Income heterogeneity and voter turnout in the 2000 presidential election, counties

heterogeneity (or what some authors call "birthplace fragmentation"). Always a tricky concept to measure, for this purpose ethnicity is operationalized using seven broad ethnic categories: Anglo-American, Western European, Scandinavian, Latino/Hispanic, Mediterranean, Eastern European/ Balkan, and West Indian, which mirror the categories used by other researchers. I have created an index of ethnic heterogeneity, in which a higher number represents a greater degree of heterogeneity. *Racial heterogeneity* is measured in a manner comparable to *ethnic heterogeneity*, only with racial categories in the place of the ethnic groups.[6] *Income heterogeneity* is operationalized with the Gini coefficient, a standard measure of the income distribution within a community. The greater a county's Gini coefficient, the greater its degree of income inequality, or income heterogeneity. To simplify the graphical presentation, for all three figures the counties have been divided into deciles based on their level of heterogeneity (thus, the value for each decile represents the mean level of heterogeneity for roughly 300 counties).

The figures clearly show that as each type of heterogeneity increases, voter turnout decreases.[7] If one has the perspective that voting is a form of civic participation, this negative relationship should not be surprising. The explanation for why heterogeneity dampens civic activity—whether voting, volunteering, or some other form of publicly spirited collective action—rests on two premises. The first is that a primary reason people engage in civically oriented collective action is in adherence to a social norm encouraging it, which is another way of saying that people vote out of a sense of civic duty. The second is that norms are more easily enforced in homogeneous communities.

What do I mean by a social norm? Like any term employed in social science, the definition is contested. For some, a norm is simply a behavioral regularity, something people generally do. The definition I employ, however, specifies that a norm is rooted in a sense of obligation. My use of the term concurs with two other definitions, one more formal, the other less so. Sociologist Thomas Voss defines a norm as "a regularity such that members of [a population] expect that nonconformity will (with positive probability) be punished with (negative) sanctions" (2001, 109). (More on sanctions below.) Legal scholar Richard McAdams defines a social norm as a "decentralized behavioral standard that individuals feel obligated to follow" (1997, 381).[8] In a memorable turn of phrase, some authors refer to a norm's "oughtness"—it is something members of a community feel they ought to do, even if they do not always do it (Hechter and Opp 2001).

It is in the seminal work of James Coleman that we find the theoretical tools to understand how civic norms are propagated, and why those norms are likely to be more effectual in homogeneous communities. A norm exists, Coleman suggests, when individuals willingly transfer some authority over their behavior to fellow members of their community: "[A] norm concerning a specific action exists when the socially defined right to control the action is held not by the actor but by others" (1990, 243). A norm is enforced within a community through the use of social sanctions. The term "sanctions" may seem vaguely sinister, but it refers to nothing more than the signals people send to one another in everyday social interactions. These sanctions are typically subtle—a disapproving look, a raised eyebrow, the whispered label of "shirker"—but are nonetheless effectual (Knack 1992). They are also largely a matter of anticipated reactions; I anticipate how my neighbors will perceive my behavior and act to meet their assumed approval (or avoid their disapproval). Robert Putnam uses the example of a neighborhood in which there is a norm to rake one's leaves to illustrate this type of social sanction.

> The norm of keeping lawns leaf-free is powerful in my neighborhood . . . and it constrains my decision as to whether to spend Saturday afternoon watching TV. This norm is not actually taught in local schools, but neighbors mention it when newcomers move in, and they reinforce it in frequent autumnal chats, as well as by obsessive raking of their own yards. Non-rakers risk being shunned at neighborhood events, and non-raking is rare. (1993, 171)

This process of norm enforcement through social sanctions will only occur when three conditions hold. First, the prescribed behavior must be generally recognized as something that individuals ought to do (or, as the case may be, not do). In Putnam's example, leaf-raking is widely accepted as normative within his neighborhood. Analogously, voting is deeply ingrained as normative within the collective American psyche and thus clearly meets this condition.

The second and third conditions apply not to the norm but to the people potentially subject to it. They must recognize the legitimacy of other members within their community to enforce the norm, and they must have social relationships with those people for sanctions to be applied. Again returning to Putnam's example, the leaf-raking norm is only effectual because residents of his neighborhood care what the others in the area think of them, and interact with them in order that sanctions for non-raking can be applied. Homogeneity within a community facilitates all three of these conditions. First, people with common backgrounds and beliefs are more likely to arrive at consensus over normative behavior. Second, commonality among members of a community enhances the legitimacy with which they view one another's opinions. Third, people generally associate with others who are "like them."

The mechanism of enforcing norms through social sanctions has been labeled *social capital*. Coleman originally employed the concept of social capital to explain the high academic performance and low dropout rates of students in parochial schools (Coleman and Hoffer 1987). Putnam (1993) applied the concept to explain the performance of Italian regional governments, and then to an array of social indicators in the United States in areas as diverse as education, economics, and public health (Putnam 2000). Over the last few years, the term "social capital" has been adopted in many literatures and has even entered the popular lexicon. Unfortunately, different authors use it to mean different things, which has cast suspicion on the term in some scholarly circles (Skocpol and Fiorina 1999). For this reason, I will define my terms carefully.

It is important to stress that the collective aspect of social capital is critical to its analytic utility, as communities are more than just the sum of their parts. As Stephen Knack explains, even people with a low sense of duty have a higher likelihood of voting in a place populated with duty-bound compatriots: "Social sanctions . . . permit a certain amount of 'substitutability' of feelings of duty, as someone with a low sense of civic obligation may nonetheless vote to avoid displeasing a friend or relative with a stronger sense of duty" (1992, 137–38).

Theory thus predicts that community homogeneity feeds social capital, which is consistent with the empirical observation that the American states Putnam identifies as high in social capital are also homogeneous racially, ethnically, and economically. Contrast Minnesota, the "social capital capital," and Mississippi, one of the lowest-scoring states on

Putnam's social capital index. In the former, 95 percent of the population is of the same race; in the latter, the percentage is only 64 percent. Likewise, Utah is relatively high in social capital and has a high level of income equality, whereas Louisiana is low in social capital and has the widest income divide in the United States. Similarly, Stephen Knack and Philip Keefer (1997) report that the nations with the highest levels of social capital are also very ethnically homogeneous and have high levels of income equality.

Alberto Alesina and Eliana La Ferrara (2000) provide more detailed evidence for the claim that civic participation increases as a function of a community's homogeneity. They model one of the most common measures of civic participation, membership in voluntary associations, as a function of the income, racial, and ethnic heterogeneity in a respondent's metropolitan area. Their results for group membership mirror those we have just seen for voter turnout. They find that heterogeneity is negatively related to group membership, as measured at the individual level by the General Social Survey.

The striking empirical parallels between the findings regarding group membership and voter turnout suggest that they have a common cause, and thus compel a careful look at the theoretical mechanism Alesina and La Ferrara develop to explain why heterogeneity is negatively related to civic activity. Working in a framework drawn from the social capital literature, they present a complex formal model premised on the assumption that "individuals prefer to interact with others who are similar to themselves in terms of income, race, and ethnicity" (2000, 850). This in and of itself is not a terribly startling proposition, as it is just the way economists say that birds of a feather flock together. The critical element of their model for our purposes, however, is what pulls people of similar backgrounds together, as they are more specific on this point than is either Coleman or Putnam. Alesina and La Ferrara go on to state, "If *preferences* are correlated with these characteristics [that is, ethnicity, race, and income], then our assumption is equivalent to saying that individuals prefer to join groups composed of individuals with *preferences* similar to their own" (ibid., emphasis added).

In other words, Alesina and La Ferrara measure heterogeneity along the dimensions of ethnicity, race, and income because they are proxies for what economists typically call "preferences," political scientists call "interests," and the layperson calls "values." For consistency's sake, and to emphasize the connection between my work and that of Alesina and La Ferrara, I will stick to using the term "preferences," but the reader should keep in mind that these other terms are just as applicable. Admittedly, Alesina and La Ferrara's strategy of using these demographic characteristics to proxy preferences has some intuitive appeal as well as empirical traction. Nonetheless, these particular characteristics seem to be blunt indicators of preferences. Given that Alesina and La Ferrara are referring to preferences with policy relevance, it seems logical that a better indicator would more closely correspond to individuals' political opinions. Consider the following thought experiment. Imagine that you were asked to predict whether two randomly selected people had similar preferences on a particular issue. You can only know one thing about them, and you do not know ahead of time the specific issue. What is the one thing that you would want to know about them? I might suggest that more than their ethnic group, income level, and even their race, you would do well to find out their partisanship (that is, whether they identify as a Republican or a Democrat), as this is the single best predictor of preferences across a wide range of issues. Partisanship, I contend, is an even better predictor than race, which is undeniably a salient factor in American politics (Carmines and Stimson 1989; Kinder and Sanders 1996). While race certainly shapes much of American politics, a measure of racial heterogeneity will not necessarily reflect the racial divide. This is because white voters are not simply the inverse of African American voters. While African Americans consistently favor liberal policies, whites are not uniformly conservative (even on issues related to race).

In determining the best measure of an individual's preferences, we need not rely on thought experiments, however, as this is an intrinsically empirical question. Which characteristic best predicts an individual's preferences—ethnicity, race, income, or partisanship? To answer this question, I have used the 1996 National Election Study to examine individuals' positions on eleven disparate issues: the general level of government spending, the environment, gay rights, health care, moral traditionalism, government assistance for African Americans, defense spending, the death penalty, abortion, working mothers, and crime.[9] This is a wide spectrum of issues, ranging from fiscal questions to so-called culture war issues to foreign policy. Some of these issues are overtly related to public policy, like the appropriate level of government spending, while others are not so closely related to the actions of government, like whether mothers with children should work outside the home. In short, these eleven questions tap into a wide range of preferences. I have run one linear regression model for each issue, each with the same set of independent variables: income, dummy variables for ethnicity, a dummy variable for race (white or black), and a dummy variable for partisanship (Republican or Democrat).[10] The way to interpret these results is by keeping your eye on the statistical significance of the variables, particularly partisan affiliation. If a variable is statistically significant, that means we can conclude it predicts attitudes on that particular issue.

In Table 2.1 we see that among these variables *only* partisanship

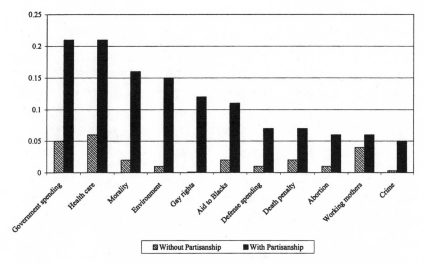

Figure 2.4. Explaining variation in preferences: adjusted R^2 with and without partisanship

consistently reaches statistical significance, and always at the .01 level. Income is sporadically significant, as are some of the ethnic classifications. Race, however, never clears the bar for significance. In sum, across these eleven issues, preferences are better predicted by partisanship than by income, ethnicity, or race.

Further underscoring the relative predictive power of partisanship over these other characteristics, Figure 2.4 displays the change in the adjusted R^2 value of each regression model when partisanship is added to an equation containing the variables for income, ethnicity, and race. The value of the adjusted R^2 reflects the percentage of the variance in the dependent variable the model explains, accounting for the number of independent variables in the model. Loosely speaking, a high R^2 value means a "better" model, at least in the sense that it explains more variance in the dependent variable. In each case, the adjusted R^2 increases substantially with the addition of a term for partisanship. For a model predicting attitudes toward government spending, for example, the adjusted R^2 jumps from .05 to .21. For a model predicting attitudes regarding homosexual rights, the R^2 increases from essentially 0 (.001) to .12. We see that partisanship is a much better predictor of preferences across a wide range of issues than the measures of heterogeneity employed in the literature to this point.

The fact that these other characteristics so poorly track political preferences explains why turnout is not high in communities that are ethnically,

TABLE 2.1
Predicting Preferences

	Gov't spending	Health care	Morality	Environment	Gay rights
Republican•	−1.198***	1.470***	2.528***	1.235***	0.876***
Income	−0.027***	0.047***	0.003	−0.009	−0.008
W. European†	0.117	−0.056	−0.057	0.067	0.153
Scandinavian	−0.120	0.237	−0.057	0.007	−0.305*
E. European	0.096	0.019	−0.220	0.074	0.007
Mediterranean	0.185	−0.166	−0.834*	−0.266	−0.162
Latino	0.346*	−0.208	−0.338	−0.239	0.327**
White‡	−0.256	−0.219	0.467	0.540	0.537
Constant	6.102***	1.538**	10.317***	1.315**	0.462
Observations	628	638	640	591	611
R² (adjusted)	0.21	0.21	0.16	0.15	0.12

Source: 1996 National Election Study.
Note: Results from linear regression. Standard coefficients.
• Excluded category is Democrat
† Excluded category is Anglo-American
‡ Excluded category is Black
* significant at .10   ** significant at .05   *** significant at .01

racially, or economically heterogeneous. If these characteristics did accurately reflect political opinions in the contemporary United States then we would expect heterogeneity to spark political conflict and thus high voter turnout driven by a Madisonian motivation. Eric Oliver, in his insightful book *Democracy in Suburbia* (2001), has identified just such a situation. Oliver finds that turnout in local elections, as well as other forms of localized political participation, is a function of the economic heterogeneity within a municipality. This is because preferences on the narrow bundle of issues that dominate local politics—zoning laws, school financing, and the like—are often proxied by an individual's income level. As we have seen, however, income is not a good predictor of preferences on a general bundle of issues. This conclusion is reinforced in Oliver's work by the fact that, unlike local political engagement, interest and engagement in national politics are not related to the degree of economic heterogeneity within one's community.

A superficial reading of Oliver's *Democracy in Suburbia* and my work might make it appear that we are in disagreement. In reality, however, we agree to a greater extent than we disagree, although the common

(continued from pg 30)

Gov't aid to blacks	Defense spending	Death penalty	Abortion	Working mothers	Crime
0.963***	0.679***	−0.438***	−0.523***	−0.408***	0.849***
0.003	0.010	0.003	0.023***	0.050***	−0.026**
0.144	−0.040	−0.042	−0.058	−0.211	0.240
0.055	−0.096	0.023	0.094	−0.178	0.281
0.334	−0.242	−0.168	−0.272*	−0.128	0.684**
0.248	−0.503***	−0.402***	0.156	0.015	−0.079
−0.231	0.240	0.271*	−0.362**	0.112	0.287
0.276	0.175	0.368	−0.249	−0.160	0.068
3.071***	2.746***	1.883***	3.599***	2.929***	3.413***
644	625	625	685	642	667
0.11	0.07	0.07	0.06	0.06	0.05

ground we share is obscured by differences in our terminology. Oliver describes his dependent variables as "civic participation," whereas I would define them as "political participation." Specifically, his dependent variables include contacting elected officials, attending a board meeting, attending an organizational meeting, and voting in local elections. As he discusses these measures, it seems clear that he thinks of them as expressions of political preferences. For example, he describes community board meetings as a means of "gathering citizen input and ensuring institutional accountability" (19). Later on, he states that "conflict is essential for fueling civic participation" (86), a statement that underscores the differences in how we define our terms (since I have defined civic participation as that which is fueled by consensus, not conflict). I acknowledge that it is insufficient for me to wave my hands at the definitional differences between Oliver's study and my own, as that skirts the real issue. Clearly Oliver and I are addressing similar, although certainly not identical, questions. Both of us are interested in how individuals' social contexts shape their involvement in various forms of collective action, although his focus is specifically on the impact of living in a suburban community. The key difference between his work and mine is that I introduce an alternative type of collective action, that which is not motivated by the expression of preferences but rather by what I have described as civic considerations. If we accept that his dependent variables capture collective action that is primarily motivated by political considerations, then his basic finding—that politically motivated participation is greater where preferences are heterogeneous—is consistent with mine. Further illuminating the similarities between Oliver's work and my own, his unpublished doctoral dissertation shows that economically homogeneous communities have higher rates of membership in voluntary associations, one form of civic participation (Oliver 1997). This is fully consistent with my general claim that homogeneity facilitates civic norms.

Even if the reader accepts that partisanship is an important predictor of issue preferences, the theory at work rests on people choosing to associate with others of similar political views. I concede that for many—perhaps most—Americans the partisanship of their friends and acquaintances is not something that occupies much of their attention. Americans are not likely to ask one another about their partisan preferences in casual conversation. This might suggest, therefore, that the partisan composition of a community is not terribly relevant for the process by which social norms are reinforced. Is partisanship really a salient social marker? The answer lies in what partisanship is really measuring. I contend that in the contemporary United States partisanship is actually a good proxy for one's cultural outlook, which in turn corresponds to a bundle of issue preferences. You may not know whether your neighbors are Republicans, but you are likely to know something about their lifestyle (whether both husband and wife work outside the home or whether they attend church regularly). People who have similar lifestyles are, in turn, likely to form networks of reciprocity with one another. And matters of lifestyle, or what some might call cultural values, are increasingly related to partisanship in America (Layman 2001). As detailed in chapter 4, Americans' friendship networks tend to include people with similar political views.

A careful reading of the literature on community heterogeneity thus leads us through the following chain of logic:
If

a. social norms facilitating civically motivated collective action are stronger in places characterized by homogeneity of preferences
and
b. partisanship is our most consistent measure of preferences
and
c. voting is a civically motivated activity
then
d. voter turnout should rise with partisan, or political, homogeneity.

And if places with homogeneous political preferences also tend to have noncompetitive elections—an almost self-evident claim—it follows that voter turnout should rise in places where elections are won by wide margins. It all fits together in a tidy, logical package. The catch, of course, is

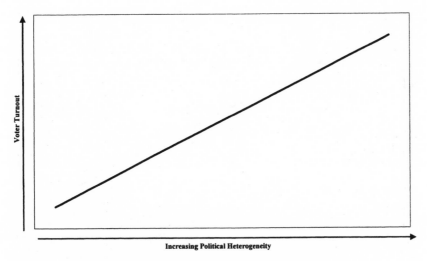

Figure 2.5. Hypothesis 1: political heterogeneity ignites voter turnout

the long line of research that argues exactly the opposite: that turnout rises where elections are competitive.

We are thus left with competing expectations about the relationship between political heterogeneity and turnout. On the one hand, the literature on competitive elections, bolstered by the conventional wisdom among lay observers of the political scene, suggests that political heterogeneity should ignite turnout. Graphically, the relationship would resemble Figure 2.5. On the other hand, the literature on community heterogeneity suggests the opposite relationship, namely that increasing heterogeneity will extinguish turnout, as depicted in Figure 2.6.

POLITICAL HETEROGENEITY

Having laid out the sharp contrast between these two theoretically driven expectations, we can turn to the data for an empirical test. Figure 2.7 plots county-level voter turnout in the 2000 presidential election against the level of political competition in each county (calculated so that the higher the number, the more competitive the county). Counties are again divided into deciles, in this case of political heterogeneity. We see that the figure resembles neither Figure 2.5 nor Figure 2.6, but is instead a synthesis of both. Rather than a linear relationship in a positive or negative direction, instead we see a curvilinear relationship. As predicted by the literature on turnout and competitive elections, voter turnout is high

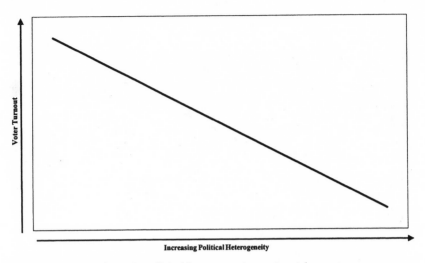

Figure 2.6. Hypothesis 2: political heterogeneity extinguishes voter turnout

in communities with a high degree of political heterogeneity, or where presidential elections are most competitive. And as I have inferred from the literature on community heterogeneity, voter turnout is equally high in communities with a high degree of political homogeneity, or where presidential elections are least competitive. Assuming that this relationship

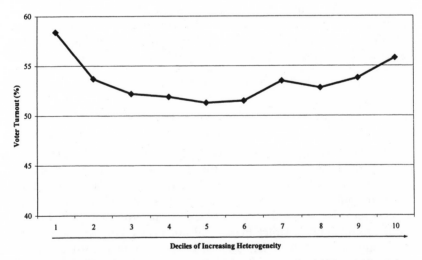

Figure 2.7. Political heterogeneity and voter turnout in the 2000 presidential election, counties

holds up when we control for other factors, we see evidence that *both* causal mechanisms drive voter turnout. In the notation of the calculus of voting, in homogeneous communities people are more likely to vote out of a sense of duty (the "D" term is higher). Conversely, heterogeneity, or electoral competition, spurs voters to the polls because they believe that their individual vote has a greater chance of affecting the election's outcome (the "p" term increases).

Because the theory at work is that the level of political diversity in a community measures the general level of commonly held preferences, political heterogeneity is better measured as an average of election results over multiple elections. Similarly, previous evidence suggests that political mobilization is most likely to occur in places that are historically competitive (Patterson and Caldeira 1983). Therefore, in order to reduce the risk that the results are driven by the idiosyncrasies of a particular election, I have constructed a *political heterogeneity index* by averaging a county's mean level of electoral competition in presidential elections over multiple elections, beginning in 1980. The measure is computed with this simple formula:

$$h_{pc} = \frac{\Sigma(100 - K_i)}{N}$$

where k_i represents the share of the vote taken by the prevailing party in each county in year i, and N is the number of years. Of course, subtracting from 100 means that h_{pc} increases as counties are more competitive.[11] As an example, in 2000 Al Gore took 61 percent of the vote in Mercer County, New Jersey. The score for Mercer County, therefore, is $100 - 61$, or 39. Its average level of competition from 1980 to 2000 is 46.8. The year 1980 is a logical starting point for the data series, since Ronald Reagan's election is often described as the beginning of a political epoch in American politics (Miller and Shanks 1996). Figure 2.8 displays turnout in the 2000 election, this time as a function of the political heterogeneity index. Again, we see the same curvilinear relationship.[12]

While the curvilinear relationship between political composition and voter turnout is unmistakable, is it meaningful? That is, does the relationship clear the bar for both statistical and substantive significance? In statistical terms, we will see a series of models which demonstrate that the impact of political heterogeneity on turnout meets conventional levels of statistical significance, which simply gives us confidence that the impact can be distinguished from zero. Perhaps more important, however, is the question of whether these differences are substantively important, the evaluation of which is not simply a matter of convention. To gauge whether the differences in turnout are substantial, consider that the absolute difference in the mean turnout rate from the least to the

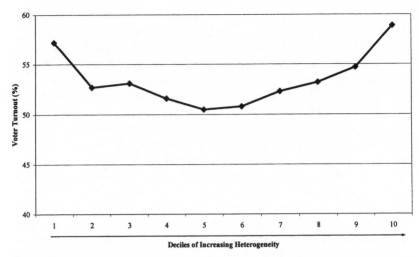

Figure 2.8. Average political heterogeneity (1980–2000) and voter turnout in the 2000 presidential election, counties

most competitive decile is between 5 and 8 percentage points. In the context of presidential elections, this is a range that would get a candidate's attention. As a rough benchmark for comparison, at the national level turnout rarely fluctuates by that much from one presidential election to another, notwithstanding all of the discussion surrounding declining voter turnout that ritualistically follows almost each election.[13] Similarly, in the early 1990s Congress was sharply divided over allowing voter registration in conjunction with renewing a driver's license, a provision that typically boosts turnout by between 3 and 6 points (Knack 1995; Rhine 1995, 1996; Franklin and Grier 1997; Highton and Wolfinger 1998).

It is also reasonable to ask what the counties at the extremes of the distribution are like. Can their high turnout be attributed to other factors, such as socioeconomic status? Take two counties in the first (most homogeneous) decile, Roberts and Brooks Counties. Both are in Texas, but besides this and their low degree of heterogeneity, they have little else in common. In Roberts County, 25 percent of the population has a college degree while the 1999 average family income was $50,400.[14] In 2000, George W. Bush won 86 percent of the vote. In Brooks County, there are less than a third as many college graduates (7 percent) and less than half the average family income ($22,473). In 2000, Bush only won 23 percent of the vote (even though it is located in his home state). At the other end of the distribution, in the top decile for political heterogeneity, contrast two other Texas counties: Hays and Liberty. In Hays County, which is close to the state capital of Austin, 31 percent of the population has a college degree and average family income is $56,000. Bush won the county with 59 percent of the vote. Situated east of Houston, Liberty County is similar in the share of its vote that went for Bush in 2000, 62 percent. However, only 8 percent of the population has a college degree, and the average family income is $43,000. Obviously, a more rigorous analysis requires simultaneously controlling for an array of possibly spurious factors, but these brief profiles hopefully provide the intuition that the relationship displayed in Figure 2.5 is not simply a function of socioeconomic variables.

Figures 2.9a, 2.9b, and 2.10 provide a different perspective on the same data used to construct Figure 2.8. These three figures display the mean levels of, first, political heterogeneity (electoral competition) and then voter turnout for every county in the continental United States in 2000. Figure 2.9a displays the average level of competition in the 2000 presidential election, with counties divided into deciles. Figure 2.9b does the same, but averages electoral competition from 1980 to 2000. The patterns are as Figure 2.8 would suggest—the areas of the country that are very light (low level of political heterogeneity) and very dark (high heterogeneity) in Figures 2.9a and 2.9b are dark (high voter turnout) in Figure 2.10. It is particularly striking to see a vertical swath of white— indicating a low level of political heterogeneity—in the center of the United States, stretching from almost the forty-ninth parallel into Texas. With only a few exceptions, counties in this area have comparatively

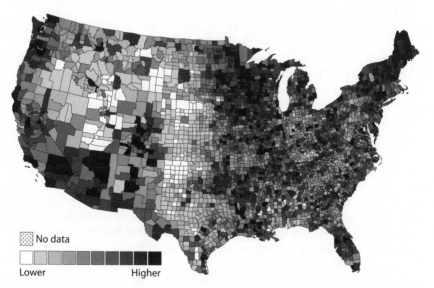

No data

Lower   Higher

Figure 2.9a. Political heterogeneity (electoral competition) in 2000

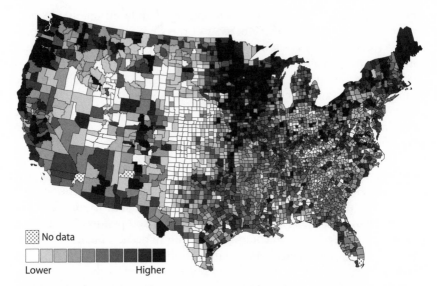

Figure 2.9b. Average political heterogeneity (electoral competition) in 1980–2000

high voter turnout. The regional patterns suggested by these maps also remind us that counties do not exist in isolation, and so possible regional effects need to be accounted for as we move to a multivariate test of the relationship between the political composition of counties and their level of voter turnout.

The first, and most critical, step in conducting a multivariate test is calculating a measure that captures the curvilinearity of the heterogeneity-turnout relationship. This has been accomplished by breaking the political heterogeneity index into two. One variable captures the impact of moving from the mean to the minimum level of political heterogeneity, the other is the inverse and thus measures the effect of moving from the mean to maximum level of heterogeneity. Intuitively, think of the heterogeneity measure as being "folded" at the mean.

More technically, these measures are derived from the equation:

$$Political\ Heterogeneity\ Index = (h_{pc} - \mu_p)^2$$

where μ_p is the mean political competition across all counties, and h_p is the mean level of competition for each county, c. Squaring the term serves two purposes. First, it ensures that values on either side of the mean are positive. Second, it captures the fact that the bivariate relationship shows the increase in turnout as accelerating the farther political composition gets from the mean (the "curve" in "curvilinear"). Figure 2.11 provides

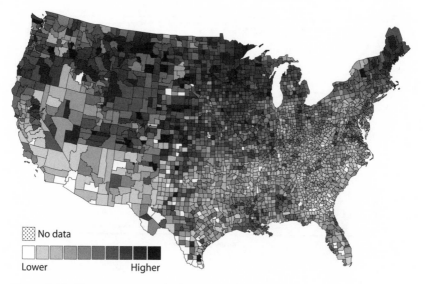

Figure 2.10. Voter turnout in the 2000 presidential election

a graphical display of how the two terms have been generated. The first has a score for the counties below the mean, with those above the mean coded as zero, while the second does the opposite. All counties above the mean receive a score, with the others set to zero.

Splitting the political composition measure in this way makes it easy to compare the relative impact of the "political homogeneity effect" versus the "political heterogeneity effect." If the relationship observed in Figure 2.6 is truly curvilinear once other controls are introduced, then both terms should be positive. Furthermore, by coding both terms on the same scale (0–1), we can easily compare the magnitude of their relative impacts. Likewise, all the other variables in the model have been coded 0–1.

Table 2.2 displays the results of a model that estimates county-level voter turnout in the 2000 presidential election. In addition to the measures of political homogeneity and heterogeneity, the model also controls for an array of factors that previous research has suggested affect turnout, including the county's mean education level, household income, its level of urbanization, population density, residential mobility, and the region of the country in which it is located.[15] It also includes ethnic, racial, and income heterogeneity to ensure that any effect attributed to political heterogeneity is not actually owing to these other dimensions of diversity. A measure of the state's level of political competition is also included, owing to the reasonable assertion that the relevant unit for political heterogeneity is the state, not the county. Because the electoral

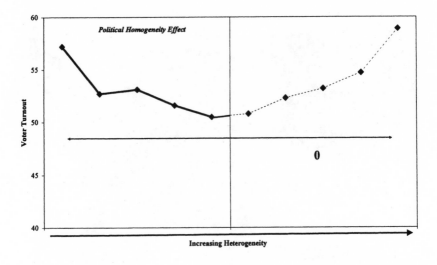

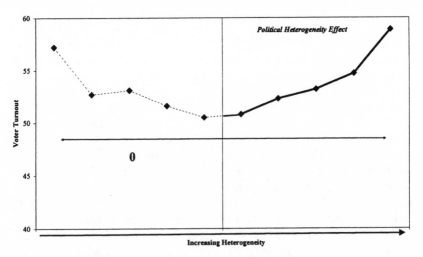

Figure 2.11. "Folding" the political heterogeneity measure

college system means that the relevant jurisdiction in presidential elections is the state, it could be that voter mobilization is a function of the statewide electoral margin. State political competition is thus measured as the closeness of the presidential election at the state level in that particular election, again calculated by subtracting the percentage of the vote taken by the winning party in that state from 100.[16]

TABLE 2.2
Political Heterogeneity and Voter Turnout, Counties

	2000	2000	1996	1992
Political Context				
2000 Political homogeneity (mean to minimum)	13.163*** (1.478)			
2000 Political heterogeneity (mean to maximum)	1.848** (0.789)			
1980–2000 Political homogeneity (mean to minimum)		8.547*** (1.742)	6.784*** (2.040)	4.823*** (1.701)
1980–2000 Political heterogeneity (mean to maximum)		4.111*** (0.854)	2.079** (0.817)	4.128*** (0.757)
County Characteristics				
% with college degree	33.125*** (1.770)	33.790*** (1.733)	33.182*** (1.948)	37.272*** (1.903)
Mean household income (log)	6.770*** (2.340)	5.757*** (2.310)	-3.104 (2.424)	-4.710* (2.467)
Urbanicity	-7.140*** (0.558)	-7.738*** (0.552)	-9.583*** (0.616)	-9.839*** (0.603)
Population density	-37.183*** (8.511)	-32.860*** (6.670)	-33.193*** (4.332)	-30.839*** (3.945)
Residential mobility	-28.593*** (1.597)	-28.297*** (1.582)	-24.984*** (2.226)	-26.678*** (2.204)
Racial heterogeneity	-8.240*** (0.719)	-8.170*** (0.718)	-3.318*** (1.222)	-5.820** (1.148)
Ethnic heterogeneity	-1.831 (2.007)	-1.585 (2.023)	-6.485** (2.049)	-7.032*** (1.928)
Income heterogeneity (Gini coefficient)	-3.177** (1.415)	-3.925*** (1.417)	-5.667 (4.451)	-11.039** (4.389)
State Characteristic				
State political competition	3.900*** (0.576)	2.214*** (0.559)	1.439 (1.906)	15.772*** (1.815)
Region				
Southern state	-4.565*** (0.301)	-4.542*** (0.309)	-5.897*** (0.388)	-5.045*** (0.377)
Upper midwestern state	1.316*** (0.300)	1.148*** (0.300)	1.754*** (0.398)	0.071 (0.372)
Constant	59.363*** (1.939)	61.175*** (1.931)	71.676*** (4.349)	71.218*** (4.275)
Observations	3,104	3,104	3,104	3,102
R^2	0.60	0.60	0.47	0.52

Note: Results from linear regression. Robust standard errors in parentheses. Independent variables standardized on 0–1 scale.

* significant at .10   ** significant at .05   *** significant at .01

We see that moving from the mean to the minimum level of political heterogeneity (the "homogeneity effect") results in a 13 percentage-point increase in turnout. This compares to a 7-point drop in turnout when moving from the least to the most urban county, a 4-point gain when comparing the state with the least degree of electoral competition with the one that has the most, and a 29-point drop in turnout between a county with the lowest level of residential mobility versus the highest. In a pattern that will become familiar, we also see that the homogeneity effect is greater than the heterogeneity effect. While the former is 13 points, the latter is slightly less than 2.

The second column of Table 2.2 is similar to the first, but substitutes results from a model using the mean level of political heterogeneity, averaged over presidential elections from 1980 to 2000 (just as was done for Figure 2.8). Again, the political heterogeneity index has been split into separate variables for the homogeneity and heterogeneity effects. The same control variables have been included in the model. Again, we see that that both the homogeneity and heterogeneity effects are positive. And once more, the homogeneity effect exceeds heterogeneity's impact, although the gap is narrower (about 4 percentage points).

Given that the data thus far have come exclusively from the 2000 presidential election, it is natural to ask whether there was something idiosyncratic about that particular contest that has led to these results. To examine whether 2000 differs from other years, Table 2.2 also presents results from the 1996 and 1992 presidential elections from models that are identical to the one used in 2000 (although with census data collected in 1990 rather than 2000). In each case, we see both the homogeneity and heterogeneity effects, and in each case the former is slightly larger than the latter.

It is worth stressing that the similarity across the three models is striking, especially given that these three elections were very different. Nineteen ninety-two was an unusual election featuring a heated race, with Ross Perot mounting a serious third-party challenge to the Republican and Democratic standard-bearers. In 1996, a popular incumbent faced lackluster Republican opposition, with Perot largely irrelevant. The 2000 election, in turn, was the closest in modern history, with Ralph Nader's third-party candidacy playing the part of the spoiler.

The bottom line from the county-level results thus far is it does not appear that the curvilinear relationship between political heterogeneity and voter turnout is simply owing to these other factors that are known to influence turnout. Nevertheless, we should be wary of an inference based exclusively on aggregate-level data. Individuals, not collectivities, vote, and individual-level relationships inferred from aggregate-level data are potentially limited by the ecological fallacy, which occurs when an individual-level relationship is unobserved in aggregate data (King 1997; Robinson 1950). However, while generally ignored in survey research, it is equally true that inferences based on individual-level data are potentially limited by the individualistic fallacy. This occurs when an observed individual-level relationship is actually due to unobserved aggregate-level characteristics (Huckfeldt and Sprague 1993). To assuage concerns about both challenges to inferring causality, the best strategy is to replicate aggregate findings in individual-level data, and vice versa (Achen and Shively 1995). However, the appropriate individual-level survey for this analysis must meet a number of criteria. It has to include a large number of respondents, sampled from a wide array of geographic jurisdictions. In addition, it has to be possible to link survey respondents to their geographic location, something not possible with all publicly accessible data.

Fortunately, the Current Population Survey (CPS) meets all of these criteria, allowing for confirmation of the county-level results with individual-level data. Conducted by the U.S. Census Bureau and the Bureau of Labor Statistics, each CPS consists of a nationally representative sample of about 50,000 respondents for whom their geographic location is identified.[17] After every biennial election, the CPS includes a small battery of questions about voter turnout in its Voter Supplement. Beginning with Wolfinger and Rosenstone's *Who Votes?*, for over two decades the CPS has been a mainstay in analyses of voter turnout. Its large N, high response rate (over 90 percent), and the fact that it is administered within a month of the election in question bolster confidence in its results. Unlike smaller-scale surveys like the National Election Studies, the expansive sampling frame of the CPS means that it has a representative sample of respondents in each state. One disadvantage of the CPS is that owing to the federal government's extreme sensitivity to confidentiality concerns, the analyst can only identify the geographic location of respondents who live in what the Census Bureau designates a metropolitan statistical area. This obviously leads to biased estimates, although the bias presumably works against my hypotheses since we would expect counties with a small population to be more homogeneous.[18]

The individual-level models employ all of the same variables as the previous county-level estimation, with the addition of both individual-level and state-level characteristics known to affect the likelihood of turning out.[19] Instead of ordinary least squares regression, the binary dependent variable (either the respondent voted or not) is more appropriately modeled using logistic regression. Consequently, the resulting coefficients cannot be interpreted as straightforwardly as with linear regression.[20] The variables have again been coded on a 0–1 scale to provide a rough sense of their comparative magnitude.

Table 2.3 reports results for 2000, 1996, and 1992. Again, the first

TABLE 2.3
Political Heterogeneity and Voter Turnout, Current Population Survey

	2000	2000	1996	1992
Political Context				
Political homogeneity in 2000 (mean to minimum)	0.097*** (0.035)	0.213* (0.125)	0.498* (0.255)	0.390** (0.170)
Political heterogeneity in 2000 (mean to maximum)	0.154*** (0.057)	0.134* (0.080)	0.215** (0.083)	0.242*** (0.059)
Mean political homogeneity (mean to minimum)		0.213* (0.125)	0.498* (0.255)	0.390** (0.170)
Mean political heterogeneity (mean to maximum)		0.134* (0.080)	0.215** (0.083)	0.242*** (0.059)
Individual Characteristics				
Education level	3.718*** (0.081)	3.719*** (0.081)	3.403*** (0.074)	3.859*** (0.075)
Family income	1.177*** (0.050)	1.177*** (0.050)	1.117*** (0.045)	1.039*** (0.041)
Age	4.127*** (0.341)	4.080*** (0.343)	3.608*** (0.170)	4.681*** (0.324)
Age squared	−0.852** (0.316)	−0.803** (0.318)	−1.141*** (0.196)	−1.594*** (0.302)
Married	0.343*** (0.026)	0.345*** (0.026)	0.281*** (0.024)	0.180*** (0.024)
African American	0.518*** (0.039)	0.517*** (0.039)	0.497*** (0.037)	−0.275*** (0.085)
Female	0.198*** (0.023)	0.198*** (0.023)	0.160*** (0.021)	0.159*** (0.021)
County Characteristics				
% with college degree	0.726*** (0.150)	0.664*** (0.154)	0.107 (0.122)	0.139 (0.110)
Mean household income (log)	−0.464** (0.195)	−0.356* (0.204)	0.160 (0.114)	0.510*** (0.156)
Urbanicity	0.160 (0.142)	0.058 (0.142)	−0.101*** (0.035)	0.441*** (0.105)

	(1)	(2)	(3)	(4)
Population density	0.189 (0.171)	−0.047 (0.213)	−0.460** (0.186)	−0.331*** (0.098)
Residential Mobility	−0.641*** (0.084)	−0.658*** (0.085)	−0.086 (0.157)	−0.079 (0.090)
Ethnic heterogeneity	0.079 (0.186)	0.235 (0.191)	−0.853*** (0.189)	−1.406*** (0.170)
Racial heterogeneity	−0.026 (0.085)	−0.006 (0.087)	0.602*** (0.190)	0.507*** (0.109)
Income heterogeneity (Gini coefficient)	0.217 (0.156)	0.277* (0.162)	2.208*** (0.316)	0.726*** (0.122)
State Characteristics				
State political competition	0.324*** (0.058)	0.253*** (0.057)	−0.383*** (0.101)	−0.010*** (0.002)
Ease of voter registration	−0.358*** (0.061)	−0.378*** (0.061)	−0.296*** (0.054)	−0.526*** (0.062)
Region				
Southern state	0.004 (0.030)	0.005 (0.031)	−0.045 (0.029)	−0.080** (0.032)
Upper midwestern state	0.166*** (0.053)	0.156*** (0.053)	0.159*** (0.049)	0.093* (0.051)
Constant	−4.351*** (0.196)	−4.354*** (0.200)	−5.242*** (0.355)	−3.064*** (0.197)
Observations	43,528	43,210	46,895	51,513
Pseudo-R^2	0.15	0.15	0.14	0.14

Note: Results from logistic regression. Robust standard errors in parentheses. Independent variables standardized on 0–1 scale.
* significant at .10   ** significant at .05   *** significant at .01

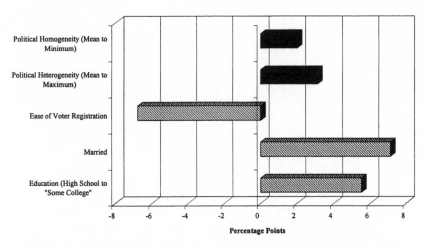

Figure 2.12. Impacts on the probability of voting. First differences generated from logistic regression; all control variables set at their means. Current Population Survey, 2000.

column predicts turnout in 2000, with political heterogeneity measured using data from 2000 only, while the remaining columns use the mean level of political heterogeneity to predict turnout in 2000, 1996, and 1992 respectively.[21] The results should look familiar, as they largely mirror those reported at the county level. About the only exception is the fact that in 2000, the heterogeneity effect is slightly larger than that for homogeneity, a slight deviation from the pattern we saw in the earlier table.

Because the substantive meaning of logit coefficients is not easily decipherable, Figure 2.12 converts them into a more intuitive metric—the impact on the probability that an individual will vote as the values of selected variables change. Each impact is calculated by holding the other variables constant at their means. These results are derived from the model of turnout in 2000, with the measure of political heterogeneity calculated using data from 2000 (in other words, from column 1 of Table 2.3). We see that the probability of an individual turning out to vote increases by 2 percentage points as one moves from the mean to the minimum level of political heterogeneity (the homogeneity effect), while the heterogeneity effect is slightly higher at 3 points. The impacts of some other variables are also included in Figure 2.12, in order to gauge the relative magnitude of these increases in probability.[22] As shown, they are a little smaller than the increase in education from high school graduate to attending "some college."

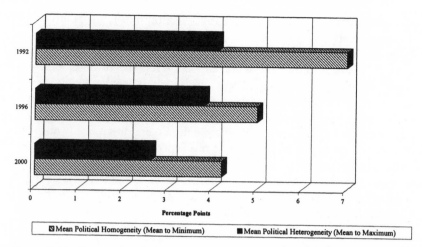

Figure 2.13. Comparing the impact of political heterogeneity and homogeneity on voter turnout. First differences generated from logistic regression; all control variables set at their means. Current Population Surveys.

Figure 2.13 similarly converts the results from Table 2.3, this time comparing the impact of mean political heterogeneity across the three presidential elections. For each, the story is extremely similar in kind, and only slightly different in degree. While the magnitude of the specific impacts varies a bit, in each case we see that the homogeneity effect is larger than that for heterogeneity. In 1992, for example, the homogeneity effect was almost 7 percentage points, compared to just under 4 points for the heterogeneity effect.

So What?

Amid these trees of statistical results, it is easy to lose sight of the forest of the overall theory. Essentially, the curvilinear relationship between political heterogeneity and voter turnout is evidence that voter turnout is driven by two motivations—civic and political—each of which is facilitated by the composition of an individual's community. If this is the case, it is logical to ask why the two effects do not simply cancel each other out. The reason they do not is that the causal processes leading to civic and political motivations are not simply the inverse of one another, which would imply that an increase in one means a decrease in the other. Recall that in Figure 2.5, the hypothesis is that we observe a rise in turnout as political heterogeneity increases because places where people have differing political views also have competitive elections. Returning to the calculus of voting, a competitive election means that individuals are more likely to believe that their vote will make a difference (a higher value for the "p" term), a perception facilitated by the mobilization efforts of political elites. In Figure 2.6, however, the turnout increases where there is political homogeneity because this is where civic norms are stronger. People in these communities have a stronger sense of civic duty (a higher value for the "D" term), as suggested by social capital theory. Because the belief that one's vote will make a difference is not precluded by a sense of duty, we should not expect a zero-sum trade-off between the two motivations for voting. It is just that, on average, people in politically homogeneous communities have a moderately stronger sense of civic duty, while people in heterogeneous communities have a moderately stronger sense that their vote will affect the outcome of the election.

CONCLUSION

This chapter's objective is to demonstrate that whether you vote depends on where you are. We have seen empirical results that are, I argue, a synthesis of two literatures that, taken alone, would each lead us to opposite conclusions about the relationship between the political composition of a community and its level of voter turnout. A longstanding body of research concludes that voter turnout is high in places characterized by political heterogeneity, where elections are most competitive. The social capital literature, however, suggests voter turnout should be high where political preferences are homogeneous. We have seen that both expectations are met. There is a curvilinear relationship between heterogeneity and turnout—it is high in the most homogeneous counties, dropping off toward the mean and then increasing as counties become more heterogeneous. This relationship holds across multiple years, in both aggregate- and individual-level data, and upon controlling for a host of rival causes. The explanation for the curvilinear relationship between heterogeneity and turnout rests on understanding the dual motivations for voter turnout. In homogeneous communities, turnout is *civically motivated*. On average, voters are more likely to go to the polls out of adherence to a civic norm. In places that are heterogeneous, however, people are more likely to vote because they feel their interests are threatened. Turnout in these communities is *politically motivated*.

Thus far, we have been able to reject a plausible alternative explanation for the curvilinear relationship between political heterogeneity and turnout—that it is simply due to other characteristics of those counties, or the people who reside in them. But it is one thing to demonstrate what does not explain a statistical relationship, and quite another to show what does. To this point we have seen that the contour of the data is consistent with the theory that voter turnout is driven by dual motivations, and that those motivations are more or less likely to be propagated in some places over others. The next step is to present some affirmative evidence in support of this theory, to show that *why you vote* depends on *where you are*. Chapter 3 takes up that task.

CHAPTER THREE

Further Implications of the Dual Motivations Theory

After having been introduced to suggestive evidence supporting the dual motivations theory in chapter 2, this chapter tests further implications of the theory. First, people are more likely to report having a civic motivation for voting in communities that are politically homogeneous, and more likely to cast a policy-motivated ballot in heterogeneous places. Next, multiple sources of data demonstrate that political homogeneity facilitates civically oriented public engagement, namely community voluntarism, while heterogeneity sparks political engagement, like marching in political protests or working on political campaigns. Finally, we also see microlevel evidence for the theory—interpersonal trust is higher in politically homogeneous communities, and the farther individuals are out of their community's ideological mainstream, the less they trust their neighbors.

CHAPTER 2 PRESENTS EVIDENCE that the dual motivations theory of public engagement could explain an otherwise unexpected relationship between political heterogeneity and voter turnout. Voter turnout is high in both homogeneous and heterogeneous places, or where elections are both the least and the most competitive. Figure 3.1 is a graphical reminder of the essentials of the theory. Voter turnout in politically homogeneous communities is more likely to be motivated by a sense of civic duty, while in heterogeneous communities people are more likely to vote because they feel they have a stake in the election. Chapter 2 also considered but discarded the possibility that the curvilinear relationship between political heterogeneity and voter turnout is owing to other characteristics of the high-participation communities.

A case has thus begun to be built for the dual motivations theory. However, if this evidence were presented in a court of law, a jury would likely not be willing to convict. While we have seen some evidence about who is not guilty, reasonable doubts remain about the suspect, as the evidence in favor of the theory is largely circumstantial. This chapter presents evidence explicitly implicating the dual motivations theory, hopefully enough to get a conviction. The case will be built by testing a series of observable implications that follow logically from the premises of the theory. As has been and will continue to be the case, wherever possible multiple

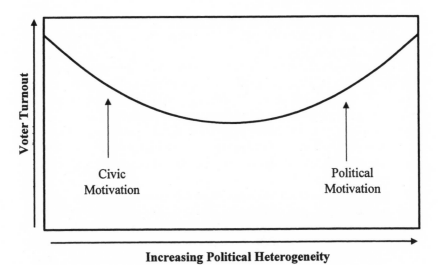

Figure 3.1. The dual motivations theory applied to voter turnout

sources of data will be brought to bear to answer the questions at hand. This way, we can be confident that any observed patterns are not idiosyncratic to one source of data, which in turn enhances our confidence in any conclusions about the general applicability of the theory.

The first test is perhaps the most straightforward—we will examine what people say motivates them to vote. Given that there is some controversy among social scientists over the attribution of motivations, however, the analysis also draws on data about people's behavior. As we will see, the dual motivations theory finds support in both types of data—attitudinal and behavioral. Standing alone, each would constitute fairly persuasive evidence in favor of the theory, but in tandem they make a more convincing case that voter turnout is driven by different processes in different places.

WHY PEOPLE SAY THEY DO WHAT THEY DO

Perhaps the most straightforward test of a theory that makes claims about motivations is simply to ask people what motivates them to do what they do. According to the dual motivations theory, people in politically homogeneous and heterogeneous communities should, on average, be more likely to offer different explanations for voting. Where it is homogeneous, civic norms are hypothesized to be stronger, meaning that we should expect voters to report that they vote for Tocquevillian reasons—out of a sense of duty. Heterogeneity, on the other hand, spurs Madisonian motivations; people vote because they wish to advance their policy interests.

It is possible to test whether voters' motivations differ with data from the Citizen Participation Study.[1] This extensive analysis of Americans' civic and political engagement included asking people to report their motivation for participating in various forms of collective action, or *why they do what they do*. Most important for our purposes, the survey asked voters about their motivations for turning out at the polls, with a question that succinctly captures the essence of civically motivated participation as I have defined it. Voters who cast a ballot in the most recent local or national election were asked whether they voted because it was their "duty as a citizen," indicating whether this was a "not very, somewhat, or very important" reason. Conversely, voters were also asked to indicate the importance of the "chance to influence government policy" as a motivation, which reflects a vote motivated by political concerns.

Although these two questions are ideally worded for testing the self-reported motivations of voters in different communities, the format in which they were asked nonetheless sets the bar extremely high for a test of the dual motivations theory. The theory predicts that duty trumps policy in homogeneous communities, and policy trumps duty in heterogeneous communities. This implies that the best test of voters' motivations would require them to make a trade-off between the two motivations. In the Citizen Participation Study, however, voters were asked about each motivation serially, and could thus report that each one was equally important. As a result, very high proportions of voters reported that both duty and policy motivated their decision to vote. Sixty-one percent of voters indicated that influencing government policy was a very important reason that they voted, with another 28 percent saying that it was somewhat important. The distribution of responses is even more skewed for the question about duty. Seventy-seven percent of voters reported that civic duty is a very important reason for casting a ballot, while only 5 percent reported that it is not very important. That such a high percentage of respondents reported voting because of these two motivations makes them difficult to model, as it is hard to explain variation when there is little variation to explain. A more refined measure of voters' motivations would allow for a better test of the dual motivations theory. On the other hand, if we are able to discern a relationship with such a skewed dependent variable, this should only bolster our confidence that we have found evidence in support of the theory.

The hypotheses are straightforward. First, voters should be more likely to cite a civic motivation for turning out at the polls in communities that are politically homogeneous, with civic motivations declining as

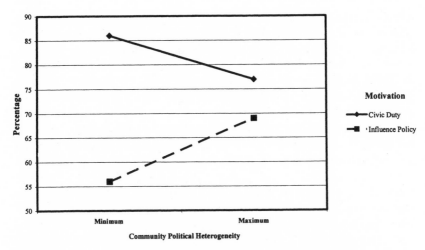

Figure 3.2. Impact of community political heterogeneity on motivations for voting

heterogeneity rises. Concomitantly, a political motivation should be least common in homogeneous communities, rising with heterogeneity. These hypotheses are tested by regressing each of the two self-reported motivations on community-level political heterogeneity, controlling for every variable used in the models we saw in chapter 2, as well as a few more.[2] Because the hypotheses are linear in nature, political heterogeneity has been coded as a single linear term, ranging from the most homogeneous to the most heterogeneous.[3]

Figure 3.2 displays results from the two models.[4] Each line in the figure represents the predicted probability that the given motivation is a "very important" reason for voting. Along the horizontal axis the level of heterogeneity in each county varies from its minimum to its maximum. For both motivations, the impact of political heterogeneity is as hypothesized. Ceteris paribus, moving from the least to the most competitive county results in a nine-point drop in the probability a voter reports that duty was a very important reason for casting a ballot. The impact of political diversity on casting a politically motivated vote is of a comparable magnitude, but in the opposite direction—an increase of thirteen points.

These results are compelling evidence in favor of the dual motivations theory. As preferences within a community become more homogeneous, people are more likely to report voting out of a sense of duty. As preferences become more heterogeneous, voting is more often driven by a political motivation. Yet while there is an attractive simplicity to self-reported motivations as evidence for the dual motivations theory, many social scientists will nonetheless reject it as unconvincing. There is considerable dispute over whether we should believe people when they tell us why they do what they do.[5] It turns out that sometimes people lie. Or, to put it more charitably, sometimes their responses to a survey question reflect their interpretation of what is socially desirable—they say what they think they are supposed to say. Social desirability bias of this sort plagues survey research, as evidenced by the effort devoted to the accurate measurement of such socially desirable behavior as voter turnout and church attendance (Abramson and Claggett 1986, 1989, 1991; Anderson and Silver 1986; Silver, Anderson, and Abramson 1986; Hadaway, Marler, and Chaves 1993). In this case, however, bias due to what people perceive to be normative is less of a problem than usual, since we are actually interested in what people believe to be so-cially desirable—that is, after all, what it means to say that something is a social norm.

WHAT PEOPLE ACTUALLY DO

Even though social desirability bias may not be a fatal flaw in a study of norm-driven behavior, the dark cloud of questionable validity that hangs over self-reported motivation nonetheless compels another perspective on the question. To assuage concerns over the validity of self-reports, I also turn to an alternative method of uncovering voters' motivations. Rather than overtly asking them why they voted, we can ask them about their other behavior. Voting, according to the dual motivations theory, can be driven by both political and civic motivations. If we could iden-tify a form of collective action that was predominantly *civic* in its moti-vation, then it should be common where voter turnout is primarily civi-cally motivated and less so where turnout is driven by political considerations. In operational terms, it should have a very different rela-tionship to a community's level of political heterogeneity than voter turnout. The relationship should be negative, not curvilinear. Similarly, if we could identify collective action that is best characterized as politically motivated, it should be more common in heterogeneous than homoge-neous communities. It should be positively related to political hetero-geneity.

The advantage of behavioral measures is that they allow us to skirt the question of whether people are accurately telling us why they do what they do. The catch, however, is that the whole exercise rests on identify-ing behavior that is primarily civically motivated and that which is largely political in nature. Because this distinction is critical to the analysis that follows, I draw on multiple sources in order to classify activities as falling into one category over another.

One source of data that provides some purchase on the question of what motivates different forms of collective action is the aforementioned Citizen Participation Study. In addition to being asked why they vote, participants in this study were also asked why they engage in a host of other activities, including contributing money to a political party and working on a political campaign. Activities like these are "political" in nature by the definitions undergirding the dual motivations theory, since influencing government action is their primary motivation. Thus we would not expect them to be motivated by civic considerations to the same extent as voting. This expectation is borne out by the data. For example, while 77 percent of voters said that acting out of duty was a very important reason for turning out to vote, only 43 percent of those who contributed money to a political party said the same. This difference is particularly notable given the fact that participants in the study were not asked to make any trade-offs among the possible motivations or to choose the most important motivation. Presumably the percentage choosing "civic duty" as a reason for giving money to a political party would be much lower if the survey forced a choice of one's primary motivation. Significantly, among the activities included in the study, none is as civically motivated as voting.[6]

The Citizen Participation Study allows us to compare the degree to which the various activities included within the survey have a civic or political motivation, and thus provides empirical support for a claim that sits at the foundation of the dual motivations theory—when it comes to their motivations, not all forms of public engagement are alike. However, for our purposes the study nonetheless has its limitations, as it was specifically designed to examine participation in activities that are motivated by the advancement of political preferences. In other words, it focuses on political engagement and thus contains no measures of civic engagement as it has been defined here.

Finding a civically motivated form of public engagement will thus require us to look beyond the Citizen Participation Study. The challenge is to find a type of engagement that is public—directed beyond oneself or one's immediate family—but without the influence of public policy as its objective. One form of engagement that meets these criteria is community service, or volunteering for charitable causes. Because the behavioral test of the dual motivations theory rests on this claim, namely that volunteering is primarily motivated by civic and not political concerns, it thus warrants some justification.

VOLUNTEERING

I am not the first to make the claim that there is a qualitative difference between community service and political activity. Numerous other observers have recently made the same observation, noting that at the same time Americans' political participation has been declining, their participation in community service is on the upswing (Putnam 2000; Crenson and Ginsberg 2002). The increasingly common concern among many knowledgeable observers is that one-on-one volunteering has begun to supplant action directed at policy solutions to social problems, particularly among younger Americans (Walker 2002). In other words, community voluntarism has begun to crowd out political activity—a claim that only makes sense if the two really are distinct types of activity. The National Association of Secretaries of State, for example, has released a report that expresses precisely this concern, presenting evidence that most people view volunteer service as the antithesis of political activity (National Association of Secretaries of State 1999). A similar report by Harvard University's Institute of Politics comes to the same conclusion (Institute of Politics 2000), as does yet another study by the Panetta Institute (Leon and Sylvia Panetta Institute for Public Policy 2000). In a thorough review of the literature on civic education, William Galston characterizes community voluntarism as "an alternative to official politics" (2001, 220). The Panetta Institute is more colorful, concluding that young Americans "are turned off by politics, turned on by other public service." Typically, this discussion of whether community voluntarism supplants political activity has a subtle ideological tone to it. Liberals are more likely than conservatives to believe that it is a problem if people are turning away from government to effect social change (Barber 1992). My point here is not to weigh in on either side of this normative debate, but rather to point out that there can only be a debate because both sides agree that there is something different about community voluntarism and political activity. The difference is that voluntarism is not directed at affecting public policy while political activity is—the fundamental distinction between civic and political participation as I define them.

Empirical evidence supports the intuitive distinction between the motivations for community voluntarism versus what Galston refers to as official politics. For example, Independent Sector, an organization that tracks Americans' rates of voluntarism, commissioned a comprehensive survey of Americans on their frequency of and motivations for volunteering and found that fewer than 4 percent of Americans reported volunteering for political organizations and/or causes within the previous year.[7] For the purposes of this analysis, however, even this number is inflated. In an example of the conceptual confusion surrounding the terms "civic" and "political," Independent Sector's political volunteering category includes activities that are more appropriately labeled civic, like volunteering for "community groups."[8]

The best evidence for the civic/political divide among types of participation comes from a classic study by Sidney Verba and Norman Nie (1972), and an equally ambitious new one by Cliff Zukin, Scott Keeter, and their colleagues (Zukin et al. 2006; see also Jenkins et al. 2003). In their exhaustive *Participation in America*, Verba and Nie draw a distinction between activity that is conflictual and nonconflictual, contrasting electoral activities like political campaigning with intrinsically cooperative activities like membership in (most) voluntary associations (53). The distinction between conflictual and nonconflictual activities should seem familiar, as it parallels the differences between civic and political participation as I define them. Much like Verba and Nie over thirty years ago, more recently Zukin and Keeter's research team set out to measure the full array of participation in the United States. And, much like Verba and Nie's study, Zukin, Keeter, and their colleagues have found a fundamental distinction between civically and politically motivated activity. The innovation of the Zukin-Keeter study is that it did not presuppose the activities in which Americans participate. The project was designed to ensure that the measures of participation in the usual sources of data employed by social scientists were not missing anything. Thus, rather than start with the batch of activities that are typically included in studies of participation, the Zukin-Keeter team convened a series of focus groups to ask people to describe the ways in which they are publicly engaged. From these sessions, they constructed a scale of nineteen activities, which has been tested and retested in surveys with nationally representative samples. Great care has been taken to maximize the validity of the scale, including experiments designed to lessen the problems of social desirability bias and faulty memory.

Zukin, Keeter, and their colleagues have produced an extremely thorough array of almost every imaginable form of participation. Using factor analysis—a statistical technique that allows the analyst to see how variables, in this case types of participation, are related to one another—they have found that these activities cluster into three groups. One they label *civic* activity, which includes regular "community service or volunteer activity."[9] In fact, community voluntarism has the highest loading on the civic dimension.

Zukin, Keeter, et al. find that the remaining activities can be grouped into two factors. One they call the *electoral* dimension, the other *political voice*.[10] They are similar in that both have the objective of influencing public policy, and thus constitute different types of politically motivated participation. They only differ in the means through which that objective

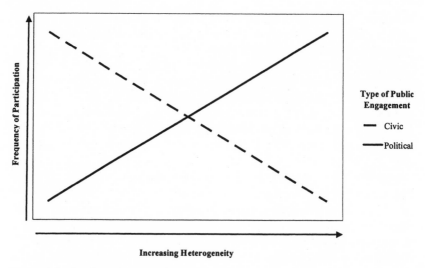

Figure 3.3. Dual motivations theory

is sought. Electoral activities, as their name implies, involve participation in a political campaign. Expressing political voice, on the other hand, constitutes activities outside of a campaign setting.

The Zukin-Keeter study allows us to pull together the strands of evidence from other sources that community voluntarism represents one type of participation, and actions taken to influence government represent quite another. The bottom line is that we have seen consistent evidence from multiple sources that this intuitive distinction holds up under empirical scrutiny. With that distinction in sharp relief, the theory of dual motivations then leads to the following hypotheses, again displayed graphically in Figure 3.3. As political heterogeneity within communities rises, we should expect civic participation to fall. Likewise, Figure 3.3 also shows us the hypothesis for the relationship between heterogeneity and the two dimensions of political participation, electoral activity and political voice. Here the slope of the line is positive.

CIVIC PARTICIPATION

The first step is testing the relationship between political heterogeneity and community voluntarism. Fortuitously, this analysis can be performed with the same source of data used to model voter turnout in chapter 2, the Current Population Survey. In September 2002 the CPS included a short battery of questions regarding participation in volunteer activities.[11] Recall the virtues of the CPS, which is an unparalleled source of data because of its enormous sample size and extremely high response rate. By using the CPS to model both voter turnout (see chapter 2) and volunteering, we do not have to worry about so-called house effects when comparing results from different surveys, which can result in systematic differences in measurement across surveys.[12] The CPS maintains an identical interview protocol and sampling frame from year to year. To ensure that the volunteering being measured is truly civic in nature, all volunteering for a "political party or advocacy group" has been excluded (although this represents a miniscule 0.8 percent of all volunteering reported in the CPS). As with the models in chapter 2 that use CPS data, again we have reason to think that the impact of political heterogeneity on voluntarism is understated, given that the CPS only allows the analyst to identify the location of respondents who live in metropolitan areas, while some of the most homogeneous communities are outside a metropolitan environment.

The model for volunteering parallels the models we have seen before and includes all of the same control variables at both the individual and aggregate levels.[13] Once more, political heterogeneity is a linear term, as the theory of dual motivations leads us to hypothesize that as political heterogeneity rises, the rate of volunteering falls. Note that the models also account for ethnic, racial, and income heterogeneity in each respondent's community, owing to the extant research which suggests that these alternative ways of measuring heterogeneity have an impact on civic activity (Alesina and La Ferrara 2000; Costa and Kahn 2003a). To ensure that the relationship between political heterogeneity and volunteering observed in 2002 is not somehow idiosyncratic to one particular year, this model has also been replicated for a similar measure of volunteering in the 1989 CPS. Table 3.1 presents the results, displaying the relationships between political heterogeneity and voluntarism in 2002 and 1989.[14]

As predicted, we find that partisan heterogeneity has a negative, statistically significant relationship to volunteering. Reinforcing the conclusion that 2002 is not somehow anomalous, the same result is observed in 1989.[15] Figure 3.4 provides a graphical display of the 2002 results. Again setting all of the control variables at their means (or modes, for categorical variables), we see that the predicted probability of volunteering declines as communities become increasingly heterogeneous, in this case by a sizable seventeen percentage points. Another way of tracking the decline in volunteering is to note that, all else equal, residents of homogenous places annually spend an average of sixty-three hours volunteering, contrasted with forty-one hours for people who live in the most heterogeneous communities.

Consistent with the principle that multiple sources of data brought to

TABLE 3.1
Political Heterogeneity and Volunteering

	Volunteer at least once in previous year, 2002	Hours spent volunteering in previous week, 2002	Volunteer at least once in previous year, 1989	Hours spent volunteering in previous week, 1989
	Logistic regression	Ordered logistic regression	Logistic regression	Ordered logistic regression
Political Context				
Mean political heterogeneity (minimum to maximum)	−0.716*** (0.090)	−0.608*** (0.084)	−0.193** (0.080)	−0.304*** (0.099)
Observations	54,466	54,467	58,156	58,156
Pseudo-R^2	0.09	0.06	0.08	0.06

Source: Current Population Survey.

Note: Robust standard errors in parentheses. Independent variables standardized on 0–1 scale. Models also control for individual-and community-level variables. Individual: education, income, age, age squared, marital status, race, and gender. Community: % with a college degree, mean household income (logged), urbanicity, population density, residential mobility, mean commuting time, ethnic heterogeneity, racial heterogeneity, income heterogeneity, South, Upper Midwest. ‘See Table C2 in appendix C for the full results.

* significant at .10   ** significant at .05   *** significant at .01

bear on a question strengthen the certainty of our conclusions, Figure 3.4 also presents the results of an essentially identical analysis from an entirely different data set, the National Household Education Survey (NHES). In 1996, the National Center for Education Statistics surveyed a representative sample of parents of school-age children by telephone and asked an array of questions pertaining to their civic attitudes and behavior. These data are presented here to foreshadow chapter 5, in which this same survey is used to examine adolescents' civic behavior, as parents and their children both participated in the study. For the topic at hand, the relevant inquiry was simply whether the adult respondents are involved in any ongoing community service work.[16] As has been the standard practice thus far, the individual-level survey data of the NHES was merged with information about each respondent's county. Unlike the CPS, in this case there is no artificial truncation of partisan heterogeneity, as there were no restrictions placed on identifying the

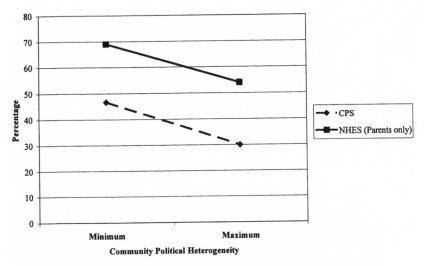

Figure 3.4. Impact of community political heterogeneity on civic participation (volunteering). All control variables set to their means. Current Population Survey, 2000, and 1996 National Household Education Survey.

location of each respondent. With the NHES it is possible to replicate the essentials of the analysis done with the CPS data, including a similar dependent variable and a parallel set of control variables. Recall, however, that unlike the CPS this was not a survey of the U.S. population in general, but parents of school-age children. Also, the CPS is a face-to-face interview, while the NHES was conducted over the telephone. While the different populations from which the samples were drawn and the different modes of survey administration mean that we cannot make precise comparisons between the results from these data and those from the CPS, there are enough similarities to warrant some general comparisons.[17]

It turns out that the differences between the two surveys are overshadowed by their similarities. We again see the same downward-sloping line—as political heterogeneity goes up, volunteering goes down. Presumably owing to the different populations from which their samples were drawn, the absolute frequency of self-reported volunteering is considerably higher in the NHES than the CPS. We would expect parents of school-age children to have a higher rate of voluntarism than the population in general, although some of the difference between the two surveys is undoubtedly due to differences in sampling and question wording (that is, house effects). Even though the two surveys show a marked gap in the absolute level of volunteering, both show an unmistakable similarity in the *relationship* between heterogeneity and the rate of voluntarism. In other words, the CPS findings have been replicated in a survey with a different sampling frame, a different means of administration, and even a different question wording for the measure of the dependent variable.

Owing to the existing literature that has shown the impact of ethnic, racial, and income heterogeneity on civic activity, county-level measures of these were also included in the CPS and NHES models. The results are mixed. In the CPS model all three have the expected negative sign, but only income heterogeneity is statistically significant. In the NHES model none of the three reaches statistical significance, and ethnic heterogeneity even has the wrong sign. Compared to partisan heterogeneity, in other words, these other forms of heterogeneity are inconsistently related to voluntarism. Once again, we see that political heterogeneity provides more empirically robust results than these other dimensions of heterogeneity.

POLITICAL PARTICIPATION

Having seen evidence supporting the hypothesis that greater heterogeneity leads to less civic activity, the analysis turns to testing the second hypothesis: as political heterogeneity goes up, so does political participation. Unfortunately, it is not possible to draw on the CPS to do so, as it has never included measures of either electoral activism or political voice. However, the source on which the analysis draws is nonetheless familiar—the Citizen Participation Study introduced earlier. This survey includes measures that correspond to both the electoral and voice dimensions of political participation. Regarding their participation in recent political campaigns, respondents were asked whether they had (a) given money; or (b) contributed time to a political party or candidate within the previous election cycle. Electoral activism is thus defined as having done either (or both) of these things. For political voice there is only a single measure, whether the respondent has taken part in a protest, march, or demonstration in the previous year.[18]

The analysis parallels what we have seen already, with partisan heterogeneity the key independent variable and a slate of control variables at both the individual and aggregate levels.[19] In both models, the relationship between partisan heterogeneity and political activity is positive and statistically significant.[20] In other words, both forms of political participation increase as heterogeneity increases—precisely as hypothesized. The results are displayed graphically in Figure 3.5. The effects are notable.

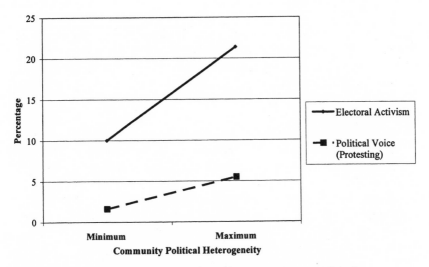

Figure 3.5. Impact of community political heterogeneity on political participation. All control variables set to their means. Citizen Participation Study.

There is an increase of about 11 points in the probability of electoral activism as heterogeneity moves from its minimum to its maximum value, and roughly 4 points for protesting over the same range. As an uncommon activity, the probability of marching in a protest has a relatively low rate of incidence. Another perspective on that 4-point gain is that it represents a threefold increase.

Once again, it is worth taking a look at how the other measures of heterogeneity fared. Does increasing ethnic, racial, or income heterogeneity lead to more politically motivated activity? The story with political participation parallels what we see for civic participation—the other measures of heterogeneity have what can only be described as an inconsistent relationship with electoral activism and the expression of political voice. In this case, the inconsistency is not across different data sets but rather within one data set across the two types of activity. Racial heterogeneity does not have an impact that even approaches statistical significance in either model. Ethnic heterogeneity is positive and significant for protesting, but not for electoral activism, while income heterogeneity has a positive and statistically significant impact on electoral activism, but no effect on protesting. Table 3.2 summarizes the results for the different types of heterogeneity across the models of civic and political participation, underscoring the point that while partisan heterogeneity behaves as

TABLE 3.2
Summary: Impacts of Heterogeneity on Civic and Political Participation

	Civic Participation		Political Participation	
	Volunteering	Volunteering	Electoral Activism	Political Voice
	Current Population Survey, 2002	National Household Education Survey, 1996	Citizen Participation Study, 1990	Citizen Participation Study, 1990
Type of Heterogeneity				
Partisan	−	−	+	+
Ethnic	−	nr	nr	+
Racial	nr	nr	nr	nr
Income	−	nr	+	nr

+ relationship is positive and statistically significant
− relationship is negative and statistically significant
nr no statistically significant relationship

expected in every case, the effects for the other forms of heterogeneity are sporadic at best.

RECAP

It is perhaps useful to pause and recap what we have learned from the fore-going analysis. The empirical findings are clear. Civically motivated partici-pation is high in politically homogeneous places, falling as communities be-come more heterogeneous; politically motivated participation is low in politically homogeneous communities, rising along with heterogeneity. The theoretical importance of these two inverse relationships is that they offer evidence for the dual motivations theory of voter turnout. In homogeneous communities, where the theory of dual motivations leads to the hypothesis that we observe high voter turnout because of strong civic norms, we also observe a high rate of civically motivated participation. In heterogeneous communities, where the hypothesis is that we observe high voter turnout because of political motivations, we also observe a high rate of politically driven participation. This evidence, in turn, is consistent with the self-reported motivations for voter turnout in homogeneous versus heteroge-neous communities. In sum, we have seen two disparate streams of evidence converge in favor of the dual motivations theory.

Variations on a Common Theme

In social science, there is inevitably slippage between a theoretical concept and its empirical measurement. This analysis began with the basic idea that in communities where people are more likely to disagree with one another, they are also more likely to turn to politically motivated collective action. And where they are more likely to agree with one another, they more frequently engage in civic forms of participation. In order to test these propositions the analysis rests on two fundamental decisions, each of which affects the other. First was the decision about how to measure commonality of preferences, and second was what constitutes a reasonable approximation of community. Any measure of the former had to be available for the latter and, obviously, vice versa. The degree of consensus, or heterogeneity, was thus operationalized as the mean level of competitiveness in presidential elections, while the county (and in some cases the metropolitan area) was used as a reasonable approximation of community.

Admittedly, the measure of political heterogeneity and the definition of community are both open to reasonable criticisms. While heterogeneity has been measured using an average of the presidential vote, clearly two people can agree on their vote for president and disagree on myriad other policy-relevant matters; of course, the inverse is equally true. An even more damaging criticism, perhaps, can be leveled at the county or the metropolitan area as the boundary for an individual's community. Across the states, counties vary widely in size (in terms of both area and population) as well as their political and social significance. Although, all things considered, counties give us a reasonable sense of an individual's mid-range social context, doubts may nonetheless linger.

Legitimate objections can thus be raised as to how the two fundamental components of the dual motivations theory have been defined. To ensure that these results are not merely a statistical artifact of how either community or heterogeneity has been operationalized, the analysis turns to a very different type of data. With these data, both community and heterogeneity are *operationally distinct from* but *theoretically consistent with* what has been used thus far. If we see the results take the same shape, the evidence in favor of the theory of dual motivations is strengthened.

The data to be used are from the Social Capital Community Benchmark Survey (SCCBS), which has a very different structure than the other data sets employed to this point. So far, each of the individual-level data sets used has consisted of a survey administered to a representative sample of the U.S. population, to which data about the geographic areas represented in the sample were appended retroactively. The SCCBS, however, uses an alternative research design. Rather than interviews conducted with a single nationally representative sample, it consists of representative samples drawn from forty-one different communities. For the purposes of the SCCBS, community is not defined as a single geographic unit like county, but instead includes geographic areas that are more naturally thought of as constituting communities.[21] The chief advantage of this two-level design is that for every survey question asked of an individual, it is possible to construct an aggregate measure for that community. With the other surveys employed to this point, we are limited to merging data that have been collected at the appropriate level of aggregation, mostly by the U.S. Census Bureau. With a survey like the SCCBS, however, you can ask individuals whether, say, they prefer Coke or Pepsi, and then also calculate the percentage of people within a given community who are Coke or Pepsi drinkers.

With the SCCBS, we need not rely on the average presidential vote in a community as a gauge for political heterogeneity. Instead, political heterogeneity is defined as the distribution of ideological preferences within a community, which is arguably closer to its theoretical roots. Recall that partisanship, operationalized as how one votes in presidential elections, has been shown to be a better predictor of preferences (or interests, or values) than the demographic measures that have been employed in the literature thus far. But an alternative—and arguably better—measure of preferences than partisanship is a person's ideology.[22] At the least, ideology is a good complement to presidential voting, since we would expect it to be correlated with an array of preferences. Empirically, this is what we observe. When ideology is used instead of partisanship to predict the eleven issue preferences we saw in chapter 2 (Table 2.1, Figure 2.4), it performs just as well. Even a cursory familiarity with American politics makes clear, however, that they are not exactly the same thing (although they are becoming increasingly aligned). Again, empirical evidence confirms the intuition. In fact, when party identification and ideology are put side by side in each of the same eleven models, in most cases they both remain statistically significant. Given that our ideal measure of preferences should maximize leverage or, in other words, will have the most explanatory power over a wide array of issues, ideology perhaps has a slight edge over partisanship. Across these eleven models, in no case is partisanship statistically significant when ideology is not. In a few cases, however, the coefficient for ideology clears the bar for statistical significance when partisanship does not (specifically, for the issues of abortion, whether mothers should work outside of the home, and the best approach to fighting crime). The consistent results for ideology are intuitively appealing, as the very concept of ideology connotes a unity of opinion across a range of issues.

The SCCBS asked respondents about their ideology with a straightforward question.

> Thinking politically and socially, how would you describe your own general outlook—as being very conservative, moderately conservative, middle-of-the-road, moderately liberal, or very liberal?

By wording the question about ideology this way, the SCCBS corrects for a potential problem with using partisanship to measure heterogeneity, namely that the measure has an overly narrow focus on political opinions. Respondents are asked about their "general outlook" on both political and social matters, thus encompassing their views more broadly.[23]

Given the nested design of the SCCBS, this five-point measure of ideology not only can tell us the respondent's personal ideology. It is also possible to calculate the *distribution* of ideological preferences in each community. Ideological distribution is simply calculated as the standard deviation of ideology within each community. The greater the standard deviation, the greater a community's ideological heterogeneity.[24]

We now have a measure of political heterogeneity that is conceptually consistent with the theoretical framework but nonetheless operationally distinct from a community's partisan composition. Furthermore, the designation of "community" is quite different than in the previous models, as no longer is the county or MSA the level of aggregation. Referring back to Figure 3.3, where the hypothesized relationships between heterogeneity and participation—both civic and political—are illustrated, we are reminded of the observable implications stemming from the dual motivations theory. Civically motivated participation, namely volunteering, should be negatively related to the standard deviation of ideology within a respondent's community. Politically motivated participation, on the other hand, should be positively related to it. In other words, where the distribution of ideological preferences is broad, the likelihood of political conflict should increase, and consequently we should observe a high rate of political participation. Conversely, where the distribution is narrow, civic norms should be stronger and civically motivated participation should be more common.

Figure 3.6 ranks, in descending order, the ideological heterogeneity of the forty-one communities included in the SCCBS. Glancing down the list, the measure of ideological heterogeneity would seem to have face validity. The most homogeneous community in the sample is rural South Dakota, while the most heterogeneous is Boston. Presumably these are two areas of the country that the casual observer would expect to vary considerably in the degree of their heterogeneity. Knowing only the communities at the end points of the distribution might leave one with the

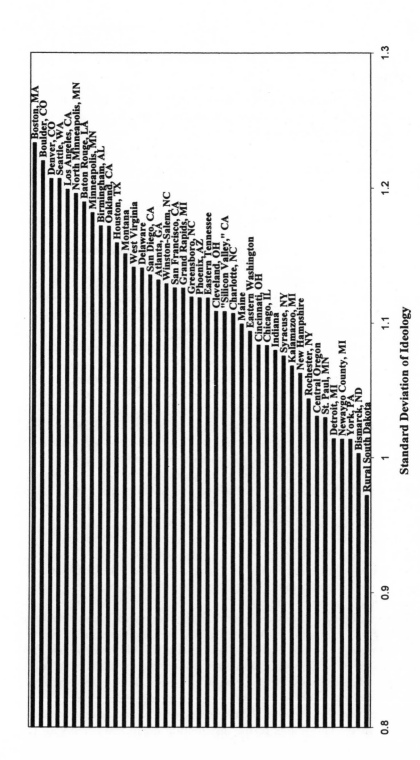

Standard Deviation of Ideology

Figure 3.6. Comparing communities' ideological heterogeneity in the social capital community benchmark survey

impression that ideological heterogeneity is simply determined by the percentage of a community's population that is urban. A closer inspection, however, reveals that this is not the case. Among the most homogeneous communities we find St. Paul, Minnesota, and Rochester, New York, as well as Bismarck, North Dakota, and metropolitan Detroit.[25] Among the most heterogeneous are Baton Rouge, Louisiana, and Boulder, Colorado. Interspersed are urban areas like Chicago and the state of Montana, which is predominantly rural. Some readers may be surprised at some of the relative rankings, but in looking them over it is important to remember that this is a measure of these communities' ideological— not racial, ethnic, or economic—heterogeneity.

The hypotheses are as before. Civic and political activity should move in opposite directions as ideological heterogeneity rises: civic participation increases, political participation decreases. Volunteering is again the measure of civically oriented participation. In this case respondents were asked how many times in the past twelve months they volunteered,[26] resulting in a scale from 0 to 60.[27]

On the political side, the SCCBS has multiple measures of political voice, all of which have been combined into an index.[28] These include

1. signing a petition within the past twelve months
2. attending a political rally within the past twelve months
3. participating in a demonstration, protest, boycott, or march within the past twelve months
4. belonging to a political organization
5. belonging to an organization that has taken local action for social or political reform within the past twelve months

There are, unfortunately, no measures of explicitly electoral activity in the SCCBS.

The test of whether ideological heterogeneity dampens voluntarism will parallel the analyses that we have already seen. However, it is necessary to account for the nested, or hierarchical, nature of the SCCBS data, and thus diverge from the methodology of the previous models. This requires a different econometric strategy than has been used to this point, a technique known as hierarchical modeling. A hierarchical model essentially consists of multiple models, one for each level at which we have data. In this case, one level is the individual, and the other is the community. The level-1 model thus includes an array of individual-level independent variables, just as we have seen before. The innovation of using a hierarchical model is that it is possible to let the intercept of the individual—or level-1—model be a function of the community—or level-2—variables. The resulting parameter estimates thus account for the impact of individual and community variables simultaneously.[29] As it is a

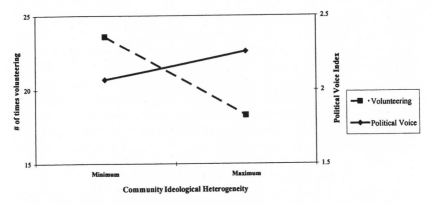

Figure 3.7. Impact of community ideological heterogeneity on public engagement. All control variables set to their means. Social Capital Community Benchmark Survey.

count, the distribution of the volunteering data is estimated with a poisson model. The political voice index is estimated with a linear model.[30]

The hypotheses for both civic and political activity find support. Volunteering falls as communities become more heterogeneous, while political activity rises. Figure 3.7 displays the impact of ideological heterogeneity on both volunteering and the political voice index, as calculated from the two hierarchical models (and holding every control variable at its mean). As expected, the lines move in opposite directions. Ceteris paribus, someone volunteers about five times fewer per year in the most heterogeneous community compared to the place that is the least heterogeneous. By way of comparison, this is about twice the impact of getting married (2.5), roughly the same as moving from a place with the greatest to the least residential stability (5.7), but a little less than the impact of increasing one's education from a high school diploma to a college degree (7.4). The impact of ideological heterogeneity on the political voice index is about 0.19 of the scale, which by itself is not a terribly informative number. Again, comparing this variable with the impact of other variables is perhaps the most illuminating way to interpret its magnitude. Ideological heterogeneity's impact is roughly the same as the impact of residential stability (0.16), but less than the gap between a high school diploma and college degree (0.35).

Both of these models also test whether racial and/or income heterogeneity has an impact on civic and political activity. (Since the SCCBS did not include any questions about ethnicity, it is not possible to construct a measure of ethnic heterogeneity.) Racial heterogeneity for each SCCBS community was calculated in the same way as it was for each county in the models presented earlier, except that instead of external census data, the analysis relies on data internal to the SCCBS (that is, the question on the SCCBS questionnaire that asked people to identify their race). Heterogeneity of income is measured like it was for ideology, as the standard deviation of income within each community.

In the above models, again we find that these other measures of heterogeneity are not related to civic and political activity in any theoretically satisfying way. Racial heterogeneity is negative in both cases, although it does not reach the conventional level of statistical significance. Income heterogeneity is a statistically significant predictor of political activity, but in a negative, not positive, direction. It has a positive sign in the volunteering model, but the coefficient is miles away from statistical certainty.

In summary, even though it is a different type of data analyzed using a different statistical methodology, results from the SCCBS lead us to the same conclusions as those drawn from the previous models we have seen. Civically motivated participation is more common in places characterized by homogeneity, and politically motivated activity is more common in places characterized by heterogeneity. These findings hold under two very different specifications of heterogeneity, and two very different ways of operationalizing an individual's community.

Hints of the Causal Mechanism

Even though our focus has been on the level of political heterogeneity within a community, it is important to remember that the causal mechanism in question is actually *not* the level of heterogeneity per se. Rather, the mechanism underlying dual motivations theory—particularly the explanation of why homogeneity leads to civic behavior—is very much a microlevel process, as it is built on suppositions regarding the nature of interpersonal interaction. Trust among people is the social lubricant that smooths the way for collective action. In a nutshell: when you perceive yourself as being like your neighbors you are more likely to trust them. Trust leads to shared norms, like a norm of reciprocity, which in turn facilitates collective action.

A large literature on interpersonal trust has developed, most of which has found that people who are more trusting are more likely to engage in civic participation (Wuthnow 1999), although there is disagreement over which way the causal arrow runs (Brehm and Rahn 1997; Uslaner 2000, 2002). Therefore, one implication of the claim that homogeneity leads to civically motivated behavior is that people in homogeneous communities should be characterized by, relatively speaking, a high degree of interpersonal trust. The SCCBS allows us to test that proposition, which if it holds is another piece of evidence in support of the dual motivations theory.

In addition to its sampling methodology, another innovation of the SCCBS is the care that was taken in asking questions about various facets of trust. Omnibus surveys like the General Social Survey and National Election Studies have longstanding time series on what is often labeled generalized trust, questions that ask respondents about whether they trust "people in general." For the purposes of the question at hand, interpreting the relationship between homogeneity and responses to these questions would be problematic. Perhaps people in homogeneous communities trust their neighbors but are suspicious of outsiders. Later on, in chapter 5, we will see evidence consistent with this claim. Uslaner (2000) argues that the standard trust items are correlated with trust in strangers, not neighbors, suggesting that a different measure of trust is needed.

The SCCBS allows us to skirt the ambiguity in interpreting the questions about trust, as it includes a question that specifically asks whether you trust "people in your neighborhood." Respondents could respond that they trust them a lot, some, only a little, or not at all. Since the theory at work specifically predicts that trust in one's neighbors should decrease as heterogeneity rises, we should find that this measure is negatively related to the dispersion of ideological preferences in one's community. More heterogeneity, less trust.

We turn to the same type of hierarchical model introduced earlier, now with the measure of trust in one's neighbors as the dependent variable. In addition to the relationship between ideological heterogeneity and trust, however, the SCCBS allows us to push a little further in understanding the individual-level processes that result in the low level of civic activity in heterogeneous communities. To this point, the explanatory factors in focus have been the aggregate characteristics of an individual's community, whether it was the community's partisan composition or ideological distribution. The analysis has not dealt with the characteristics of individuals, except as control variables. The causal process that has been described, however, occurs among individuals. Social capital theory states that norms of reciprocity strengthen as individuals come to trust one another, and that trust is driven, at least in part, by individuals' perceptions that they share preferences with their neighbors. We would expect, therefore, that individuals whose preferences are not held in common within their community are less likely to have a place in the virtuous circle of trust and reciprocity that has come to be described as social capital. Operationally, we should thus observe that the farther individuals' own ideologies fall out of the mainstream within a community,

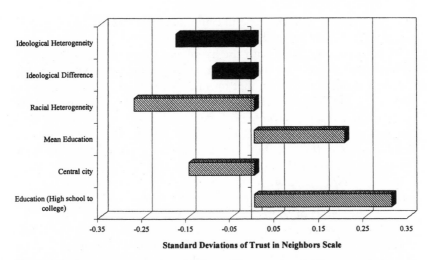

Figure 3.8. Impacts on trust in neighbors. All control variables set to their means. Social Capital Community Benchmark Survey.

the less trusting they are of their neighbors. It is important to note that this hypothesis does not rest on an individual's absolute degree of ideological extremism, nor its direction. Thus, being a moderate in San Francisco might make you a radical in Salt Lake City. And being a conservative in Berkeley should make you just as distrustful of your neighbors as being a liberal in Boise.

The test of this hypothesis is straightforward. I have constructed a measure of relative ideology as a function of an individual's own ideology in comparison to the mean ideology within the community. Specifically, it is the absolute difference between an individual's self-reported ideology score and the mean within the community. If the hypothesis is correct, the impact on trust should be negative. The greater the distance between an individual's own ideology and the prevailing ideology in her community, the less trust she places in her neighbors.

Figure 3.8 displays the relative impact of a number of statistically significant variables in this model, displayed in standard deviations of the trust scale.[31] We see that at both the individual and community level, more education means more trust, while living in the central city of an urban area leads to less trust. Racial heterogeneity also has a negative impact on trust, with its negative impact (0.27 of a standard deviation, or SD) essentially equaling the positive impact of increasing one's education from being a high school to a college graduate (0.31 SD). Of course, the fact that racially heterogeneous places have lower levels of neighborhood trust is consistent with the general claim that civic norms are more difficult to foster where people have divergent preferences.

We see that, consistent with the hypothesis, ideological heterogeneity within a community also has a negative impact on trust, with a magnitude that is slightly less than that for race (0.15 SD). Furthermore, as expected, the coefficient for relative ideology is negative, meaning that the farther one is from the ideological mean, the less trust one has in one's neighbors. The impact, which far exceeds the threshold for statistical significance ($p = .002$), is about half that for community-level ideological heterogeneity (-0.08 SD).

In other words, here we have evidence of *why* homogeneous communities have higher levels of cooperative behavior and heterogeneous places higher levels of conflictual activity. Where people differ from their neighbors, they are less likely to trust them, which means that social norms are less likely to be enforced. A lack of trust would also imply that they are more likely to have kindling for a political conflagration within their communities.

CONCLUSION

The primary objective of this chapter has been to bolster the case for the theory of dual motivations. In places characterized by partisan and/or ideological consensus, public engagement has a civic flavor and is thus motivated by a social norm. In places marked by conflict, engagement is more likely to be politically motivated and thus directed at influencing public policy. First, we saw that the more politically homogeneous a community, the more likely voters there report turning out because they feel it is their duty to do so; participation in these places has a Tocquevillian cast. And the more politically heterogeneous a community, the more likely voting is to be motivated by Madisonian interests. Second, behavioral evidence from multiple data sets collected using different methodologies is consistent with these self-reported motivations. Civically motived participation, namely volunteering in the community, is more common in homogeneous environments, while politically motivated activity is more common in places that are heterogeneous. Even when the critical concepts of community and heterogeneity are operationalized in distinct ways, the results hold up with remarkable consistency. Furthermore, while we saw that other forms of heterogeneity (ethnicity, race, and income) sometimes appear to have an effect on either civic or political participation, those impacts are inconsistent. Only partisanship and its close cousin, ideology, show consistent results across the different types of participation and multiple sources of data. We were also reminded that the causal process described by the theory of dual motivations rests on a microfoundation of individuals' behavior, as we saw that individuals are less likely to trust their neighbors in heterogeneous communities and report even less trust the farther they are from the ideological mean.

It is important to underscore just what we have learned thus far. In toto, this array of empirical findings provides support for the theory of dual motivations, and thus can explain the otherwise puzzling observation that presidential voter turnout rises where elections are not competitive. Turnout in presidential elections aside, however, a more fundamental purpose of this chapter is to explore how it is that the communities in which we live affect our public engagement. Simply put, living in different places has different consequences for participation. With this insight, it is possible to reconcile a seeming contradiction in the current literature on community heterogeneity. On the one hand, one line of research (conducted mainly by economists) has found that "heterogeneity reduces civic engagement" (Costa and Kahn 2003a). On the other hand, another line of research (primarily done by political scientists) has found that heterogeneity fosters engagement (Oliver 2001; Gimpel, Lay, and Schuknecht 2003). Who is right? The answer is both. While at first glance these conclusions appear empirically incompatible, they are actually theoretically consistent with one another, once we recognize that they are looking at different forms of participation. Participation motivated by the advancement or defense of political interests is sparked within heterogeneous communities—places where people have divergent interests or preferences. Places where interests or preferences are held in common facilitate publicly spirited collective action that is outside the arena of political combat. As the United States becomes increasingly heterogeneous (or in the vernacular outside of social science, diverse), increasing attention will be paid to heterogeneity's consequences. The lesson of the foregoing analysis is that, at least when it comes to public engagement, those consequences do not lend themselves to simplistic assertions. One should be wary of claims to the contrary.

While the analysis of individual-level trust begins to get at the process by which heterogeneity affects public engagement, there are admittedly still a few gaps in the theoretical chain linking the characteristics of communities with their residents' behavior. The next chapter fills in some of those gaps by examining how an individual's social network affects voter turnout, and is in turn affected by the composition of the wider community.

CHAPTER FOUR

Social Networks

Thus far, we have seen evidence that politically homogeneous communities facilitate civically motivated public engagement, while political heterogeneity leads to politically motivated activity. In chapter 3, I argued that homogeneous communities breed civic norms. Implied, but as yet untested, has been the hypothesis that civic norms are enforced through personal interactions among like-minded people. The first half of this chapter examines whether the homogeneity of one's social network increases the likelihood of turning out to vote. It does. The second half then tests whether the homogeneity of social networks is in turn a function of the partisan composition of one's wider community. It is.

IN CHAPTERS 2 AND 3 the analysis focused on how communities qua communities affect the likelihood of individuals' engaging in various forms of collective action. While "community" has been defined in different ways—metropolitan areas, counties, cities—each is a relatively large conglomeration of people. The civic motivation side of the dual motivations theory, however, has as its underpinning the behavior of individuals within their own social network. Our understanding of many political phenomena is enhanced when we couple the study of individuals with the study of groups of individuals. Thus, individuals are ideologically inconsistent (Converse 1964), but when viewed in the aggregate, public opinion is stable (Page and Shapiro 1992). Conversely, partisanship is very stable at the individual level—once a Democrat, always a Democrat (and once a Republican, always a Republican) (Green, Palmquist, and Shickler 2002; Jennings and Niemi 1981)—but fluctuates when we view the electorate as a whole (Erikson, MacKuen, and Stimson 2002). In this case, our understanding of a macrolevel phenomenon is dependent on the workings of a microlevel process. Viewed close up, we should observe essentially the same picture as at a distance. Testing the theory, therefore, requires some consideration of how individuals' own personal networks affect their likelihood of engaging in collective action. This chapter examines, first, whether the degree of homogeneity within an individual's own social network facilitates voter turnout and other forms of public engagement. Second, it tests whether the composition of individuals' microenvironments (their immediate friends and acquaintances) is a function of the composition of their macroenvironments (community). The evidence suggests that the answer to both questions is yes. Whether you vote depends on who you know; and who you know depends on where you are.

Contextual Effects

In the existing literature on what have come to be known as "contextual effects,"[1] there are two different perspectives on how human behavior is affected by social forces, represented by research into *social context* and *social networks*, respectively.[2] While the language employed by different researchers varies, for the most part "social context" is used to refer to the characteristics of a relatively large geographic area. Because they employ data collected for counties and metropolitan areas, chapters 2 and 3 fall squarely into the social context literature. "Social networks," on the other hand, simply refer to the family, friends, and acquaintances with whom each of us has regular interaction.

A focus on either contexts or networks requires an analytical trade-off. Social context research emphasizes breadth, as the analysis typically employs nationally representative samples of individuals. The empirical strategy mirrors the previous chapters. Individual respondents are matched with the characteristics of their social context—say, their county. Everyone in a single county is assigned the same value for any county-specific measures, like the average education level or degree of political homogeneity. One advantage of this methodology is that because it usually employs data collected on a national scale, any findings are generalizable to the American population. The disadvantage is simply that any analysis is restricted to data collected consistently across the nation, and at a relatively broad level of aggregation. We might say that these studies tell us a little about a lot. In contrast, social network research sacrifices breadth in the interest of depth. It generally uses a different methodology. Rather than matching individuals to information about their community, individuals are asked about their own social network (family, friends, acquaintances). In some studies, the members of the networks are also interviewed (known as "snowball sampling" because the sample starts out small and then snowballs). These studies have typically been conducted in a particular community, and so they are usually not generalizable to a wider population in a strict sense. Even when they do entail a national sample, however, they are still limited to measuring a relatively small portion of any individual respondent's social network (Knoke 1990; Lake and Huckfeldt 1998). That is, these studies tell us a lot about a little.

More important than the methodological differences in how contexts and networks are studied are the conceptual differences in how their effects are understood. While they obviously share common theoretical roots, generally speaking a focus on contexts is thought to capture more involuntary social interaction than the study of networks. Social networks, especially when defined as people with whom individuals discuss important matters, are almost entirely a matter of personal volition and thus predominantly consist of voluntary interaction. We choose our spouses, friends, hairdressers, and bartenders. Social contexts, on the other hand, are not characterized by individual choice to nearly the same extent. While we choose where we live (within obvious constraints), once made that choice results in exposure to people and information over which we have little control (Huckfeldt and Sprague 1993). To take a typical example, consider how people choose where to buy a home. Many Americans select their neighborhood based on the quality of the local public schools. However, since liberals and conservatives presumably place the same value on a quality education for their children, this process of self-selection does not guard a staunch Republican who has sought out a good school from living next to a Democratic party activist, who also moved in because of the local school. A Republican voter may thus have voluntarily chosen where to live, but in doing so can be involuntarily exposed to signs advocating Democratic candidates on his neighbor's lawn.

For the most part, the study of the relationship between social environments and political activity (as compared to attitudes) has largely been conducted within the literature centered on social contexts, not networks. In fact, the research into social networks sheds light on the dual motivations theory. When put side by side, two of the earliest examples of studies relating social context to political participation speak to both the civic and political motivations for voter turnout. It appears that the first examination of how social context affects voter turnout was published by Herbert Tingsten in 1937 (1963). He demonstrated that turnout among individual working-class voters in Sweden was positively related to the proportion of working-class voters in their precinct, yet more evidence that birds of a feather vote together (see chapter 2). In the United States, V. O. Key's work on the politics of the South devoted considerable attention to the impact of black population density on white voter turnout (1949). Key demonstrated that white turnout increases as the black population within a county increases, a finding replicated by others as well (Matthews and Prothro 1966; Alt 1992). He convincingly theorized that the increase in turnout was owing to white hostility toward African Americans—another manifestation of how political motivations can be spurred by community heterogeneity.

In the decades following these seminal works, there has only been sporadic attention paid to how individuals' social contexts affect their levels of participation.[3] One notable exception can be found in Sidney Verba and Norman Nie's *Participation in America* (1972). They found that community size and character affect rates of participation; people who live in small, independent (that is, not suburban) communities had the highest level of political activity. A few years later, Robert Huckfeldt (1979) found an interaction between the socioeconomic status of individuals and the average status within their communities when modeling different types of participation. He observed that highly educated people participate more in collective activities when surrounded by people of a similar educational background; similarly, voters with low levels of education participated more when surrounded by others with limited education.[4] In other words, Huckfeldt found evidence that is at least broadly consistent with the claim that civic motivations are greater when people find others with common preferences. Even more supportive of the argument that voter turnout is often driven by the strength of civic norms within a community is a study in which Stephen Knack and Martha Kropf (1998) use an innovative measure of civic norms at the county level—census return rates—to argue that such norms facilitate voter turnout. Certainly, these contextual studies have advanced our understanding of how social environments affect participation. But they share a common liability. Each is limited to inferring microlevel processes from data collected at a considerably higher level of aggregation.[5]

Studies in the social networks literature, on the other hand, have the analytical tools to examine microlevel processes. For the most part, this vein of research has been directed at explaining the effect of social networks on political opinions, not participation. Perhaps this is not surprising, given that much of this literature has focused on studies of particular communities, where the variation in participation is relatively limited. The Columbia School's landmark studies of Elmira, New York, and Erie County, Ohio, are cases in point (Lazarsfeld, Berelson, and Gaudet 1948; Berelson, Lazarsfeld, and McPhee 1954), as is the work by Robert Huckfeldt and John Sprague in South Bend, Indiana (Huckfeldt and Sprague 1995).[6] Diana Mutz's recent research is a notable exception, as she has carefully examined the ways that politically diverse social networks affect political participation (2002a). I will discuss Mutz's work in more detail below.

The existing literature thus leaves us with a considerable gap. Contextual studies that examine participation have not had much to say about individuals' social networks. And the studies that examine social networks have had little to say about participation. Perhaps owing to this gap, and at the very least exacerbated by it, is an ambiguity within the social capital literature. As a theoretical concept, social capital is a collective phenomenon; it is, after all, known as *social* capital. But those collectivities are obviously composed of individual people. Since many studies of social capital focus on individuals' behavior (Brehm and Rahn 1997; Schneider et al. 1997; Lake and Huckfeldt 1998; Stolle and Rochon 1998), it is easy for the casual consumer of this literature to forget that social capital theory is primarily an explanation of how webs of social relationships have consequences for the enforcement of social norms. The better scholarship on social capital–related topics is careful to strike a balance between the individual and the aggregate. For example, while John Brehm and Wendy Rahn model social capital at the individual level, they take pains to specify that "social capital is an aggregate concept that has its basis in individual behavior, attitudes, and predispositions" (1997, 100). Likewise, Putnam (2000) measures social capital both among individuals and within collectivities.

Stemming as it does from the social capital literature, this study shares the same duality of studying both individuals and collectivities. On the one hand, the fundamental claim is that what we do depends on where we are: the volume and nature of our public engagement is shaped by our social environments. But on the other hand, the topic at hand is the explanation of individuals' behavior, and so it is not enough to leave the analysis at the aggregate, that is, community, level. Thus far, this duality has been accommodated in the manner of social context research, matching individuals with the characteristics of their communities. The preceding analysis therefore shares the same weakness as social context research generally, namely that the microlevel process by which norms are enforced is only inferred, not observed. The analysis to follow hopefully shores up this weakness by turning to social network data.

A Microlevel Test

To review, thus far we have seen evidence that voter turnout is driven by civic motivations in politically homogeneous communities. Likewise, other forms of civic participation—such as voluntarism—follow from political homogeneity. Fundamentally, the explanation for these observations is simply that civic norms are stronger where individuals share common preferences (opinions, values, and so forth). Civic norms are enhanced where people trust one another, and trust is easier to build when people feel that they are surrounded by like-minded compatriots. Such norms are enforced through social sanctions. Sanctions and trust are really two sides of the same theoretical coin. The former result when people do not adhere to a norm; trust results when they do.

While the earlier analysis of trust serves as a girder buttressing the theoretical framework (see chapter 3), it nonetheless shares the same liability as most social context research. Left unexplored is an examination of individuals' social networks as facilitators or inhibitors of collective action, like civic and political participation. As mentioned above, the data demands for such an analysis are high. Obviously, the relevant data must include measures of individuals' public engagement, specifically turning out to vote, which implies that a sample across a wide geographic area is advantageous (to ensure that there is enough variation to model). Since we are interested in individuals' social networks, we also need information about the people in the survey respondent's immediate environment. Specifically, we need to know the extent to which members of an individual's social network have common preferences.

Fortunately, a source of data exists that meets these criteria. In 1987, the General Social Survey (GSS) included a series of questions about each respondent's personal social network.[7] First, respondents were asked about their network of discussion partners.

> From time to time, most people discuss important matters with other people. Looking back over the last six months, who are the people with whom you discussed matters important to you? Just tell me their first names or initials.

Up to three names were recorded. Then, the respondent was asked about a few characteristics of the discussion partners, including whether they were family members or not. Most important for our purposes, the respondent was asked to identify the partisan affiliation of each partner.[8]

With these data, we can examine whether *micro*environments facilitate voter turnout in a manner analogous to that of *macro*environments. Granted, these data fall short of an ideal test of the causal mechanism at work. For one, the discussion partners themselves were not interviewed. This certainly introduces bias into the measurement of network homogeneity, since other research has found that individuals are likely to misperceive the commonality between themselves and their friends and acquaintances (Huckfeldt and Sprague 1995). Also, we only have a thin measure of commonality—partisanship. A richer analysis would incorporate opinions on a wide variety of issues. These social network data also focus attention on only a few people specifically identified as those with whom the respondent discusses important matters. Social capital theory suggests that the subtle process of norm enforcement through social sanctions (and the subsequent thickening of bonds of trust) occurs as much through "weak" as "strong" ties (Granovetter 1973).[9] Socially approved behavior is facilitated not only through deep conversations with close friends, but also through brief encounters with casual acquaintances. Indeed, a common theme in the contextual effects literature is that intimates are not the only source of social influence. Unfortunately, these data do not permit gauging the impact of such casual encounters.

These GSS data do have their share of advantages as well, however. Most important, they obviously have a measure of individuals' social networks. They also bear a close resemblance to the data employed in earlier chapters, making comparisons across the data sets feasible. Notably, in 1987 the GSS questionnaire included a series of inquiries about various forms of political participation beyond voting. Respondents were also asked a host of demographic questions, meaning that we can account for the same potentially confounding factors as in previous chapters. It is also important that the GSS question about social networks did not mention politics per se but rather people with whom the respondents discuss important matters, which might have nothing to do with politics. This feature of the question lessens the concern that the tally of discussion partners is simply another way of measuring political interest, which is the fear when surveys ask respondents to list the people with whom they converse about politics. (The analysis nonetheless accounts for each respondent's level of political interest.) Finally, the GSS shares the critical criteria of being representative of the nation as a whole, as well as identifying the geographic location of most respondents (specifically, those who live in metropolitan areas). Therefore, as with the other surveys examined to this point, data about the broader social context of the individual respondents can be incorporated into the analysis (although this feature will not be necessary until the second half of this analysis). The bottom line is that while these data have their flaws, they do allow for preliminary tests of hypotheses stemming from the civic side of the theory of dual motivations.

Table 4.1 displays the distribution of discussion partners who share a common partisan affiliation. Commonality was defined as a respondent and a partner who are both Republicans or Democrats;[10] because of the ambiguity surrounding the term, these figures do not reflect pairs in which both the respondent and partner are political independents (Keith et al. 1992).[11] We see that 39 percent of Americans report having no discussion partners with the same partisan affiliation. (Keep in mind that in many cases this means that respondents do not know the partisan affiliation of their partners. Undoubtedly, there is commonality in many of these dyads.) Fifteen percent report that all three of their most important discussion partners identify with the same party, while 61 percent of Americans have at least one discussion partner who shares the same partisan affiliation.[12] The main point to be drawn from Table 4.1 is simply that there are considerable differences in the political homogeneity of individuals' social networks. This is a variable, not a constant.

Before turning to the analysis of social networks, it is worth revisiting

TABLE 4.1
Political Homogeneity in Social Networks

Number of discussion partners with same partisan affiliation	Percentage
0	39 (664)
1	26 (452)
2	20 (351)
3	15 (254)

Source: 1987 General Social Survey.

just what the theory of dual motivations leads us to expect. When it comes to civically motivated participation, the hypothesis is clear. If partisan homogeneity leads to the enforcement of civic norms, then the greater the number of discussion partners who share a respondent's partisan affiliation, the greater the likelihood that person turns out to vote, owing to the fact that voting is often a civically motivated act. However, the impact of a politically heterogeneous social network on politically motivated public engagement is not so clear. Perhaps being in a network characterized by opposing partisans stimulates a sense of political conflict, thus driving politically motivated turnout. Or perhaps political motivations are spurred solely by the wider social context, resulting in no impact for interpersonal relationships characterized by political disagreement.

In any discussion of social network research, the proverbial elephant sitting in the middle of the room is the fear that any impact we attribute to the social network is really owing to the characteristics that lead people to be embedded within that social network. We need to be sure that any effects attributed to individuals' social networks are not simply a function of personal characteristics that in turn shape those networks. People who like *Star Trek* often spend a lot of time with other people who also like *Star Trek*, but this does not mean that hanging around with Trekkies leads one to become a fan—in this case, the relationship almost certainly runs the other way. Therefore, in an effort to isolate the impact of the political diversity within one's social network, the following models contain an array of control variables above and beyond the standard set of demographic measures. For example, in addition to a count of discussion partners whose partisan affiliation matches the respondent's (the critical independent variable), the model also includes a measure of how many discussion partners the respondent named in the first place. This is because the measure of social network homogeneity essentially captures two pieces of information simultaneously. As discussed already, we know the number of discussion partners who share the same partisan affiliation as the respondent (up to three). This means we also know how many discussion partners each respondent has. There is good reason to think that a wider social network means a higher likelihood of voting, independent of the network's political composition. More socially connected people are probably more attuned to social pressures to vote. Including a count of discussion partners with a common partisan affiliation in the model might conflate the number of *matching* partners with simply the *number* of partners. Including them both in the model allows us to focus on the impact of the number of discussion partners with a common partisan affiliation.[13]

We also need to be sure that any effect attributed to the partisan homogeneity of the social network is not just a function of the fact that the respondent herself is a partisan. Therefore, the model controls for whether the respondent identifies as either a Democrat or a Republican. The model further controls for whether the respondent simply knows the partisan affiliation of her discussion partners, regardless of whether they have it in common.[14] This is because we might expect that politically attentive individuals—those most likely to turn out to vote—are also likely to know the partisan leanings of their acquaintances. Similarly, the model also controls for the extent to which the respondent discusses political matters with each discussion partner. Frequency of political discussion is measured with a six-point scale for each discussion partner, from which an overall additive index was constructed. In the same vein, the model accounts for the respondent's own level of political interest. The model also includes the same demographic measures that we have seen in previous chapters: education, income, age, marital status, race, and gender.[15]

Table 4.2 displays the results of a logistic regression model predicting voter turnout in the 1984 election. All of the variables have been coded using a 0–1 scale, so the magnitude of their impacts on turnout can be compared.[16] We see that, as expected, the coefficient for political homogeneity within a social network is positive (and statistically significant). Figure 4.1 translates the results into the estimated level of voter turnout as a function of political homogeneity within one's social network (as usual, holding all control variables at their means).[17] The estimated probability of someone turning out to vote climbs roughly thirteen percentage points as the level of social network homogeneity climbs from having no politically like-minded discussion partners to having three. As is suggested by a glance down Table 4.2, the impact of political homogeneity within one's social network is comparable to having adopted a partisan affiliation, long recognized as an important factor leading to political involvement. Social network homogeneity, however, has a

TABLE 4.2
Social Network Political Homogeneity and Public Engagement

	(1) Logistic regression	(2) Ordered logistic regression	(3) Ordered logistic regression
	Voted in presidential election	Frequency of voting in local elections	Electoral activism
Social network homogeneity	0.748*** (0.252)	0.382** (0.190)	0.209 (0.197)
Number of discussion partners	0.261 (0.418)	−0.254 (0.292)	−0.249 (0.340)
Knowledge of network members' partisanship	−0.575* (0.305)	−0.293 (0.221)	0.246 (0.208)
Frequency of political conversation	1.260*** (0.455)	0.931*** (0.313)	1.017*** (0.376)
Partisan identifier	0.859*** (0.211)	0.717*** (0.210)	0.774*** (0.202)
Interest in politics	1.944*** (0.394)	2.249*** (0.320)	2.736*** (0.320)
Observations	1,497	1,594	1,599
Pseudo-R^2	0.22	0.12	0.10

Source: 1987 General Social Survey.

Note: Robust standard errors in parentheses. Weighted data. All independent variables coded 0–1. Model also controls for education, income, age, marital status, race, and gender. See Table C5 in appendix C for the full results.

* significant at .10   ** significant at .05   *** significant at .01

smaller impact than the frequency of political conversation and level of interest in politics.

A disadvantage of the measure for voter turnout in this particular survey is that it refers to an election held three years prior. This introduces considerable measurement error in the dependent variable, almost certainly biasing it upward. To ensure that the results are not idiosyncratically a function of the poor measurement of the dependent variable, Table 4.2 also displays the results of regressing a different dependent variable—frequency of voting in local elections—on exactly the same set of independent variables.[18] The results are scaled into an index ranging from 1 (never vote) to 4 (always vote), and so ordered logistic regression is used as the estimator. Once more, we see that social network homogeneity is positive and statistically significant. This is as expected, for

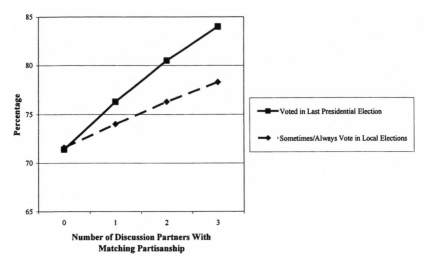

Figure 4.1. Impact of social network homogeneity on voter turnout. All control variables set to their means. General Social Survey, 1987.

while our attention in this study has been directed primarily at turnout in presidential elections, civic norms should motivate turnout in other types of elections, too. In Figure 4.1, we see that participation in local elections rises at a slightly lower rate than for presidential elections.[19]

We have thus seen support for the hypothesis that political homogeneity within a social network leads to voter turnout, the explanation for which is that civic motivations are fostered within such social networks. Admittedly, though, this relationship is not necessarily due to the fact that civic norms are stronger within a homogeneous environment, since these data provide no direct measure of what motivated the vote. It could be that small networks of like-minded partisans are likely to vote to further their *political* objectives, rather than out of a civic motivation. Using the analysis in chapter 3 as a template, we can perform at least one test of whether civic motivations drive voter turnout among people enmeshed in a homogeneous network. If the mechanism linking social network homogeneity and turnout is a civic motivation, then we should *not* observe a relationship between network homogeneity and politically motivated (that is, noncivically motivated) collective action. Fortuitously, the 1987 GSS includes a series of questions that measure electoral activism, as in chapter 3. Specifically, respondents were asked about three activities: contributing money to a political party or candidate, working on a political campaign, and attending a political meeting or rally.[20] These three items have been combined into an additive index of electoral activism. If it is the case that social network homogeneity fa-cilitates civic, but not political, motivations, we should observe that when regressed against the same array of independent variables as the two measures of voter turnout, political activism is not predicted by so-cial network homogeneity. In Table 4.2, we see that it is not. While the coefficient is positive, its standard error is large enough that it does not approach statistical significance.

Stepping back from the specifics of the statistical models, these results essentially show us that the more you are engaged with individuals who share your political preferences the more likely you are to engage in civi-cally motivated collective action. This parallels the observation that liv-ing in a community with people who share your preferences leads to high voter turnout, but not other forms of participation with a predomi-nantly political motivation. We thus have a microlevel confirmation of the macrolevel results from chapters 2 and 3.

Since we have seen that being situated in a social network with like-minded partisans facilitates voter turnout, it is logical to ask about the impact of a network composed of people who have a partisan affiliation that differs from yours. Is the lonely Democrat in a crowd of Republi-cans spurred to vote, perhaps because her partisan sympathies have been stimulated or simply out of spite? In this case, the dual motivations theory does not lead to an obvious hypothesis, as it is not clear whether political (that is, preference-driven) motivations can be ignited in small-scale social networks.

To test which of these processes is at work (or both), I have con-structed a measure that is the mirror image of social network homogene-ity. In this case, the count is of discussion partners who have a different partisan affiliation than the respondent, and is labeled social network heterogeneity.[21] Note that because the partisan identity of discussion partners is often not known, social network homogeneity and hetero-geneity are not simply the mirror images of one another. These data con-firm what we have known since the early Columbia School research—few Americans are ensconced in an environment characterized by partisan dispute. Only 16 percent of Americans have even one discussion partner whom they know to have a different partisan affiliation than they do. Only 2 percent have three such partners. However, while the distribution of the data is skewed, there is nonetheless reasonable variation in the degree to which social networks are politically heteroge-neous. This still leaves open the question, therefore, whether the degree of partisan disagreement within a social network stimulates political participation.

It would appear that it does not. In a parallel set of models (not shown), I have tested whether social network *hetero*geneity predicts presidential voter turnout, turnout in local elections, and electoral activism respectively (with every other variable exactly the same as the models in Table 4.2). In each case, the coefficient for social network heterogeneity has a negligible magnitude and is far from statistical significance, suggesting that political motivations are not stimulated within relatively intimate social networks.

What has this microlevel analysis taught us? First, homogeneity within intimate social networks is positively related to voter turnout. This relationship cannot be explained by the size of the network, an individual's awareness of her associates' partisan leanings, political discussion within the networks, or an individual's own interest in politics. Instead, the working hypothesis is that it is due to the civic norms fostered within networks of like-minded associates, an explanation consistent with the macrolevel data we have already seen. Second, the degree of heterogeneity within a social network does not seem to foster political activism, suggesting that political motivations are not ignited within small-scale social networks.

It is worth noting how these results overlap with and diverge from other research on the subject. Diana Mutz (2002a), building on the classic work done by the Columbia School researchers, similarly finds that people embedded in a politically homogeneous network are more likely to vote, although she frames her results by emphasizing that heterogeneity—or "cross-cutting networks"—drives turnout down, rather than that homogeneity drives turnout up. Mutz, however, offers a different (although not necessarily contradictory) explanation than I do. She stresses the ambivalence of people whose social networks are politically diverse, and their desire to avoid political conflict among friends and acquaintances. I would add to that explanation the complementary observation that civic norms are likely to be weaker in heterogeneous social environments. In referring to the literature on cross-pressures, James Coleman puts it well:

> The reduced likelihood of voting among persons who are in surroundings different from those to which their background or interests predispose them may result from reduced application of normative sanction that would lead to voting. (1990, 292)

Linking Networks and Context

The goal of this chapter has been to bridge the gap between macrolevel evidence, like that used in chapters 2 and 3, and a microlevel theory. Thus far, one half of that gap has been bridged, as we have seen how the impact of political homogeneity within a social network parallels the impact of political homogeneity within a community. The other half of the gap is simply whether the political complexion of one's social network is in any way related to the political composition of one's community. The relationship between network homogeneity and turnout might not be related at all to the broader context in which respondents live, but instead be a process totally driven by self-selection. Individuals who are predisposed to vote might also be likely to seek out intimates with common political preferences, irrespective of their context.

A classic study by Ada Finifter (1974) provides reason to think that individuals, particularly those with minority political opinions, carve out social enclaves of friends with common preferences. She found that Republican autoworkers in a Detroit plant sought out Republican coworkers for friendships on the job, whereas Democrats (the overwhelming majority) were not so selective in forming friendship groups. While this is only one study in one particular social context at one point in time, it does raise the question of whether social network homogeneity can be explained wholly as a matter of individual choice and is therefore unrelated to the wider social context in which one is situated. In the words of Robert Huckfeldt and John Sprague:

> If we think of a friendship group as one part of a social network, this means that networks are subject to individual control in a way that contexts are not. Indeed, the network can be seen as the end result of efforts made by individuals to impose their own preferences upon their social contexts, and the composition of networks is subject to the multiple, interdependent, cascading choices of people who share the same social space—the people who compose the context. (1993, 290)

Indeed, the self-selected nature of social networks speaks to the conceptual difference between networks and contexts. The critical question, however, is the extent to which people's choice of discussion partners is shaped by the wider community, over which they have less immediate control. Huckfeldt and Sprague convincingly argue that social networks are contingent on the choices made available by the broader social context: "Personal choice is not determinant in the construction of a social network. . . . [T]he choice of an associate operates within constraints imposed by a context" (ibid). In a sense, this is the principle guiding contextual effects research—social influences are not totally endogenous to an individual's own preferences.[22] That is, we may have some control over our social environment, but it is far from total control. The question at hand is the extent to which the partisan complexion of an individual's community is reflected in her immediate social network. We turn, therefore, to explicitly testing the link between the composition of individuals' social contexts and their social networks. Does partisan homogeneity in the former lead to the same in the latter?

Answering this question is straightforward. It is simply a matter of seeing whether the political homogeneity of individuals' social networks is related to the partisan composition of the community in which they live. This has been tested with a model that resembles what we have seen previously. On the lefthand side is the count of like-minded partisans in an individual's personal social network. On the righthand side is the array of individual and contextual demographic variables used previously, as well as a measure of the overall size of the respondent's network of discussion partners. The critical independent variable is the mean level of partisan competition in a respondent's metropolitan area,[23] as this is the lowest level of aggregation for which the General Social Survey recorded the geographic location of its respondents in 1987.[24] Recall that the metropolitan area is a very unrefined level of aggregation, introducing noise into the analysis. Furthermore, as noted above, we would expect metropolitan areas to be more heterogeneous than rural communities. By excluding rural areas, we limit the range of the independent variable and bias the analysis against the hypothesis.

Our expectation is that the more politically heterogeneous an individual's community (context), the fewer her like-minded discussion partners (network). In operational terms, the coefficient for community partisan heterogeneity should be negative. And, it is.[25] Figure 4.2 displays the impact of community-level political heterogeneity on the political complexion of social networks, based on the results of the model. All else equal, we see that the estimated percentage of people who do not have a single discussion partner with a matching partisan affiliation rises from 28 percent in the most politically homogeneous community to 35 percent in the most heterogeneous. Conversely, the percentage with three discussion partners with whom they share a partisan affiliation drops from 19 to 14 percent. By way of comparison to other variables in the model, these are impacts of a moderate range—less than, say, the mean income of a community, but comparable to its population density.

Another way to read this model is that the partisan complexion of an individual's community is one factor—but only one factor—affecting the partisan composition of her social network. At first blush, it may appear that this is an example of social science data confirming a commonsensical expectation. The more diverse someone's environment, the more diverse her personal social network. Put another way, it is harder for a Democrat to find and thus befriend fellow Democrats in Casper, Wyoming, than Cambridge, Massachusetts. Given the existing literature on the way individuals construct their social networks, though, it was not clear at all that this bit of common sense would prevail. If birds of a

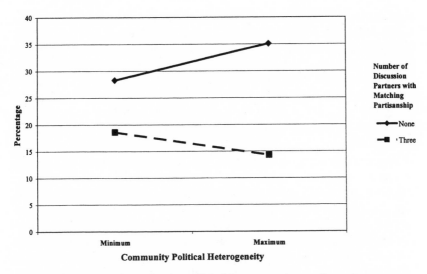

Figure 4.2. Impact of community political heterogeneity on discussion partners. All control variables set to their means. General Social Survey, 1987.

feather truly do flock together, then (as Finifter found) we might expect them to seek each other out wherever they are. That we find an effect for the community's political composition demonstrates that networks are not independent of context, an important piece of evidence supporting the hypothesized microlevel foundation of the theory that civic motivations drive voter turnout. That this effect is moderate in its magnitude reminds us that context by no means determines the makeup of one's social network.

CONCLUSION

The two main findings of this chapter are complementary, as the theoretical significance of each is dependent upon knowing the significance of the other. We have seen that the political homogeneity of an individual's community influences the degree of homogeneity within her social network, and in turn that the makeup of her social network affects the likelihood of turning out to vote. In tandem, these two observations flesh out the process by which individuals in a community with homogeneous political preferences come to have a relatively high level of voter turnout.

Understanding this process is only a means to a greater end, however. More fundamentally, the previous three chapters have demonstrated that simply viewing voter turnout as a response to the stimuli of political conflict does not do justice to the mix of motivations that bring people to the polls. Our Madisonian impulse toward faction is balanced by our Tocquevillian sense of duty. Furthermore, empirically oriented scholars need not throw up their hands at the very mention of civic duty as hopelessly tautological, or somehow too "squishy" a concept to incorporate into our models of political behavior. There are good, theoretically grounded reasons to expect the social contexts in which people live to affect their motivations for engaging in collective action, and there is considerable evidence that this expectation is met.

Yet even "bringing duty back in" to our understanding of collective action with political consequences is not my ultimate objective. Many pages ago, we were introduced to Traci Hodgson, the woman who voted alone in Boston. Her ballot was cast almost purely out of civic motivations, I suggested, since she was totally unaware of any information pertaining to the candidates whose names appeared on the ballot. And her sense of civic duty, I further suggested, sprang from the characteristics of the community in which she was raised. In other words, it was not the social context in which she was currently living that motivated her to turn out, but the context in which she was socialized as a youth. Simply put, the argument is that social context *then* affects behavior *now*. That claim, though, rests on the even more fundamental premise that place matters at all—social context *now* affects behavior *now*. And so, in chapters 2 through 4, we have seen evidence for why this is the case. While this has been an essential theoretical step, it is only the first. Establishing that attributes of one's community affect the public engagement of adults serves as a foundation for exploring its impact on young people. Do communities similarly shape the engagement of adolescents as they do for adults? The next chapter takes up that question, whether what you did then depends on where you were then.

PART TWO

What You Did Then Depends on Where You Were Then

CHAPTER FIVE

Social Environments and Adolescents' Public Engagement

To this point, the analysis has dealt only with the behavior of adults. Now, we turn to adolescents. Are young people affected by their environment in the same manner as their elders? If so, this suggests that socialization experiences differ across community contexts, with potential consequences for public engagement as people age. This chapter begins by demonstrating that adolescents are more likely to engage in civic activity in homogeneous environments, which are hypothesized to have strong civic norms. Furthermore, both schools and families in homogeneous communities foster two components of civic norms—voice (allowing youth to participate in decision making) and order (discipline). However, civic norms are a double-edged sword. For while homogeneity facilitates voluntarism, voice, and order, it also appears to contribute to relatively low levels of political tolerance. Political heterogeneity, on the other hand, leads to a greater sense of political efficacy.

SO, WHERE ARE YOU FROM?

I am hard-pressed to come up with a meaningful question asked as frequently in conversation as this one. "How are you?" is probably heard more often, but rarely has much meaning. Nobody asks how you are because he really wants to know the answer. In contrast, it often seems to be the case that people have a genuine interest in knowing where others are from.

A personal anecdote makes the point. On my first day of graduate school, all of the incoming doctoral students filed into a small seminar room. While some of us had met one another briefly, no one yet knew each other well. We sat down, unsure of what to do or what to say. Soon a few professors from the department joined us. And, in a reassuringly familiar ritual, one of them asked us to introduce ourselves and tell everyone else where we were from. Like a grammar school roll call, one by one each of us took our turn. No one wanted to say too much, so we all stuck to the basics: just our names, the vaguely defined area of political science we wanted to study, and—significantly—our hometowns. By the time all of us had taken our turn, the professor who initiated the introductions was smirking. Speaking with just a touch of haughtiness, she remarked that we would all soon learn that in academic circles, "Where are you from?" really means, "Where did you go to college?"

It is very telling that we all chose to introduce ourselves to our peers and our professors by indicating where we were born and/or raised. Even in a setting where we might have been expected to talk up our accomplishments, if only to assuage our own insecurities, there was no mention of who graduated from which college. When asked, "Where are you from?" we all just naturally responded with our hometowns. The question's ubiquity is owing to its utility. For good or bad, we often learn a lot about people when we learn where they are from.

This chapter examines what we can learn about civic and political behavior by knowing where someone is from. Thus far, the evidence brought to bear on the analysis of civic and political participation has focused on adults. However, you will recall that the theoretical framework initially described in the opening pages specifies that it is not only adults whose participation is shaped by their communities, but also adolescents. The analysis that follows, therefore, turns our attention to the public engagement of young people. This chapter applies the theory of dual motivations to adolescents, testing the extent to which the complexion of their communities affects both their civic and political involvement. As we will see, the evidence suggests that place matters for adolescents as well as adults.

Why focus on adolescents? While the early studies on political socialization examined preadolescent children (Greenstein 1965; Easton and Dennis 1969; Hess and Torney 1967), later research settled on adolescence as the critical period for the development of civic and political attitudes (Jennings and Niemi 1974). Adolescence represents the critical period of what Erik Erikson (1968) famously described as identity formation. One review of the developmental psychology literature aptly characterizes Erikson's influential perspective on the importance of adolescence as a "crucial bridge between the rules-oriented morality of childhood and the deeper ethical sense that orients adult life" (Perlmutter and Shapiro 1987, 187). It is because adolescence is a bridge between childhood and adulthood that it draws our attention. Ideally, we would know more about the development of civic and political orientations over the entire life span, as it is likely that the early studies of political socialization were on to something by focusing on children. However, perhaps as a consequence of the fact that the study of socialization largely withered away, a complete theory of how civic and political orientations develop over the entire course of life is yet to come. And even if we did have the theory, we do not currently have the data to test it. Therefore, in the absence of a more developed theory and more extensive data, I focus on the period of life where we are most likely to see connections with adult-hood, namely adolescence. In this chapter, we will examine young people in grades nine through twelve; chapters 6 and 7 will center on high school seniors only.

POLITICAL SOCIALIZATION AND SOCIAL ENVIRONMENTS

Given the frequency with which informal conversations turn to where someone was raised, you might think that this would be a natural area of research for political scientists. If so, you would be wrong, as the topic has rarely been addressed. The study of how local communities shape the political development of young people could potentially be of interest to two groups of scholars. The first group consists of scholars primarily interested in the political development of young people, for whom community-level factors are one possible influence among many on the preparation of young people for public engagement. The second comprises scholars whose main interest is in the impact of local communities on individuals' political behavior, for whom young people are one population among many to be studied.

Although there is a voluminous (if dated) literature on the political socialization of youth, this body of research has paid virtually no attention to how the context of one's local community might affect the development of civic orientations and habits. Studies exploring questions pertaining to young people's civic engagement have largely missed the significance of community by having a scope that is either too wide or too narrow—on the one hand, the nation, on the other, the home and/or school. Cross-national studies like Gabriel Almond and Sidney Verba's *The Civic Culture* (1989 [1963]) are in one sense obviously an analysis of social context as a factor influencing political socialization. However, because Almond and Verba's focus was on differences *across* nations, they are silent on the impact of local communities *within* a nation. Their interest was in context *writ large*. More studies have been limited to a single country (most often, the United States) but typically have not examined social context. Their analysis has been restricted to the influence of families and schools, communities *writ small* (Merriam 1934; Hyman 1959; Greenstein 1965; Easton and Dennis 1967, 1969; Hess and Torney 1967; Langton and Jennings 1968; Dawson and Prewitt 1969; Merelman 1969, 1971, 1973; Andrain 1971; Jennings and Niemi 1974). Few studies have examined the impact of context *writ medium*. While some have hinted that place, defined locally, matters for understanding youths' attitudes (Jaros, Hirsch, and Fleron 1968), there has been little theoretical development of how this occurs.

In recent years, increasing attention has been paid to the study of political socialization, although this new wave of research does not always use that term. Fortunately, this new generation of youth-oriented research is considering fresh answers to old questions. To that end, two recent studies are notable for their attention to local communities as influencing the civic and political development of young people. The scarcity of such research warrants careful consideration of the few studies of young people that take community-level factors into consideration. These two studies are discussed in depth below, as each offers insights to ground and guide the analysis at hand.

While scholars primarily interested in the political development of young people have paid some (limited) attention to local communities, researchers in the "contextual effects" school have historically paid little attention to young people. It is significant that in their exhaustive review of extant research into the effects of social context on political behavior, Huckfeldt and Sprague (1993) do not cite a single study that pertains to political socialization. Since then, as detailed below, there have been a few studies linking context and socialization, but they are still relatively rare.

Social Capital

Perhaps one reason that studies of context have not generally paid much attention to socialization and vice versa has been the absence of a theoretical framework linking the two. That has begun to change, as the social capital literature provides such a framework. In fact, James Coleman's early work on social capital specifically addresses how small-scale communities affect young people. Though not often recognized by contemporary social capitalists, he and Thomas Hoffer initially drew on the concept of social capital to explain the academic performance of students in Catholic secondary schools (1987).[1] Catholic schools, Coleman and Hoffer argued, are tightly embedded within an ethnoreligious community. Not only do members of this community share common values, they also have social relationships with one another. These personal interactions, in turn, produce "closure" within social networks: each member of the network knows every other member. Under this condition, "two can discuss a third's behavior and develop consensus about what is proper or appropriate behavior, that is, develop social norms" (1987, 222). Coleman and Hoffer describe how parochial school students are likely to be enmeshed within a closed network where norms are developed and enforced. In subsequent work, Coleman (1990, 1988) then extended the application of social capital to subjects other than education and people other than adolescents, including voter turnout among adults.

Fundamentally, social capital refers to the mechanism by which social norms are enforced. Thus far, the focus has been on how those norms are enforced in real time—the social sanctions that guide human behavior. Eventually, however, norms can become internalized. In other words, norms need not guide an individual's behavior strictly through the fear of facing some sort of immediate social punishment, but rather through habituation. The internalization of a norm means "that an individual comes to have an internal sanctioning system which provides punishment when he carries out an action proscribed by the norm or fails to carry out an action prescribed by the norm" (Coleman 1990, 293). We might say that a norm has been internalized when you act in accordance with it even when no one else is looking. The term "socialization" aptly refers to the process by which a norm is internalized—one learns what is socially desirable. As young people undergo socialization, they are imprinted with norms that have the potential to guide their behavior throughout their lives.

Coleman's work on social capital is a theoretical tour de force, bridging the ever-widening divide between sociology and economics. However, he left the empirical refinement of his ideas to others. Coleman provides no empirical test, for example, of the basic notion that social norms are more efficacious in communities with closed social networks. Nor does he offer any analysis of the factors that influence the degree of closure within social networks.

Putnam's (1993) research into governmental performance in Italy was among the first to put social capital to the empirical test, and the first to bring the concept to the attention of most political scientists. Adapting Coleman's fundamental insight about the importance of social networks and the norms they foster, Putnam argues that the varying performance of subnational governments in Italy is related to the different levels of social capital across Italy's regions. In particular, Putnam draws attention to participation in voluntary associations as an important indicator of the social networks, and thus norms, within a community. And though he does not address the influence of these norms on young people specifically, socialization of youth is nonetheless an implicit theme in his story. Putnam notes that civic norms have deep roots, even suggesting that they can persist for centuries. Reasonable people can disagree about the specific length of time that the civic character of a region persists, but it seems clear that it is not invented ex nihilo with each successive generation. Somehow, the norms that guide one generation come to guide the next, an observation that is not limited to Italy. In the United States, civic differences among the states have sustained themselves over many decades, and perhaps even centuries (Elazar 1972; Sharansky 1969). Political scientists Tom Rice and Jan Feldman have even found that European immigrants to the United States carry with them the civic templates of their homelands, which persist over multiple generations (1997). Thus, fifth-generation Americans of Scandinavian descent share the civic attitudes of contemporary Scandinavians, perhaps suggesting quite a different answer to "So, where are you from?" than most people naturally offer.

Coleman and Putnam have reminded us that, to some extent, the child is father to the political man. And they are not alone, as a growing chorus of scholars has returned recently to the subject of adolescent paths to adult participation. After having ebbed for a number of years (Cook 1985), research into political socialization has begun to flow again (Sears and Valentino 1997; Niemi and Junn 1998; Rahn and Transue 1998; Galston 2001; Bartels 2002; Campbell 2002; McDonnell, Timpane, and Benjamin 2002; Plutzer 2002). In revisiting the subject of how young people develop (or not) into active citizens, this new wave of research has been informed by theoretical developments in the study of political behavior that have emerged since the early work on political socialization, including (in at least two cases) attention to community-level factors.

Notably, one recent study has acknowledged the local community as an important factor in the preparation of adolescents for engagement in a participatory democracy. Pamela Conover and Donald Searing (2000) have explicitly incorporated differences across local communities into their study of "how citizens are made." Recognizing the diversity in the composition of communities across the United States, they sought to interview young people in a variety of local settings, ranging from a rural, racially homogeneous farming community in the Midwest to an urban environment with a significant Hispanic population in the Southwest. Conover and Searing describe how the character of the local community is an important factor in the civic development of adolescents. Take, for example, the description they offer of the midwestern farming community in their sample. It succinctly captures what is meant by a community characterized by political homogeneity, and thus strong civic norms:

> Politically, the citizens proudly identify themselves as conservatives; the majority are Republicans, although partisan politics is not salient at the local level. The citizens are enthusiastically patriotic, especially about their own town. Their love of community—love of place—is reinforced by clear social norms and a sense of civility and decency. In daily life, this strong sense of community is focused on the churches and schools rather than on politics. (95)

Note the stress on the lack of political rancor, and the presence of civic norms animating residents' behavior. Nor do Conover and Searing suggest that civic norms are restricted to communities that are rural and/or Republican. The urban, southwestern community included in their study is "overwhelmingly Democratic," its residents share a strong sense of community, and like its midwestern counterpart "boasts relatively high participation rates" (96).

Conover and Searing's work is commendable for stressing that place matters for understanding how young people develop habits of engagement. Nonetheless, their research design does not provide leverage on just what it is about place that matters. With only four cities represented in their sample, it does not take long to identify more relevant factors of a community to test than they have communities with which to test them. Nonetheless, their careful attention to community context provides empirical support for the strong theoretical claim that a youth's local context shapes her preparation for civic life.

A second and even more recent study picks up where Conover and Searing's work leaves off. James Gimpel, J. Celeste Lay, and Jason Schuknecht have examined how adolescents' local political environments affect their development as active citizens. They surveyed thousands of high-school-age adolescents in a single state (Maryland), using a research design that ensured they included rural, urban, and suburban communities within the study. Among their many insights, they conclude that partisan heterogeneity at the community level "enhances internal efficacy by giving young people the impression that participation matters to electoral outcomes, and it increases knowledge by stimulating the flow of information" (Gimpel, Lay, and Schuknecht 2003, 55). In other words, political heterogeneity acts as a stimulus for politically motivated engagement. Gimpel, Lay, and Schuknecht note, however, that because their data are limited to a single, Democratic-leaning state, questions remain about the generality of their conclusions. The analysis of national-level data below provides evidence to complement theirs, although it also highlights that political homogeneity leads to an increase in civically motivated engagement.

DUAL MOTIVATIONS THEORY APPLIED TO ADOLESCENTS

This chapter's task is to see what happens when we take the basic model that has been used for adults and apply it to adolescents. To do so, this chapter relies on two different sources of data. The reason for using both is similar to the justification for the research strategy in chapter 3, where the analysis included data on self-reported motivations and behavior. Each has its weaknesses; in tandem they tell a more convincing story than either could alone. For example, the first source of data employs a measure of adolescents' projected public engagement—what they say they are going to do as adults. When adolescents are asked about their future behavior, we have no way of knowing whether they will actually do what they say they will do. However, when these results converge with adolescents' reports of the behavior they are currently engaged in, we have good reason to believe that both stem from a common cause.

The first source of data employed in the analysis is the Civic Education Study (CES). The CES is the U.S. component of a twenty-eight-nation study of civic and political attitudes among adolescents, conducted by the U.S. Department of Education under the auspices of the International Association for the Evaluation of Educational Achievement (IEA).[2] As before, data collected from individuals have been merged with their community-level characteristics, with county serving as an approximation for community.[3]

The CES survey contains a series of questions asking, "When you are an adult, what do you expect you will do?" Respondents are then given a list of activities, like "join a political party" and "volunteer time to help poor or elderly people in the community." For each one, they indicate the probability that this is something they see themselves doing, with options ranging from "I will certainly not do this" to "I will certainly do this," with "I will probably not" and "I probably will" in between. Admittedly, we should maintain a level of healthy skepticism regarding statements from adolescents about what they intend to do in the future. Rather than treat these questions as windows into the future, however, it might make more sense to think of them as providing insight into adolescents' *present* state of mind. By asking them whether they expect to be involved in one form of engagement or another, we gain insight into how they currently perceive such activity.

From this array of questions, it has been possible to construct three indices that parallel the measures used in chapter 3. One is for civically motivated activity, two others for the different forms of politically motivated participation: voice and electoral activism. The civic index consists of the aforementioned question about volunteering in the community, as well as one that asks about "collecting money for a social cause." Political voice is measured with questions about three political activities: collecting signatures for a petition, writing letters to a newspaper about social or political concerns, and participating in a peaceful protest march or rally. The electoral index has two items, joining a political party and running for local or city office.[4]

Because these three indices so closely resemble the data used in the previous analyses, we can examine whether community context has the same impact on adolescents' expectations as it does on adults' behavior.

Does political homogeneity lead to the anticipation of civically motivated activity? And does heterogeneity fuel politically oriented expectations? To find out, each index has been regressed on the familiar measure of partisan composition,[5] in addition to the same county-level factors as in the models of adult behavior introduced earlier. At the individual level, the model replicates as many of the measures that are applicable to ninth-graders. These include race and gender, as well as a measure of how much education the student expects to receive (anticipated education). Owing to the fact that the CES sample uses a hierarchical design (students sampled within schools), hierarchical linear modeling is used, as in chapter 3. Recall that this means the intercept for each contextual unit (in this case, schools) is allowed to vary as a function of the aggregate-level variables.

In Table 5.1 we see that adolescents are less likely to say that they will engage in civic activity as communities become more politically heterogeneous—paralleling the effect on adults' civic behavior. While the size of the coefficient is modest, it has been estimated with enough certainty to achieve statistical significance. Because the dependent variable is an index (ranging from 0 to 6), the substantive magnitude of the impacts reflected in the model may not be intuitive. The independent variables have been coded on a 0–1 scale, however, to assist with interpreting their relative magnitudes. In substantive terms, the coefficient of −0.33 for partisan heterogeneity means that, all else equal, moving from the least to the most politically heterogeneous community translates into a drop in anticipated civic activity of one-third of a "point" on the index, or about one quarter of a standard deviation. In relative terms, this is considerably less than the impact of expecting to attend college (itself a combination of both academic achievement and socioeconomic status), and a little less than half the impact of gender (as adolescent girls are more likely to report that they anticipate being involved in civic activity as adults).

The gist of the results for the civic activity index is simply that what we saw for adults is replicated for adolescents. Being situated in a homogeneous community fosters civic involvement. The civic side of the dual motivations theory appears to apply to young people. But what about the political side? Do adolescents' expectations of involvement in politically oriented participation similarly parallel what we have observed for adults? The remaining two columns of Table 5.1 shed light on this question, as they test the link between political heterogeneity and the two indices of political activity. Both models are otherwise identical to the one for civic activity. In sharp contrast to the results for civic activity, however, there is no discernable relationship between political heterogeneity and politically motivated engagement, whether the political activity

TABLE 5.1
Political Heterogeneity and Adolescents' Anticipated Public Engagement

	Civic Activity (1)	Political Voice (2)	Electoral Activism (3)
Political context			
Mean political heterogeneity (minimum to maximum)	−0.330** (0.141)	−0.253 (0.313)	−0.082 (0.200)
Level-1 effects			
Anticipated Education	1.162*** (0.174)	1.692*** (0.239)	1.116*** (0.176)
African American	0.143 (0.101)	0.075 (0.154)	0.084 (0.102)
Female	0.793*** (0.073)	0.600 (0.095)	0.021 (0.064)
Level-2 effects			
% with college degree	0.002 (0.495)	−0.028 (0.773)	0.597 (0.640)
Mean household income (log)	−0.059 (0.592)	−0.499 (0.848)	−0.891 (0.595)
Urbanicity	0.034 (0.208)	0.244 (0.359)	−0.060 (0.270)
Population density	−1.21** (0.497)	−0.943 (0.676)	−0.660 (0.447)
Residential mobility	−0.322 (0.227)	−0.193 (0.334)	−0.082 (0.200)
Mean commuting time	0.100 (0.237)	0.415 (0.397)	0.453 (0.299)
Ethnic heterogeneity	0.664*** (0.235)	0.815** (0.387)	0.083 (0.341)
Racial heterogeneity	−0.060 (0.183)	−0.243 (0.320)	−0.101 (0.269)
Income inequality (Gini coefficient)	0.676** (0.335)	0.344 (0.499)	−0.247 (0.373)
Constant	3.028*** (0.055)	3.594*** (0.079)	1.976*** (0.057)
Number of level 1-Units	123	123	123
Number of level 2-Units	1,752	1,752	1,752
Individual-level variance explained	0.13	0.27	0.03

Source: Civic Education Study.
Note: Results from hierarchical models. Robust standard errors in parentheses. Independent variables standardized on 0–1 scale. Weighted data.
* significant at .10   ** significant at .05   *** significant at .01

in question refers to the expression of voice in the political process or electoral activism. Given that the civic side of the dual motivations theory is replicated among adolescents, while the political side is not, this suggests that civically motivated behavior is more a matter of socialization and habituation than is political involvement, although we will see subsequent evidence that political heterogeneity can nonetheless have an impact on young people's sense of political efficacy.

As before, we are again interested in the impact of the other measures of heterogeneity found in the existing research literature. What impact do ethnic, racial, and income heterogeneity have on adolescents' anticipated levels of civic and political activity? As in the models of adult behavior, we again find evidence supporting the fundamental claim woven throughout the present discussion: political heterogeneity shows more empirical consistency than the other types of heterogeneity that have drawn the attention of previous researchers. The other heterogeneity measures do not behave in any systematic manner. While both ethnic and income heterogeneity have an unexpectedly positive impact on civic behavior, racial heterogeneity has a null relationship. None of the three has a significant impact on electoral activism, while only ethnic heterogeneity appears to affect political voice (positively). In sum, there is no pattern that comports with expectations growing out of the framework of the dual motivations theory.

On the one hand, these results from the CES data have their inherent limitations. They do not reflect these adolescents' actual behavior, but rather what they anticipate doing as adults. More precisely, they rely on reports of what these young people *say* they plan on doing as adults. Because many of these activities have a normative tinge to them, we might expect these youth to report what they think they are supposed to say. However, as with the measures of motivations for participation (see chapter 3), this is still valuable information. We actually are interested in what adolescents think they are supposed to say, as this is an indication of the norms they perceive within their community, which in turn have considerable potential to shape their adult behavior.

However informative, reports of anticipated civic and political involvement are only one means of testing whether the theory of dual motivations applies to adolescents. Again, we see a parallel with the self-reported motivations modeled in chapter 3. On their own, measures of anticipated involvement are suggestive but far from definitive. But in combination with data on present behavior, they become all the more compelling. As a complement to forecasting activity in the future, therefore, the analysis turns to observations of activity in the present.

Who Volunteers?

This whole enterprise rests on finding a measure of civically motivated behavior in which we can reasonably expect teens to engage. As with adults, adolescents' community service fits the bill. Unlike voting, there is no age requirement to participate in volunteering, and considerable evidence suggests that American youth regularly engage in volunteer service within their communities (Youniss and Yates 1997). Admittedly, however, some portion of adolescents' community service is not accurately described as civically motivated, since volunteering is sometimes done for instrumental purposes. As has been noted, this is undoubtedly true of adults' volunteering as well, but seems to be a particular concern for any analysis of youth. Community service has become a virtual prerequisite for admission to America's better colleges and universities. Engaging in voluntarism primarily for an individualistic purpose like gaining admission to college is not properly characterized as civic in nature, which explicitly refers to public-spirited collective action. We are reminded that although they are the building blocks of the theory of dual motivations and thus the focus of the analysis at hand, civic and political motivations do not exhaust all of the possible reasons that someone might engage in collective action.

Fortunately, evidence exists suggesting that volunteering among adolescents is not simply a matter of perfunctorily padding a college application or résumé but is most often spurred by a genuine concern for others. For example, James Youniss and Miranda Yates, scholars of community service, argue persuasively that young people generally participate in volunteer service out of a genuine desire to contribute to the well-being of their communities (Youniss and Yates 1997). A similar conclusion can be drawn from data collected by Independent Sector, a nonprofit organization that monitors the frequency of voluntarism and philanthropy in the United States.[6] In 1996, Independent Sector commissioned the Gallup organization to survey American adolescents about their engagement in voluntary activity. In addition to being asked whether they volunteer, those who said they did were asked why. On the whole, adolescents were more likely to report that their voluntarism was motivated by considerations that are better characterized as public-spirited than instrumental. For example, 84 percent reported that their volunteering is motivated by compassion toward people in need; essentially the same percentage reported that they performed community service to "do something for a cause that is important" to them. In contrast, 63 percent said that volunteering will look good on their résumé, while 60 percent said that their community service was motivated by the possibility of making new contacts to advance their career (Hodgkinson and Weitzman

1997). Obviously, these choices were not mutually exclusive, which is entirely reasonable given that voluntarism—as with probably all human behavior—has multiple motivations. After all, there is nothing inconsistent about volunteering because one feels compassion toward the needy and recognizing that such voluntarism might impress a college admissions committee or potential employer. Because the respondents were not asked to rate the importance of these motivations, we do not have a formal test of how they rank relative to one another. Certainly, however, these results make clear that for many American teens volunteering is motivated by a desire to have a positive impact on their community. This motivation appears to outweigh the instrumental benefits, although these are certainly relevant, too.

As further evidence that volunteering performed by adolescents is often civically motivated, consider the benefits that adolescents report receiving from their volunteer service. In the same Independent Sector survey, over 95 percent of teens who reported that they had volunteered in the previous month indicated that learning to respect others is an important benefit of their voluntarism, followed closely by learning to be helpful and kind (93 percent). Comparable percentages reported that getting along and relating to others, gaining satisfaction from helping others, and coming to understand people who are different were important consequences (92, 90, and 85 percent, respectively). Notably, 83 percent of teen volunteers said that helping them understand more about good citizenship was an important benefit of their service. While objections can be raised about the validity of self-reported motivations and benefits,[7] these data are not consistent with the claim that most teenagers cynically engage in volunteer service only to add another line to their résumé. Rather, they provide support for the argument made by Benjamin Barber, who has advocated that young people engage in community service because it is a "powerful response to civic scapegoatism and the bad habits of representative democracy" (1992, 252).

The 1996 National Household Education Survey (NHES) offers an opportunity to test whether the level of homogeneity in a local community has an impact on the rate at which adolescents volunteer—whether place matters for teens. The reader may recall the NHES, as it was briefly introduced in chapter 3. In its previous appearance, the NHES was employed to test whether place matters for these teens' parents. In this case, the analysis will draw on data from both parents and their children, as the parents' interviews were accompanied by interviews with their adolescent children.

The NHES has a number of features that make it an ideal means of examining the way in which local communities shape the civic development of their young residents. For one, the respondents are located in

over 1,000 counties in forty-six states. Also, the questionnaire is extensive. Interviewers inquired about numerous matters pertaining to the
civic involvement of young people, including a wide array of information
about their schools. We can thus account for an array of school-related
factors when testing the impact of community-level political heterogeneity. Furthermore, the dual interviews with both parent and child mean
that we can also account for civic influences in the home.

The empirical attack is guided by the same strategy that we have seen
before. Once more, county is used to approximate a respondent's community. The critical independent variable is the political complexion of
the county, again measured so that the more politically heterogeneous a
county, the higher its value.[8] The other contextual measures are as described previously. This should all look familiar to anyone has read the
previous chapters, where more information about these measures can be
found.

The dependent variable also has a familiar ring to it. Adolescents were
asked:

> During this school year, have you participated in any community service activ-
> ity or volunteer work at your school or in your community?

This wording parallels the questions about adult behavior that we saw
earlier for both volunteering and voter turnout. However, a complication
arises when modeling adolescents' community service as a manifestation
of voluntarism. In recent years, an increasing number of high schools in
the United States have mandated that their students engage in community
service as a requirement for graduation (Kleiner and Chapman 1999).
There are differing opinions regarding the normative implications of the
somewhat oxymoronic phenomenon of "involuntary volunteering,"
a debate that is only tangential to this analysis. Whatever its normative
consequences, mandatory community service threatens to obscure our
ability to infer the impact of local community context on voluntary behavior. We are interested in explaining the behavior of individuals, not
the policies of schools. The two would be conflated if the analysis included students whose community service is a curriculum requirement.
Therefore, the model is restricted to only those students whose schools
do not require that they perform community service.[9]

Every effort has been taken to isolate the impact of norms within the
community, separate from the influence of home and school. Thus, the
model accounts for attending a school that advertises and arranges service opportunities, which past research has found to be an important
factor influencing young people's voluntarism (Niemi, Hepburn, and
Chapman 2000).[10] Note that *arranging* service is different than the
school *requiring* community service for graduation; this is only a measure

of whether the school has the means to assist students in finding opportunities to work as a volunteer. The model also controls for the type of school a student attends, specifically whether it is one of three types of private school: Catholic, religious but not Catholic, or private but not religious.[11] Other research has found that private schools are more likely to encourage community service than their public counterparts (Greene 1998; Niemi, Hepburn, and Chapman 2000; D. Campbell 2001b). Controlling for attending a parochial school is particularly appropriate given Coleman's focus on Catholic schools as wellsprings of social capital.

The second channel through which students could be recruited as volunteers is the home, and so the model accounts for whether the student's parent is a participant in community service. This is an absolutely critical component of the analysis, as parents who volunteer are likely to encourage their children to do so also. Even more fundamentally, controlling for volunteer activity on the part of parents is a stringent test of the relationship between the community and the individual. Quite logically, the early political socialization literature stressed the role of the family in preparing young people for a lifetime of civic activity. The objective here, however, is to test whether the community beyond the walls of one's home has an independent impact on civic engagement. Norms encouraging collective action might be communicated and enforced primarily in the home, draining away any independent effect of the community.

With a binary measure—either respondents volunteered or they did not—logistic regression is again the estimator. Table 5.2 displays the results of substantive interest (with the full results reported in Table C7, appendix C), namely the relationship between political heterogeneity and volunteering, as well as the three other types of heterogeneity. Before turning to the impact of political heterogeneity, note that neither ethnic, racial, nor income heterogeneity has any statistically discernable impact on volunteering among young people. The story, however, is quite different for political heterogeneity. It clearly is related to volunteering and, as hypothesized, that relationship is negative. The greater the degree of heterogeneity, the lower the probability that a young person performs volunteer service.

These results have been translated into a visual display of the coefficients' respective impacts on the likelihood of volunteering. Figure 5.1 compares the impact of community political heterogeneity with some other statistically significant variables in order to provide a sense of comparative magnitude. Moving from the least to the most politically heterogeneous county results in about a 13-point drop in the probability that an adolescent will engage in volunteer work. This decrease in the probability of volunteering has a slightly greater absolute magnitude

TABLE 5.2
Community Political Heterogeneity and Volunteering

	Youth (1)	Parents (2)
Political context		
Mean political heterogeneity (minimum to maximum)	−0.712** (0.283)	−1.005*** (0.258)
Heterogeneity		
Ethnic heterogeneity	0.325 (0.391)	−0.333 (0.365)
Income heterogeneity	0.575 (0.567)	0.065 (0.533)
Racial heterogeneity	−0.280 (0.335)	1.068*** (0.307)
Constant	−2.913*** (0.597)	−0.427 (0.472)
Observations	5,057	5,740
Pseudo-R^2	0.08	0.06

Source: 1996 National Household Education Survey.

Note: Results from logistic regression. Robust standard errors in parentheses. Independent variables standardized on 0–1 scale. Weighted data. Models also control for individual- and community-level variables. *Individual:* parent volunteers, parent's education, family income, two-parent household, academic performance, educational expectations, African American, female, age, Catholic school, other religious school, private secular school, racial composition of school, size of school, school arranges service. *Community:* % with a college degree, mean household income (logged), urbanicity, population density, residential mobility, mean commuting time, South, Upper Midwest. See Table C7 in appendix C for the full results.

* significant at .10   ** significant at .05   *** significant at .01

than the impact of parental education, which increases volunteering by 10.5 points as it moves from its lowest to highest value. It is a little less than the impact of having a parent who volunteers (which increases the probability of volunteering by 17 points). It is also less than another factor related to the enforcement of social norms—the mean commuting time within a community (22-point drop).

Figure 5.2 displays another comparison, this time across models instead of within one. Here we see the impact of a community's partisan composition on the voluntarism of parents and their children. The models used to generate these predicted probabilities of volunteering are essentially identical, although the youths' equation includes the extra burden of parental voluntarism as a control variable. (See Table 5.2.) The similarity is striking. While the absolute level of volunteering is about ten points lower for youth than adults, the decrease in the rate of volunteering is almost identical for both. The two lines are virtually parallel to one another.

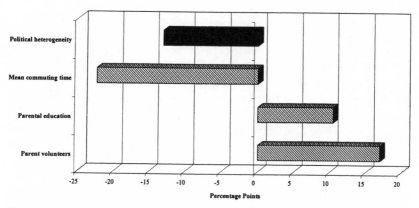

Figure 5.1. Impacts on volunteering (adolescents). All control variables set to their means. National Household Education Survey, 1996.

As with the analysis of the CES data, we again see evidence in support of the basic claim that politically homogeneous communities foster civically motivated participation among young people. This finding should seem familiar. Essentially, what we had early observed for adults has been shown to apply also to adolescents—a critical step in our exploration of how "where we are from" shapes our public engagement. Anyone who is only interested in the question of whether adolescents' civic

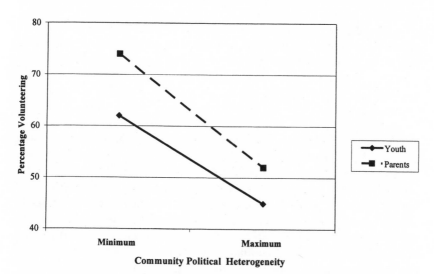

Figure 5.2. Impact of community political heterogeneity on volunteering. All control variables set to their means. National Household Education Survey, 1996.

involvement is shaped by their community in a manner comparable to adults can stop reading this chapter here and skip ahead to chapter 6. As with the examination of adult behavior, however, we need not be satisfied with only the broad contours of this analysis. The existing literature suggests that community context has a number of other consequences, all of which are woven together with a common thread drawn from the social capital literature: that social norms are stronger in some communities than others. Should we find that these further implications of social capital theory hold up, it should only bolster our confidence in the theory's explanatory ability.

The further implications of social capital theory that we can test correspond to two streams within the social capital literature, as exemplified by the work of James Coleman and Robert Putnam. In Coleman's work we find an emphasis on how social norms, a form of social capital, serve to enforce *order*—specifically, within schools and the communities in which schools are embedded. Thus, Coleman's work on Catholic schools highlights how they are often extensions of a tightly knit community in which norms are enforced through social interactions in the neighborhood, as well as at school. In Robert Putnam's work on social capital we find a different emphasis on how social capital fosters *voice*, through the norm of participation in democratic decision making. At first blush, voice and order might seem to be at odds with one another. Voice, after all, carries the connotation of freedom, while order implies constraint. Really, though, voice and order are simply the two faces of social capital, as any social norm—even one encouraging the expression of voice—involves the shaping of behavior. Therefore, the subsequent analysis will examine the impact of political homogeneity on both aspects of social capital, beginning with order.

ORDER

Building on Coleman's research into Catholic schools, sociologists Anthony Bryk, Valerie Lee, and Peter Holland have delved more deeply into the social capital found within Catholic schools. Their book *Catholic Schools and the Common Good* (1993) discusses at length the reasons for the success of Catholic school students, both academically and civically. They provide a compelling statistical analysis coupled with details gleaned from on-site fieldwork at a number of schools to make the point that Catholic schools are *communities*. That is, echoing Coleman and Hoffer, these schools benefit from the social capital found among teachers, parents, and students. Bryk, Lee, and Holland tellingly describe schools in which teachers and students interact in an atmosphere of respect, which the authors attribute to a shared commitment to common values. Like the reluctance in political science to acknowledge that duty motivates people to vote, these authors admit to being initially skeptical that a seemingly amorphous concept like "community" could ever be measured so as to serve as a rigorous explanation for the achievement levels of Catholic school students. Yet their qualitative and quantitative evidence consistently points in the same direction—there is something about the social relationships within these schools that make them distinctive. For our purposes, the essential point to distill from these works is that parochial schools are nestled within a wider community where norms are shared, trust is thickened, and order is thus enforced. The $64,000 question is whether they are sui generis, perhaps because of their religious profile generally or Roman Catholic character specifically.

We have reason to suspect that the sense of community Bryk and his colleagues found within Catholic schools can also be found in other types of schools. For example, in other research I have found evidence that the mutually respectful environments they observe in Catholic schools are replicated in public charter schools (D. Campbell 2001a). Likewise, recall Conover and Searing's description of the schools in the rural midwestern town within their study of adolescent socialization. They, too, stress that the local public schools are the focal point of what by all accounts could be described as a community rich in social capital.

Synthesizing these studies therefore suggests that a community with strong civic norms should have schools that are characterized by effective discipline, for while social norms *encourage* behavior that is, by definition, "normative," they also serve to *discourage* behavior that also, by definition, strays from the norm. Above I discussed how the behavior of adults is affected by social sanctions, which are often subtle. In contrast, adolescent behavior is often shaped by norms that are explicit and sanctions that are not so subtle. Anyone who has spent any time at all with teenagers knows that they typically do not respond to subtlety. Instead of "rake your lawn or face disapproving looks from your neighbors," it's "don't run in the hallway or risk a detention after school." The hypothesis is thus that schools embedded in communities with strong civic norms—as operationalized with the measure of political heterogeneity—engage in disciplinary efforts that parents view favorably. To the extent that teachers, principals, and parents all have common preferences (values), school officials can feel free to act in loco parentis. The process is almost certainly self-reinforcing. The greater the trust among parents, teachers, and administrators, the more that teachers and principals are willing to enforce discipline, because they know that actions at school will be supported at home. And the more rules and norms are enforced, the more parents are satisfied with the disciplinary climate in the school, and thus deepen their trust in the school's faculty and administrators.

The NHES allows us to test the extent to which a school's general disciplinary climate is related to the characteristics of the community in which it is found. Specifically, parents were asked to indicate the extent to which their child's teachers "maintain good discipline in the classroom" and "the principal and assistant principal maintain good discipline" at their child's school.[12] The questions have been combined in a simple additive index of school discipline.[13] We should expect that the more politically homogeneous a community, the more likely parents are to be satisfied with the discipline in their child's public school. As has been the modus operandi, the model includes an array of factors that could conceivably be related to a parent's perception of a school's disciplinary environment. In addition to the standard set of demographic and community-level variables, these include the size of the school as well as its racial composition. As has been the practice, ethnic, racial, and income heterogeneity at the community level are also included in the model so as to compare their impact with political heterogeneity. The dependent variable consists of seven ordered categories, and so the model has been estimated with ordered logistic regression. The model is restricted to students in neighborhood public schools (that is, not magnet schools or private schools), since the point is to test the extent to which the school's environment reflects the wider community in which it is rooted. Schools of "choice," whether they be private or public, are by design communities with shared values and thus do not constitute a test of the hypothesis (Moe 2000).[14]

Figure 5.3 shows us the impact of increasing political heterogeneity on discipline in school (Table 5.3 contains the results of the model).[15] Specifically, the figure displays the drop in the percentage of parents who have either the highest or next to highest values on the school discipline index (5 or 6 on a scale spanning 0–6). We see that as political heterogeneity increases, parents are less likely to endorse the disciplinary practices of their children's neighborhood schools. Here we have one example of how communities in which, relatively speaking, values are held in common are characterized by one type of order. A second dimension of order occurs not in school, but at home. Figure 5.3 also shows us how discipline in the home is affected by community homogeneity, since we should expect that parents find it easier to have a disciplined home in a community where they share norms—and values—with other parents. The measure of home discipline is an index constructed from the following questions, asked of students:[16]

Does your family have rules for you about:
    What time you go to bed? (asked of students in grades 6 through 8)
    What time you have to be home on school nights? (asked of students in grades 9 through 12)

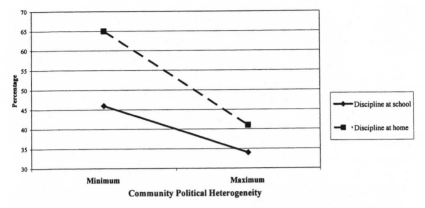

Figure 5.3. Impact of community political heterogeneity on "order." All control variables set to their means. National Household Education Survey, 1996. For discipline at school, points represent the percentage of parents who scored a 5 or 6 on the 0–6 scale. For discipline at home, the graph displays the percentage of adolescents who scored 3 or 4 on the 0–4 scale.

Doing your homework?
The amount of time you are allowed to watch television?
What television programs you are allowed to watch?

As shown in Figure 5.3, we see that discipline in the home is affected by community political heterogeneity much like discipline in school.[17] As heterogeneity increases, there is a weakening of parental discipline. Side by side, the similar results for discipline both at school and home suggest that homogeneous environments are characterized by social order, at least among adolescents. As suggested by Coleman, the intergenerational transfer of social norms is easier to accomplish in social environments where values are held in common. Presumably, these results would be even stronger if we had a more refined measure of "community" and, perhaps even more important, richer measures of common values. Partisanship is a workable approximation (see chapter 2) but is nonetheless a blunt indicator.

While imperfect, political heterogeneity nonetheless offers more analytical leverage than other types of heterogeneity. As shown in Table 5.3, ethnic, racial, and income heterogeneity show no consistent pattern across the models of order in the home and at school. None of them has an impact on discipline at school. In the model of order at home only ethnic heterogeneity reaches statistical significance, as it is positively related to family discipline. These models, therefore, lead us to the conclusion that a community's level of political homogeneity affects the degree to which

TABLE 5.3
Community Political Heterogeneity and "Order"

	Discipline at school (parents) (1)	Discipline at home (youth) (2)
Political context		
Mean political heterogeneity (minimum to maximum)	−0.523** (0.249)	−1.137*** (0.246)
Heterogeneity		
Ethnic heterogeneity	−0.135 (0.349)	0.700** (0.342)
Income inequality	−0.375 (0.513)	0.432 (0.509)
Racial heterogeneity	−0.077 (0.284)	0.066 (0.282)
Observations	4,708	4,708
Pseudo-R^2	0.01	0.07

Source: 1996 National Household Education Survey.
Note: Results from ordered logistic regression. Robust standard errors in parentheses. Independent variables standardized on 0–1 scale. Weighted data. Models also control for individual- and community-level variables. *Individual:* parent volunteers, parent's education, family income, two-parent household, academic performance, educational expectations, African American, female, age, racial composition of school, size of school, school arranges service. *Community:* % with a college degree, mean household income (logged), urbanicity, population density, residential mobility, South, Upper Midwest. See Table C8 in appendix C for the full results.
* significant at .10   ** significant at .05   *** significant at .01

order characterizes its schools and homes, while other forms of heterogeneity do not have a similarly consistent impact.

VOICE

Next we turn to the other face of social capital: voice. Does the order that characterizes politically homogeneous communities come at the expense of young people being able to give input into the decisions that affect their lives? In these communities, are parents able to guide the policies of their schools? In short, must communities choose between voice and order?

The first test of the degree to which a community's level of political heterogeneity affects the expression of political voice deals with youths' perceptions, specifically of whether they feel their opinions are valued at school. Young people were asked whether "most students and teachers respect each other" and whether "the opinions of the students are listened

TABLE 5.4
Community Political Heterogeneity and "Voice"

	Students' Voice at School (youth) (1)	Parents' Voice at School (parents) (2)	Students' Voice at Home (youth) (3)
Political context			
Mean political heterogeneity (minimum to maximum)	−0.598** (0.238)	−0.560** (0.258)	−0.548** (0.258)
Heterogeneity			
Ethnic heterogeneity	0.098 (0.350)	−0.291 (0.333)	0.151 (0.330)
Income inequality	0.249 (0.525)	−0.645 (0.514)	−0.646 (0.486)
Racial heterogeneity	−0.270 (0.265)	0.044 (0.259)	−0.150 (0.249)
Observations	4,708	4,708	4,708
Pseudo-R^2	0.03	0.01	0.02

Source: 1996 National Household Education Survey.
Note: Results from ordered logistic regression. Robust standard errors in parentheses. Independent variables standardized on 0–1 scale. Weighted data. Models also control for individual- and community-level variables. *Individual:* Parent volunteers, parent's education, family income, two-parent household, academic performance, educational expectations, African American, female, age, racial composition of school, size of school, school arranges service. *Community:* % with a college degree, mean household income (logged), urbanicity, population density, residential mobility, South, Upper Midwest. See Table C9 in appendix C for the full results.
* significant at .10   ** significant at .05   *** significant at .01

to." There is also a similar measure for parents, which includes a question about the level of respect among students and teachers, another about whether their child's school "welcomes my family's involvement with the school," and a third that asks whether the school "makes it easy to be involved there."[18] Table 5.4 displays the impact of community political heterogeneity on the degree to which students and parents feel that their schools have a participatory climate. In both cases we see that, far from being a trade-off, voice accompanies order. Greater political homogeneity leads to more voice in the local schools, for youth and adults. Figure 5.4 translates the results into a more intuitive display, with the sharp downward slope of the lines underscoring the point that as political heterogeneity rises, the perceived opportunities to express voice fall.[19]

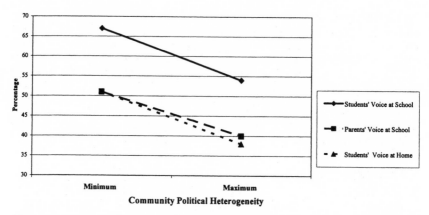

Figure 5.4. Impact of community political heterogeneity on "voice." All control variables set to their means. 1996 National Household Education Survey. For students' voice at school, points represent the percentage of adolescents who scored a 5 or 6 on the 0–6 scale, while students' voice at home displays those scoring 7 through 9 on the 0–9 scale. For parents' voice at school, the graph displays the percentage of students who scored 7 through 9 on the 0–9 scale.

Table 5.4 also includes a third model, this time of voice at home. Just as living in a community characterized by social consensus buttresses a family's efforts to have discipline in the home, perhaps it also facilitates the inclusion of young people in family decisions. Are students who have their voices heard in the classroom also able to express their opinions in the living room? Students were asked three questions, which together constitute the measure of voice in the home:[20]

> Do your parents/guardians:
>   Talk over important family decisions with you?
>   Listen to your side of an argument?
>   Let you have a say in making up rules that concern you?
>   [Hardly ever, sometimes, or often.]

As displayed in the third column of Table 5.4, more political heterogeneity means that students are less likely to report that they can express voice at home, again suggesting that interactions at home reflect interactions in the wider community. Figure 5.4 confirms that the decline in the expression of students' voice at home parallels the decline for voice at school. Once again, we also see that the political composition of a community is the only form of heterogeneity that has a systematic relationship to the three measures of voice. None of the other types of heterogeneity reaches statistical significance in any of the models.

These models, it should be stressed, are meant to test observable implications of the basic theory that some communities are more likely to foster social norms than others. Each one does not, therefore, necessarily constitute a full explanation for the particular dependent variable being modeled. Indeed, while measures of fit for maximum likelihood models like these are not easily interpretable, by any reasonable yardstick the so-called pseudo-R^2 in each model is extremely low.[21] In other words, while these models are useful to test the theory that political homogeneity fosters social norms, they nonetheless remain poor overall explanations for both voice and order.

POLITICAL EFFICACY AND TOLERANCE

The previous figures and tables make the point that a variety of civic indicators are similarly related to a community's partisan composition. Specifically, the level of partisan heterogeneity in a community has three types of effects. First, it has a direct impact on the probability that an adolescent engages in community service. Second, it leads to tighter discipline both in school and at home. Third, it fosters a participatory climate in both places as well. In other words, adolescents in homogeneous communities are subject to at least three interrelated civic influences: the home, the school, and the community. The empirical regularities in these measures should give the reader confidence in the theory that suggests they have common roots. All of these relationships, I suggest, can be explained by the presence of strong social norms.

If I left the story here, it might appear that homogeneous communities have it all—utopias where homes and schools combine to inculcate within their young people the "habits of the heart" (Tocqueville 1988; Bellah et al. 1985) that lead to a lifetime of civic involvement. But, as you might expect, there is more to the story. Politically homogeneous communities have other social consequences that many people might find troubling.

Recall that in their study of the community-level factors affecting adolescents' political socialization, James Gimpel and his colleagues found that partisan heterogeneity within community serves as a stimulus for greater political engagement (Gimpel, Lay, and Schuknecht 2003). One of their more notable findings is that adolescents have a stronger sense of political efficacy in communities characterized by political competition. Where the parties are competitive, young people see politics in action and come to learn that elected leaders respond to voters' opinions. The NHES permits a test of Gimpel, Lay, and Schuknecht's findings, as it included a question gauging young people's internal political efficacy, the sense that

TABLE 5.5
Community Political Heterogeneity and Political Efficacy, Tolerance

	Political Efficacy (1)	Political Tolerance (2)
Political context		
Mean political heterogeneity (minimum to maximum)	1.257*** (0.389)	0.568* (0.343)
Heterogeneity		
Ethnic heterogeneity	−0.224 (0.496)	0.167 (0.513)
Income inequality	−0.932 (0.680)	−0.381 (0.695)
Racial heterogeneity	−0.000 (0.412)	−0.586 (0.424)
Observations	3,161	3,161
Pseudo-R^2	0.04	0.04

Source: 1996 National Household Education Survey.

Note: Results from logistic regression. Robust standard errors in parentheses. Independent variables standardized on 0–1 scale. Weighted data. Models also control for individual- and community-level variables. *Individual:* parent volunteers, parent's education, family income, two-parent household, academic performance, educational expectations, African American, female, age, Catholic school, other religious school, private secular school, racial composition of school, size of school, school arranges service. *Community:* % with a college degree, mean household income (logged), urbanicity, population density, residential mobility, mean commuting time, South, Upper Midwest. See Table C10 in appendix C for the full results.

* significant at .10   ** significant at .05   *** significant at .01

the individual has the capacity to be engaged in politics, which has been adapted from the efficacy questions that have long been included in the biennial National Election Studies. Respondents were asked whether they agree with the statement, "Politics and government seem so complicated that a person like me can't really understand what's going on." In other surveys, political efficacy is typically measured with multiple items, each containing a range of response options, while in contrast this is simply a binary measure: either you are efficacious (1) or not (0). The model in Table 5.5 tests the relationship between community political heterogeneity and political efficacy with logistic regression, controlling for the same array of other variables we have seen before (see Table C10, appendix C for the full results). In particular, note that the model controls for the political efficacy of a youth's parent.[22] Table 5.5 displays the results of substantive interest, while Figure 5.5 presents the results graphically, displaying the percentage of youth who indicated that they feel efficacious. In sharp contrast to the figures we have seen thus far, Figure 5.5 shows us

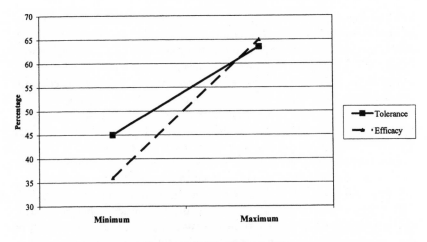

Figure 5.5. Impact of community political heterogeneity on political efficacy, tolerance. All control variables set to their means. National Household Education Survey, 1996.

an upward-sloping line. As political heterogeneity rises, so does political efficacy. It appears that the results Gimpel, Lay, and Schuknecht found in Maryland apply more generally to data collected nationwide.[23]

When political heterogeneity increases, so does an adolescent's sense of political efficacy—as does an adult's participation in politically motivated public engagement. The common relationship suggests a common cause. In both cases, it appears that political contestation within a community stimulates political engagement. Among adults, engagement leads to behavior, specifically in the form of electoral activism and expressions of political voice. Among adolescents, it manifests itself in attitudes; engagement is translated into efficacy.

We are thus confronted with what on the surface might appear to be a contradiction. Students feel that they can express voice at home and school, while also believing that they, and their family, are not able to do the same when it comes to government. Perhaps this seeming paradox can be explained if we note the differences in these measures, rather than their similarities. For while they all refer in some way to participation in decision making, the venues for those decisions are qualitatively different.

The school and the home are woven into the fabric of adolescents' everyday lives. And since—as the old saw goes about politics—civic norms are local, evidence for those norms should be reflected in individuals' local, everyday experience. People serve as volunteers close to home; the neighborhood school is a community on a small scale. The political efficacy questions, on the other hand, ask adolescents about their relationship to a much broader community. Their perception of that relationship seems to be affected by the degree of heterogeneity within their community. Being embedded in a politically competitive environment apparently fosters a sense among young people that they can successfully navigate their way through the thickets of the American electoral system, and that their efforts will be rewarded by a responsive political system.[24]

The working hypothesis, therefore, is that political heterogeneity facilitates a sense of efficacy in venues beyond the small-scale environments of home and school because it fosters an outward-looking perspective. If that is the case, we might also expect youth in politically heterogeneous environments to show other signs of looking beyond the boundaries of their community. Put another way, we should anticipate youth in politically homogeneous environments to be inward-looking, perhaps at the expense of excluding those who are not seen as members of their community. Recall that a fundamental premise underlying the analysis is that civic motivations are reinforced by commonality among members of a community. Commonality, however, is a double-edged sword. Normative democratic theory, shored up by empirical evidence, raises red flags about the potential for homogeneity to breed intolerance of people who fall outside the boundaries of whatever the homogeneous group holds in common. Birds of a feather may flock, vote, and volunteer together, but at what cost to how they perceive birds of a different feather?

The central importance of tolerance to a pluralistic democracy has led both normative and empirical scholars to contribute to an enormous—and ever-growing—literature. Over decades of research, different definitions of tolerance have been developed, but all share the fundamental insight expressed by John Sullivan, James Pierson, and George Marcus:

> Though liberal societies may be divided by intense conflicts, they can remain stable if there is a general adherence to the rules of democratic or constitutional procedure. Tolerance in this sense implies a commitment to the "rules of the game" and a willingness to apply them equally. (1982, 2)

A fundamental test of tolerance, therefore, is your willingness to grant civil liberties to members of groups who hold opinions that differ, perhaps dramatically, from yours. It is one thing to express abstract support for the right to free speech as guaranteed by the First Amendment; it is quite another to agree that neo-Nazis should be able to march in Skokie.

While it has long been hypothesized that heterogeneity fosters tolerance, Diana Mutz (2002b) provides a direct test of the connection. She finds that the greater the diversity of political opinions in people's network of political discussion partners, the greater their political tolerance. While Mutz's data deal only with social networks and not with social contexts,[25] we can infer that a heterogeneous social context will also be correlated with tolerance. Recall that in chapter 4 we saw that the heterogeneity of an individual's social network is at least partly a function of the heterogeneity within her social context. Thus, it seems likely that a heterogeneous context leads to a heterogeneous social network, which fosters political tolerance.

The NHES permits a test of how homogeneity within respondents' communities relates to their degree of political tolerance or, more specifically, their appreciation of free speech rights. To that end, the following question was asked of both parents and youth:

> Now I'd like to ask your opinion on some things. There are no right or wrong answers.
>
> Suppose a book that most people disapproved of was written, for example, saying that it was all right to take illegal drugs. Should a book like that be kept out of a public library? [Yes, No.]

This question has deep roots in generations of tolerance research, capturing the central concept of applying the "rules of the game" to everyone, no matter how unpopular their views. As with many of the other measures in the NHES, it is spartan. The fact that it is dichotomous severely limits the possible variation of the dependent variable, thus placing a significant statistical hurdle in the path of the analysis. Technical questions aside, there is also a normative debate about the value that should be placed on political tolerance, in contrast to other democratic values. While presumably every small-d democrat would agree that tolerance for opinions different than one's own is the bedrock of a pluralistic democracy, there is reasonable debate about balancing tolerance for all viewpoints with the promotion of views held to be normative within a community. Another way of looking at a question like this one, therefore, is to consider it as testing the extent to which young people are willing to permit the expression of views that diverge from their community's norms. In fact, this question offers a particularly good test, since it specifies that most people disapprove of the book in question. When put in these terms we can see how homogeneous communities, places with strong social norms, would be expected to have a low tolerance for views that deviate from those norms.

The tolerance model follows those we have seen thus far, with a tolerant response coded as 1 (the binary dependent variable means that logistic regression has been used). A positive coefficient thus means that variable is positively related to tolerance. The model is virtually identical to what we have seen before, sharing an identical set of demographic and contextual variables. Note the model controls for the type of school youth attend, given that public schools have been lauded for their emphasis on tolerance (Gutmann 1999; Macedo 2000).[26] The model also accounts for their parents' level of political tolerance, again ensuring that the model isolates the impact of the community context from influences in the home.[27]

Table 5.5 displays the model, while Figure 5.5 communicates the results in graphical form. Like efficacy, we see that political tolerance rises along with political heterogeneity. In each case, the *more homogeneous* a community, the *less willing* its adolescent residents are to permit a book with views that are out of step with the community's norms to be kept in a public library.[28] Note also that, in a refrain that should be familiar by now, we again see that none of the other heterogeneity variables achieves statistical significance in either model. Once again, the type of heterogeneity that matters most is political.

I am hardly the first to ask whether tight-knit communities foster a sense of exclusion. In *Bowling Alone*, Putnam traces this question through literature and philosophy, pointedly asking whether fraternity is at odds with liberty and equality. He concludes that community and equality are mutually reinforcing, which may appear to be at odds with my conclusion that homogeneity and intolerance move in lockstep. However, the two conclusions are not necessarily inconsistent, as they simply reflect the different ways that we have conceptualized community norms. Putnam measures social capital using an array of indicators, all measured at the state level. These include the mean volume of volunteering and level of voter turnout. Thus, two components of his independent variable constitute two of my dependent variables, which I have argued are driven by distinct motivations. Putnam thus argues that participation and tolerance go together, while I am suggesting that one factor driving civically motivated participation—community homogeneity—actually facilitates intolerance.

The patterns in the findings reported above echo a theme in Putnam's work, as he draws a distinction between two types of social capital: bonding and bridging. Social capital of the bonding variety refers to connections among people who have much in common, while the bridging variety consists of networks that are "outward looking and encompass people across diverse social cleavages" (Putnam 2000, 22). Homogeneous communities facilitate bonding, reflected in the strong civic norms found within them. Heterogeneity, however, appears to foster a mind-set conducive of bridging, as evidenced by the higher levels of political tolerance found among young people who live in heterogeneous environments.

The story told by these data reflects the thesis of Alan Ehrenhalt's poignant book *The Lost City: Discovering the Forgotten Virtues of Community in the Chicago of the 1950s* (1995). Like many contemporary declensionist authors of both the left (Bellah et al. 1985; Schudson 1998; Skocpol 2003) and the right (Gelernter 1995; Fukuyama 1999; Himmelfarb 1999), Ehrenhalt laments the fraying of civic bonds in America. In his narrative, he describes various Chicago neighborhoods as they were in the 1950s. What he finds are communities that fit a civic profile consistent with the one sketched here—places where a sense of duty was instilled at home, in school, and on the streets. These were communities with sharply defined boundaries. You knew who was from the neighborhood and who wasn't; you knew who could be trusted and who couldn't. Ehrenhalt's can be read as a cautionary tale, however, as these same neighborhoods are also characterized by an unreflexive suspicion of "the other."

CONCLUSION

It appears that there is something to asking, "Where are you from?" after all. The bottom line of this chapter is simply that the dual motivations theory appears to hold up for adolescent attitudes and behavior. Place matters for young as well as old. And since civic norms are local, evidence for those norms is reflected in individuals' local, everyday experience. Table 5.6 summarizes the plethora of results reported in this chapter. At first, it may seem that the sheer number of models estimated using two different data sets is a lot to absorb. Interpreting these results is made much easier by the fact that the theory of dual motivations ties them all together. As with adults, civic activity among adolescents is more common in politically homogeneous environments, whether civic participation is measured by what young people say that they are going to do in the future or what they are doing in the present. Furthermore, we found that partisan heterogeneity has an intriguing relationship to the environment of both home and school. On the one hand, in homogeneous communities we find schools where students can express *voice*—educators are responsive to their students and the school environment is one of mutual respect. In the home, we find a similar story. On the other hand, however, in homogeneous communities we also find homes and schools characterized by *order*, where we observe tight discipline. While voice and order may appear contradictory at first glance, social capital theory links them together. In fact, if voice is the product of social norms, then they would almost certainly have to be accompanied by order, as norms are enforced through discipline of one sort or another. The methods used to discipline teenagers

TABLE 5.6
Summary: Impacts of Heterogeneity on Volunteering, Voice, Order, Efficacy, and Tolerance

	Anticipated civic activity	Anticipated political voice	Anticipated electoral activism	Youth voluntarism	Parents' voluntarism
Type of heterogeneity					
Partisan	−	nr	nr	−	−
Ethnic	+	+	nr	nr	nr
Racial	nr	nr	nr	nr	+
Income	+	nr	nr	nr	nr

+ relationship is positive and statistically significant
− relationship is negative and statistically significant
nr no statistically significant relationship

are simply social sanctions by another name—methods of enforcing norms. To connect voice with order is to synthesize the different but complementary perspectives on social capital found in the work of Coleman and Putnam. Coleman's writings centered on order and said little about voice. Putnam's work has emphasized voice and said less about order.

Political heterogeneity, on the other hand, fosters political efficacy—a sense that one can make a difference in the wider political environment. Interestingly, political heterogeneity does not also lead young people to report that they will be more likely to engaged in politically motivated behavior as adults. While I would hesitate to make too much of this distinction, the apparently divergent results may be because there is a difference between asking young people whether they (or their families) *could* make a difference in the political arena, and whether they actually intend to enter that arena. Politically diverse communities also appear to foster tolerance, more precisely a willingness to allow unpopular opinions to be expressed within one's community. One way to read these results is that politically homogeneous environments foster tight-knit communities, which have both their virtues and vices.

THE NEXT STEP

This chapter serves to demonstrate that the renaissance of political socialization research will benefit from considering the influence of the

(continued from page 126)

Discipline at school	Discipline at home	Students' voice at school	Parents' voice at school	Students' voice at home	Youth efficacy	Youth tolerance
–	–	–	–	–	+	+
nr	+	nr	nr	nr	nr	nr
nr	nr	nr	nr	nr	nr	nr
nr	nr	nr	nr	nr	nr	

local community. However, this discussion only takes us partway to understanding what is significant about the connection between context and political socialization. "So, where are you from?" usually refers to where we *were*, not where we *are*. Recall that on my first day in graduate school, my fellow doctoral students and I identified ourselves by where we had been born and raised, even though many of us were far removed from wherever that might be. It is not enough to understand how context affects adolescents; we must also understand how the way we were as adolescents affects the way we are as adults.

Even though I suspect that few of us realize it consciously, when we ask people where they are from we are really making two intertwined claims. The first is that the local community context molds us when we are young. The second is that experiences in our youth continue to shape us as we age. This chapter has addressed the former; we turn next to the latter: what we do now depends on what we did then.

PART THREE

What You Do Now Depends on What You Did Then

CHAPTER SIX

The Links between Adolescents' and Adults' Public Engagement

In chapter 5 we saw evidence that the theory of dual motivations applies to adolescents. The next logical step is to ask whether what we do as adolescents affects what we do as adults. This chapter demonstrates that it does. Using a panel study, we see that adolescents who volunteer become adults who vote.

THE PREVIOUS CHAPTER detailed factors that lead to adolescents' voluntarism; the next step is to investigate the long-term consequences of volunteering. Does civically motivated participation among adolescents have any bearing on what they do as adults? This chapter uses longitudinal data—repeated interviews with the same people—to explore the extent to which adults' activities are shaped by their experiences as adolescents. Demonstrating that behavior in adolescence is related to behavior in adulthood is an important girder of the theoretical structure under construction. In chapter 5, we saw how adolescents' social environments affect whether they engage in community service. Since this has been billed as a study of public engagement not only among adolescents but also adults one might ask, so what? The answer, I suggest, is that what we do now depends (at least in part) on what we did then. In other words, experiences in adolescence set people on a civic trajectory that affects their level of engagement as adults.

THE LONG REACH OF ADOLESCENCE

Train up a child in the way he should go—so goes the proverb—and when he is old, he will not depart from it.[1] The sentiment is as relevant now as when it was penned. The massive investment in our education system is predicated on the fundamental belief that experiences in one's youth shape experiences in adulthood. Marketers clamor to imprint their products' brands in the consumer psyche of adolescents, expecting to reap the benefits for years to come. And what is parenthood if not the process of training up children in the way they should go, presumably owing to the hope that when they are old, they will not depart from it?

The assumption that what we do now (as adults) depends on what we did then (as youth) guides educators, marketers, and parents alike. It guides political scientists, too, or at least some of them. And it has done so since long before anyone thought to call them political scientists or their field of study political socialization. We can go all the way back to Plato's *Republic* for a discussion of young people's socialization into political roles.

In this case, the focus is how civic norms internalized in our youth can shape the nature of our public engagement beyond adolescence. Recall that our explanation for why civic participation is more common in homogeneous social environments rests on these being places with strong civic norms. These norms are enforced through sanctions—social pressure, often subtle, to behave in a certain way. And since such social pressure is more efficacious when and where people value one another's opinions, civic norms are stronger in politically homogeneous communities. If we left the explanation there, we would have difficulty explaining why many people act in accordance with social norms even when they are freed from the threat of social sanctions. Why do people brake their cars at stop signs on deserted roads in the middle of the night? Why do people like Traci Hodgson bother to vote even after moving into a new community where they are surrounded by strangers?

The answer is that sanctions need not only be applied externally, by others. They can also be applied to oneself, through the process of internalizing norms. Norm-induced behavior may begin as the product of externally applied social sanctions but eventually be rooted in something other than social pressure. Eventually, we come to sanction ourselves. While it is possible for norms to be internalized throughout one's life, perhaps the most important period of our lives for the internalization of social norms, including those relating to public engagement, is adolescence. For better or worse, this is the stretch of the life span when we are most likely to adopt—or not—society's expectations.

While it is common to encounter the claim that seeds planted in one's youth bloom in adulthood, it is less common to encounter empirical tests of the claim. Studies designed to connect adolescence and adulthood require observing the same people at more than one point in time—first as youth, then as adults. Conducting such research is difficult, expensive, time-consuming, and thus rare. For the most part, the longitudinal research that has been done focuses on the question of whether participating in extracurricular clubs and groups as an adolescent leads to participation in political activity as an adult. Consistently, the answer has been yes, it does. For example, one of the most notable and robust findings to arise from a major longitudinal study of high school seniors which began in 1965 is that participation in high school activities is a "pathway" to participation in political activity up to a decade later (Beck and Jennings

1982). Similar results have been found by other analysts using other sources of data (Smith 1999; Hanks 1981; Youniss and Yates 1997; Youniss, McLellan, and Yates 1997). Sidney Verba, Kay Schlozman, and Henry Brady (1995) asked adults to recall their experiences in adolescence in order to examine the influence of experiences in adolescence on the political participation of adults. They, too, find that some types of extracurricular activity in one's youth contribute to political engagement later on in life. Involvement in clubs and groups, but not participation in high school sports, correlates with political engagement later in life. In reviewing this literature, it seems clear that the preponderance of the evidence suggests that, all else equal, behavior in adolescence impacts behavior in adulthood. But none within this collection of studies specifically addresses my central claim, namely that being inculcated with civic norms in one's youth has a long-term effect on participation. By and large, this literature has been limited to examining the impact of participation in extracurricular groups, behavior that is similar to but nonetheless distinct from civically motivated public engagement such as community service.

It is important to stress that, for the most part, the extracurricular activities these studies link to adult participation are rarely civically motivated, as I have defined it. Generally, the activities included in these studies include such things as the school newspaper, chess club, drama club, jazz band, and so forth. It is unlikely that membership in groups like these meets my definition of civically oriented activity, for while they may teach the art of association, most extracurricular activities are not explicitly *public-spirited*—the essential element of civically motivated behavior. Certainly, some groups for adolescents are designed to connect them to their community, like scouting and student government. Most, though, are not so oriented toward civic engagement. Therefore, it follows that we should not expect involvement in traditional extracurricular activities to be related to the degree of political heterogeneity in one's community, since extracurricular activities of this sort are not the product of civic norms. Sure enough, extracurricular activities do not appear to be related to community heterogeneity. In models that test for the relationship between participating in extracurricular clubs and the degree of heterogeneity within one's community, controlling for the same array of variables as in chapter 5, none of the heterogeneity variables has an impact.[2] This null finding is in contrast to the fact that we have seen how voluntarism *is* related to a community's level of political heterogeneity, a consequence of its public-spirited—civic—nature. Significantly, the existing evidence suggests that participation in community service in high school does correlate with civic activity at least a short time after high school (Smith 1999).[3] However, given that early adulthood is a particularly disruptive period in people's lives, thus deflating rates of public engagement, a better test of the volunteering-voting link requires a longer time frame (Highton and Wolfinger 2001; Plutzer 2002).

The theoretical connection, then, between volunteering and voting is that they are both civically motivated. Civic norms spur youth to volunteer, which serves as positive feedback further reinforcing those norms. Having been internalized in adolescence, these norms motivate adults to vote. Voluntarism is therefore at least partly a reflection of the civic norms within an adolescent's community. We need not posit that volunteering per se leads people to the polls, although it certainly leaves open the possibility that engaging in community service deepens the norms that prompted the voluntarism in the first place.

The contention that extracurricular organizations and community service are different animals is underscored by the increasing attention paid to service learning in American high schools. While specifics vary in its application, essentially service learning consists of placing "students in community-based service projects" (Mann and Patrick 2000, 31). One impetus for encouraging community service is simply that traditional extracurricular activities do not engage students with their communities. For example, the National Commission on Civic Renewal, a blue-ribbon bipartisan panel of knowledgeable observers of America's civic scene, has noted that "our schools should foster the knowledge, skills, and virtues our young people need to become good democratic citizens," and then went on to single out "well-designed community work" as a means for them to do this, rather than stressing more traditional extracurricular activities (National Commission on Civic Renewal 1998).

The discussion regarding service learning is only one strand of a sustained national conversation over the plummeting levels of public engagement in the United States generally, and among young people particularly. The extent to which young people engage in the public sphere—from voting to volunteering—has come under increasing scrutiny. As noted in chapter 3, many observers have lamented the fact that while their rates of volunteering are high, American youths' involvement in other forms of public engagement is low, and getting lower. We should not be surprised that trends in community service and political engagement diverge, as volunteering for a soup kitchen and volunteering for a partisan campaign are qualitatively different activities. The former is civically motivated, while the latter is motivated by political considerations. However, voting, the reader is reminded, has a little of both. Volunteering and voting thus share civic roots, and as a consequence we should expect to see a correlation between them. A distinction between this study and much of the existing literature on public engagement among young people, therefore, is that the conventional wisdom holds that young people turn to volunteering *instead* of voting. If that is true, we should observe a negative relationship between engaging in community service and going to the polls. Instead, I suggest we should find that as a form of civically motivated behavior, serving in the community is *positively* related to another civic act, casting a vote.

MONITORING THE FUTURE

Owing to the considerable difficulties inherent in implementing a longitudinal study, few such sources of data exist. One that has remained largely unknown among scholars of politics is *Monitoring the Future: A Continuing Study of American Youth*. Primarily designed to monitor the drug and alcohol use of American adolescents, the Monitoring the Future (MTF) study contains interviews with nationally representative samples of high school seniors, and has been conducted annually since 1975.[4] Each year, roughly 15,000 students are surveyed.[5] As a study about drug use, it might not be expected to shed much light on civic and political behavior. Amid its questions about controlled substances, though, is an array of items that specifically address aspects of public engagement, including voting, electoral activism, and the expression of voice in the political process. Crucially, respondents are also asked about their involvement in community service. In addition to its cross-sectional component, MTF is also a panel study.[6] A subset of respondents is selected for follow-up surveys every two years past high school and asked exactly the same questions as at baseline.[7] As a result, MTF provides precisely the data that are necessary to test the extent to which voluntarism in adolescence leads to voting and other activities as people move into the early years of adulthood.[8]

MTF thus offers an opportunity to test a number of hypotheses. First, we can test this chapter's central hypothesis, namely whether engaging in community service as a youth leads to civic participation in early adulthood, both volunteering and voting. Since both of these activities have been described as civically oriented, we should expect to see high school voluntarism as a pathway to each. Since MTF also includes measures of behavior corresponding to both the electoral and voice dimensions introduced in earlier chapters, we can also test whether voluntarism in high school leads to political engagement in the years following adolescence.

TURNING TO THE DATA

In order to maximize the length of time included in the panel, this analysis will focus on the cohort of MTF respondents who began the study (that is, graduated from high school) in 1980. Follow-up interviews were then conducted in 1981/1982, 1983/1984, and 1989/1990. It is this final wave of the study that is of most interest, given its reach of nine to ten years following high school. Throughout the analysis, our attention will be focused on the question asked about participation in community service as the key explanatory factor. This question is one in a series, which has as its stem, "How often do you do each of the following?" Other activities in the series include watching television, getting together with friends informally, and going to parties or other social affairs. Respondents could report that they do each activity "almost everyday, at least once a week, once or twice a month, a few times a year, or never." In 1980, 29 percent of American high school seniors reported that they never volunteered in their communities. Forty-five percent said that they perform community service at least a few times per year, while another 17 percent indicated that they volunteer once or twice a month. The remainder, roughly 9 percent, reported volunteering once a week or daily.

Because it includes voluntarism among an array of other activities, MTF's method of asking students about their participation in voluntarism has certain advantages over a question that specifically draws attention to community service, as is usually the case. Most important, it probably helps keep social desirability bias in check.[9] However, there are always trade-offs. The format of the MTF question makes it impossible to distinguish between students who are required to engage in community service for school credit and those who do so for other reasons. However, it is equally important to note that 1980 predates the rise of community service as a widespread requirement in America's schools, and so very few of the youth in this panel would have been subject to service requirements as part of their schooling experience.

The first order of business is to establish that there is reason to think that civic habits form in adolescence. We begin, therefore, with the simplest possible linkage by asking whether voluntarism in high school serves as a pathway to voluntarism later in life. Table 6.1 displays a simple model that tests the relationship between high school voluntarism and participation in community service at each of the three waves in the MTF study. The dependent variable replicates the question about the frequency of volunteering asked when the respondents were in high school, producing a scale from "never" (1) to "every day" (5).[10] The model also accounts for other factors that we might think would affect the propensity to be a community volunteer, each of which will be repeated in subsequent models. These include race, gender, and family socioeconomic status (specifically, parents' education).[11] Political interest is also included, as measured contemporaneously with the dependent variable. The model also accounts for the frequency of TV viewing when the

TABLE 6.1
Voluntarism in Adolescence and Adulthood

	Wave 1 (1–2 years)	Wave 2 (3–4 years)	Wave 3 (9–10 years)
High school voluntarism	4.018*** (0.496)	3.116*** (0.496)	2.379*** (0.482)
Television viewing	−0.191 (0.656)	−0.836 (0.755)	−0.525 (0.667)
Parents' education	1.052** (0.526)	0.914* (0.531)	1.560*** (0.558)
Political interest	1.036* (0.573)	1.315** (0.600)	0.945 (0.651)
African American	0.835*** (0.299)	0.941*** (0.315)	0.087 (0.343)
Female	0.083 (0.212)	−0.252 (0.218)	0.286 (0.224)
Observations	385	354	326
Pseudo-R^2	0.11	0.08	0.06

Source: Monitoring the Future.

Note: Results from ordered logistic regression. Standard errors in parentheses. Independent variables standardized on 0–1 scale. Weighted data.

* significant at .10   ** significant at .05   *** significant at .01

respondents were in high school. Other researchers have singled out television viewing as having an especially dampening effect on levels of civic engagement (Putnam 1995, 2000; Brehm and Rahn 1997; Campbell, Yonish, and Putnam 1999).

As evidence that volunteering in the community does not necessarily reflect political engagement, note that in the third wave political interest does not have a statistically significant impact on volunteering. Also worth noting is that, while television viewing in high school is negatively related to voluntarism at all three waves of the study, at no point does it reach conventional levels of statistical significance. The primary hypothesis, however, is supported. We see that high school voluntarism is positively, and strongly, related to voluntarism at all three waves. Volunteer in high school, volunteer after high school. In substantive terms, when we hold everything else constant at their means or modal values,[12] moving from never volunteering to doing so "once or twice a month" in high school leads to a 21-percentage point increase in volunteering at least that frequently in the first follow-up study, a 14-point increase in the second wave, and an increase of 16 points in the third follow-up, a decade following high school.

Presumably, it does not come as a surprise that volunteering at one point in time corresponds to volunteering at a subsequent point in time, although neither was this a sure thing. Because of the social disruptions in early adulthood, it is also conceivable that any "volunteering habit" developed in high school would not stick during the years immediately following high school. However, this analysis only sets the stage for our central question, whether volunteering leads to voting. To the extent that volunteering is a reflection of a young person's adopting a civic orientation, we would expect a strong positive relationship between voluntarism in adolescence and voter turnout in adulthood. It is thus to such a test that we now turn.

Perhaps reflecting the fact that political scientists did not design the study and that its primary objective is not to examine civic engagement, MTF uses a unique indicator of voter turnout. Typically, surveys ask respondents if they voted in a particular election, say, the most recent presidential contest. The MTF item, however, asks whether they "have ever voted in a public election." Once respondents have cast a vote in any election their score on this measure is fixed, so we have no indication of the frequency with which they vote. And, given the question's imprecision, it is impossible to tell whether ballots were cast at the national, state, or local level. While the unusual wording of its turnout question makes comparisons between MTF and other sources of data problematic, it nonetheless provides useful information. Voting is largely a matter of habit (Green, Gerber, and Shachar 2003; Plutzer 2002), and so turning out once often marks the beginning of a lifetime of regular appearances at the polls.[13]

Table 6.2 displays results from taking the model used earlier to estimate the frequency of volunteering and applying it to voting. As expected, we see that socioeconomic status contributes to the probability of turning out. We are reminded that voting shares a political as well as civic dimension, as we see that interest in politics has a strong, positive relationship to voter turnout in all three waves. Interestingly, the frequency of television viewing among adolescents has a negative influence on voter turnout at each point in time. The impact of TV viewing is only at the edge of the conventional threshold for statistical significance ($p < 0.10$), but remains steady even to the final wave. The impact of television viewing is notable given the limited variation in the measure: the range is from "never" to "almost everyday." Since most American adolescents watch TV "almost every day" (71 percent in 1980), it would be more informative to record the duration of television viewing, rather than just its frequency. That we find an effect even with such an unrefined measure speaks to the potency of television's negative impact on public engagement.

Our main interest, of course, is in the impact of high school voluntarism on voting. We see that there is a positive relationship between volunteering and voting in all three waves. The contrast between volunteering and TV viewing is striking, and suggests that they exert countervailing forces

TABLE 6.2
Voluntarism in Adolescence and Voting in Adulthood

	Wave 1 (1–2 years)	Wave 2 (3–4 years)	Wave 3 (9–10 years)
High school voluntarism	0.822* (0.498)	1.307** (0.576)	1.862** (0.943)
Television viewing	−1.253* (0.747)	−1.766* (0910)	−3.517* (1.801)
Parents' education	1.321** (0.586)	1.477** (0.639)	2.422** (1.027)
Political interest	2.391*** (0.646)	2.449*** (0.721)	4.386*** (1.219)
African American	−0.420 (0.324)	−0.173 (0.368)	0.105 (0.508)
Female	0.109 (0.231)	0.153 (0.256)	−0.227 (0.386)
Constant	−1.329 (0.892)	−0.466 (1.094)	0.769 (1.999)
Observations	365	334	304
Pseudo-R^2	0.08	0.08	0.18

Source: Monitoring the Future.
Note: Results from ordered logistic regression. Standard errors in parentheses. Independent variables standardized on 0–1 scale. Weighted data.
* significant at .10   ** significant at .05   *** significant at .01

on adolescents. Interestingly, other analysis reveals that it is television viewing *in adolescence* that has a significant impact on voting, not time spent watching television at waves 1, 2, and 3, respectively. In other words, the contemporaneous measure of TV viewing fails to reach statistical significance as a predictor of voter turnout (although it is negative at all three points in time). If television were simply soaking up time that would otherwise be devoted to civic activity, we would expect to find the opposite: the frequency of TV viewing at the time of the survey should have a significant impact, while TV use in adolescence should not. Why would TV consumption in adolescence have such a long reach? One explanation is that just as volunteering in one's community fosters a strong sense of connection to that community, and thus a strong sense of civic responsibility, sedentary TV viewers have a tenuous connection to their communities and thus do not internalize the norm of engaging in civically oriented activity.

Figure 6.1 provides a sense of the relative magnitude of voluntarism's impact on voter turnout by comparing it to the impact of parents' education and television viewing in all three waves of the study (again, holding the other variables constant at their means or modal values). In each case, we see the increase in the probability of having voted as the frequency of voluntarism in high school increases from having never volunteered to

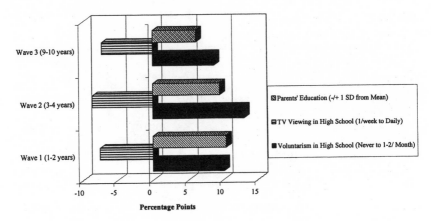

Figure 6.1. Impacts on voter turnout. All control variables set to their means. Monitoring the Future.

volunteering "once or twice per month." Similarly, we see the impact of an increase in parents' education from one standard deviation below to one standard deviation above the mean, and the impact of television viewing as it moves from watching TV once a week to daily. In all three waves, the impacts of the three variables are comparable. High school voluntarism, for example, increases the probability of turning out to vote by 10 points at wave 1, 13 points at wave 2, and 9 points at wave 3. Television viewing decreases the probability of voting by 8, 9, and 7 points, respectively.

The bottom-line conclusion from the models relating voluntarism in adolescence to behavior in early adulthood is that volunteering begets both more volunteering and voting. Both are examples of civically motivated behavior (although, of course, voting also has a political dimension), supporting the hypothesis that volunteering in high school fosters adherence to civic norms. It could also be, however, that volunteering simply fosters participation in collective action of all types, including explicitly political activity. If true, this would suggest that the causal process at work is not that adolescents develop an internalized norm toward civically oriented activity specifically, but simply that they become "doers," engaging in a wide variety of activities. Of course, these explanations need not be considered mutually exclusive either.

Sorting out the two explanations requires testing whether voluntarism impacts politically oriented activity. If so, it is unlikely that voluntarism fosters civic norms, and thus civically oriented participation, per se. Therefore, the models displayed in Tables 6.3 and 6.4 test the link between voluntarism in high school and, respectively, the expression of

TABLE 6.3
Voluntarism in Adolescence and Political Voice in Adulthood

	Wave 1 (1–2 years)	Wave 2 (3–4 years)	Wave 3 (9–10 years)
High school voluntarism	0.712 (0.521)	0.655 (0.460)	0.755 (0.488)
Television viewing	−0.917 (0.749)	−0.632 (0.675)	−1.775*** (0.677)
Parents' education	2.109*** (0.641)	0.696 (0.534)	2.136*** (0.596)
Political interest	1.881*** (0.716)	0.041 (0.569)	3.448*** (0.697)
African American	−0.089 (0.392)	−0.370 (0.338)	−0.509 (0.390)
Female	−0.303 (0.254)	0.133 (0.219)	−0.115 (0.236)
Observations	386	355	325
Pseudo-R^2	0.06	0.01	0.10

Source: Monitoring the Future.

Note: Results from ordered logistic regression. Standard errors in parentheses. Independent variables standardized on 0–1 scale. Weighted data.

* significant at .10   ** significant at .05   *** significant at .01

political voice and electoral activism. Both of these indices resemble the measures in previous chapters. Electoral activism is measured as having worked as a volunteer for a political campaign or given money to a political candidate or party, while the political voice index includes participating in a lawful demonstration, writing to public officials, and

TABLE 6.4
Voluntarism in Adolescence and Electoral Activism in Adulthood

	Wave 1 (1–2 years)	Wave 2 (3–4 years)	Wave 3 (9–10 years)
High school voluntarism	−0.342 (0.647)	0.784 (0.611)	0.332 (0.559)
Television viewing	−1.122 (0.836)	−0.693 (0.834)	−0.561 (0.809)
Parents' education	0.224 (0.724)	1.413** (0.685)	1.593** (0.678)
Political interest	2.984*** (0.839)	2.493*** (0.758)	3.443*** (0.805)
African American	−0.081 (0.444)	−0.582 (0.499)	0.020 (0.447)
Female	0.281 (0.301)	−0.222 (0.282)	−0.066 (0.274)
Observations	386	353	326
Pseudo-R^2	0.04	0.04	0.08

Source: Monitoring the Future.

Note: Results from ordered logistic regression. Standard errors in parentheses. Independent variables standardized on 0–1 scale. Weighted data.

* significant at .10   ** significant at .05   *** significant at .01

boycotting certain products or stores.[14] With only one exception (wave 2 for political voice), political interest is a consistently positive predictor of both electoral activism and political voice. Television viewing has a negative impact in every case, but only reaches statistical significance in wave 3 of the political voice model.

Most important, in no case does high school voluntarism have a statistically significant impact on either electoral activism or political voice, although we should not ignore that the direction of the relationship is positive in five of the six models. The lack of any statistical relationships that meet the threshold for statistical significance can be taken as evidence in favor of the civic norms explanation for the link between voluntarism and voting. Voluntarism appears to feed activity with a civic, but not political, orientation. However, given the tendency toward a positive link between voluntarism and these two types of political activity, we should not overstate the definitiveness of these results. After all, it could very well be that while volunteering leads to civic participation because it fosters civic norms, it also facilitates political participation through other channels, like the development of civic skills and wider social networks.

Service Learning

Since the topic arose earlier, it is reasonable to ask whether these results speak to the policy question of whether schools should adopt community service requirements. Unfortunately, at this point the answer is no better than "maybe"—although this is an informed "maybe." Recall that because of the way MTF is conducted, there is no way of knowing whether respondents' service is imposed by their school, although the baseline data were collected in 1980, before community service requirements became widespread. This is not to say, however, that these results are totally irrelevant to the question of whether high schools should adopt service learning programs. They *do* show that, in general, voluntarism impacts civic involvement, suggesting that a community service component of a high school curriculum might have a similarly positive effect. The only way to find out is with carefully designed studies that are both experimental and longitudinal—two features largely missing from the existing body of literature on community service (Nolin et al. 1997; Kleiner and Chapman 1999; Mann and Patrick 2000; Niemi, Hepburn, and Chapman 2000). These results recommend that this is research worth undertaking.

Indeed, randomized experiments would address the thorny problem of attributing a causal effect to voluntarism, as compared to examining whether the two are correlated (which is all the present analysis is able to do). For the purpose at hand, however, even the correlation between the two is telling, since the underlying theory is essentially built on the claim that volunteering and voting share a common root, namely the internalization of a civic norm. The moral of this chapter's story is simply that volunteering in adolescence leads to voting in adulthood. The significance of this statement is amplified when combined with the conclusion of the previous chapter: adolescents' voluntarism is related to the social context in which they live. Taken together, the findings of these two chapters suggest that whether you vote as an adult is related to where you lived as an adolescent. This inference can be expressed as a syllogism:

Since
a. volunteering as an adolescent → voting as an adult
and
b. community context → volunteering as an adolescent
therefore
c. community context → voting as an adult

The starkness of these expressions, however, obscures the intricacy of the theoretical latticework that connects them. For while the conclusions of each chapter thus far can stand on their own, their full significance only becomes apparent upon being viewed as a whole. We have seen that political homogeneity within a community can foster civically motivated collective action. Commonality breeds trust, at least among those perceived as being "in common." Trust, in turn, facilitates the enforcement of social norms. Those norms affect the behavior of adolescents as well as adults. And the behavior of adolescents affects their behavior as adults.

Woven together, the individual strands of the story thus give us reason to think that the community in which you were raised shapes (but does not determine) your long-term disposition toward civic participation. Nonetheless, there are still loose ends that could potentially cause everything to unravel. Even if volunteering has civic norms as a cause and voter turnout as an effect, it nonetheless could be the case that civic norms in adolescence do not have a direct influence in shaping adult behavior. After all, I have only inferred that civic norms are the link between volunteering and voting. Furthermore, even if someone's social context in the past has an effect that reaches into the future, we do not know its impact relative to factors in the present. With these questions left unanswered, the evidence presented thus far points us in the right direction, but does not represent the final destination.

Returning to the syllogism, this chapter provides evidence for (a), chapter 5 for (b). The next step is to test (c). The conclusion that civic norms instilled in adolescence lead to participation as an adult thus rests on two disconnected sources of evidence. One part of the story has been told with contextual data, the other with data that are longitudinal. The empirical gap between them can only be closed with data that have both a contextual *and* a longitudinal component. Only then will we be able to determine if what you do now depends on where you were then, the subject of the next chapter.

PART FOUR

What You Do Now Depends on Where You Were Then

Adolescents' Social Environments and Adults' Public Engagement: The Civic Motivation Model

Having seen that (a) adolescents' social environments affect their public engagement and (b) public engagement in adolescence leads to engagement in adulthood, the next step is to test (c) whether adolescents' social environments shape public engagement later in life. To do so, I introduce a new measure of "community" for adolescents—their high school. The strength of civic norms within a high school is then measured as the prevalence of the belief that to be a good citizen, one must vote. A school's civic climate is shown to have a long-term impact on voter turnout—stronger civic norms in high school increase the probability of voting fifteen years later. A school's civic climate has an equally long reach as a positive influence on civic participation like volunteering, but no effect on politically oriented engagement. Furthermore, a participatory norm in high school also exhibits evidence of a sleeper effect, having an impact that grows over time.

IN THIS PENULTIMATE CHAPTER, it is perhaps useful to remind ourselves of our ultimate objective. Remember Traci Hodgson? She was the young woman we were introduced to in chapter 1, who cast the only ballot at her precinct in a Boston city election. Our objective has been to explain why she was the lonely voter. The explanation is deceivingly simple: she voted in Boston because she had come to see voting as her duty. And she came to see voting as a civic obligation because she had internalized voting as a civic norm. Furthermore, she internalized that norm because she spent her formative years in a community characterized by strong civic norms. Over the preceding chapters, we have examined the plausibility of this explanation for her vote, building a theoretical structure to explain Traci's vote as driven by a civic motivation, implanted during her adolescent years.

First, we saw evidence that *what you do depends on where you are*. Heterogeneous communities like Boston have a very different civic character than homogeneous places like Traci Hodgson's hometown of Little River, Kansas. In politically heterogeneous communities, voter turnout is more likely to be ignited by political conflict. People vote because they see their interests threatened. In homogeneous communities, however, voter turnout is more likely to be motivated by a sense of civic obligation.

Similarly, politically heterogeneous communities are more likely to be the site of political combat, as their residents are more likely to work on political campaigns and march in demonstrations, while communities characterized by relative political homogeneity are more likely to host civically motivated activities like volunteering in the community.

Traci grew up in a community where public engagement likely had a stronger civic than political flavor, from which we can infer that her adolescence was shaped by civic norms. Rather than leave it as an inference, however, chapter 5 directly tested the claim that adolescents' engagement in their communities is affected by the degree of political heterogeneity within those communities. There, we saw that adolescents' public engagement is shaped by the communities in which they live. Or, in other words, I examined whether *what you did then depends on where you were then*. The pattern paralleled what we observed for adults. In communities with greater political heterogeneity, adolescents have a greater degree of political efficacy—the sense that engagement in politics is worth the effort because it brings substantive results. On the other hand, with political homogeneity comes a higher level of civically motivated activity, specifically engagement in community service.

The next step was to see whether civic behavior in adolescence links to adulthood. It is one thing to say that while living in some communities over others, teens are more likely to engage in civically motivated activity. It is quite another to say that once they leave those communities, they continue to be civically involved. Remember that Traci cast her solitary vote in Boston, where she was a newcomer, and not in Little River, where she spent her adolescence. And so, the analysis next turned to the question of whether *what do you do now depends on what you did then*. We found strong links between young people's participation in civically oriented activity and their civic involvement later on in life.

We have thus come a long way in explaining why Traci bothered to vote. We can say that place matters for adults, that place matters for adolescents, and that adolescence matters for adulthood. The final step is to put it all together and see whether adolescents' places matter for their behavior as adults: if *what you do now depends on where you were then*. In other words, to what extent can we explain Traci's vote *in Boston* because of a norm she internalized while growing up *in Little River*?

Adolescents' Communities

Studying the impact of different communities on public engagement is complicated by the fact that the term "community" has shifting meanings, depending on who is using the term and in what context. An experience of a friend of mine illustrates the point. One day this friend struck up a conversation with a woman in front of his home in Somerville, Massachusetts. Detecting a local accent, he asked, "So, where are you from?" assuming that he already knew the answer. He was surprised when she responded that she was "not from around here." Rather, she explained, "I'm from Medford." For those unfamiliar with Massachusetts geography, Somerville and Medford border one another. Both are working-class, ethnically heterogeneous communities in the metropolitan Boston area. When traveling from one to the other they are virtually indistinguishable, at least to me. Yet this woman has come to see differences between them. To her, they are two distinct communities, and she considers herself to be from one of them and not the other.

The "woman from Medford" has a precise definition of her community, which is different than how others may define theirs. Complicating things further, depending on the situation people will have shifting definitions of what constitutes their community. For some purposes, I might consider my city as my community, for others my neighborhood. For other purposes, it might even be my coworkers or fellow fans of the Boston Red Sox. These shifting meanings make it difficult, probably impossible, to arrive at a uniform measure of community that applies to everyone, everywhere, at every point in time. Thus, previous chapters have relied on what I readily acknowledge are imperfect measures of one's community, usually the county or metropolitan area. Counties and metro areas represent a careful compromise among a combination of factors: a clearly defined geographic area of mid-range size, applicable to essentially the whole nation, for which the relevant data are available. From one perspective, the imperfection of defining community this way means that the glass is half full—if noisy measures provide theoretically consistent, empirically robust results then presumably a more refined method of operationalizing community would only put the findings in starker relief. But the glass is also half empty, as legitimate questions remain about whether the analysis is capturing the impact of community as specified by the theory. Overall, I would hope the reader agrees that the glass is better described as full than empty, especially since different ways of measuring community produce comparable results. Nonetheless, ambiguities over the many nuances of community still cloud our understanding of how it impacts public engagement, or anything else for that matter.

The more careful the definition of the community in question, the more theoretical leverage we gain on the question of how social environments shape public engagement. This chapter narrows its scope somewhat from the earlier ones, and centers on one specific type of community. Since our attention will be directed at adolescents specifically, the community in focus will be the high school. We have already seen that schools are an extension of the communities that they serve (see chapter 5). In this chapter, we will treat schools as communities in their own right.

While, like adults, teens are also potentially members of many different communities, unlike adults virtually all of them belong to one community that encompasses several aspects of their lives—their school.[1] Obviously, they are places in which American youth spend thousands upon thousands of hours. Yet a mere tally of time does not fully capture the social significance of high school, which is why so much popular entertainment deals with the refiner's fire that is the American high school experience. In fact, the foundations of the theoretical literature upon which the present discussion is based—social capital theory—lie in James Coleman and Thomas Hoffer's early research on schools (1987).

SCHOOL AND CIVIC EDUCATION

Since this is a study of norms related to civic engagement, narrowing in on high schools is especially appropriate. Schools are a particularly critical institution affecting the state of our nation's civic health. High schools are where young people receive much of their preparation for a life of active citizenship. For in addition to subjects like algebra and chemistry, America's schools have the mandate to teach the arts of association and engagement. Although largely forgotten owing to the intense attention paid to test scores in reading and math, originally the primary purpose of America's public, or common, schools was to forge a common citizenry out of an immigrant nation. The means employed by the early common school advocates are anachronistic to our modern ears—mainly, promoting mainline Protestantism (Glenn 1988)—but the fundamental end is not (Gutmann 1999; Macedo 2000). Now, as then, American society consists of a kaleidoscope of ethnic, linguistic, and cultural groups. Somehow, unum must be found within the pluribus. Consequently, "civic education is once more on the radar screen of contemporary political science" (Galston 2001, 217). This contemporary talk of the civic objectives of the nation's schools is not merely a nostalgic nod to an earlier era, as these aspirations are widely embraced by today's general public. In a 1996 Phi Delta Kappa/Gallup poll, 86 percent of Americans reported that they feel "preparing students to be responsible citizens" is a "very important" purpose of the nation's schools, more than the 76 percent who felt that it is equally important that schools should "help people become economically self-sufficient" (Elam, Rose, and Gallup 1996). Indeed, with the eyes of the nation upon him Chief

Justice Earl Warren specifically cited the civic function of public schools when the Supreme Court ruled racial segregation to be unconstitutional, noting that education "is the very foundation of good citizenship" (*Brown v. Board* 1954, 691). Echoes of the concern over the schools' mission to provide a civic education are a subtext in the current debate over initiatives to increase school choice, such as vouchers and charter schools (Kelly 1996; Macedo 2000; Moe 2000; Gutmann 2000; Finn, Manno, and Vanourek 2000; Godwin and Kemerer 2002).

There are at least two ways that schools engage in civic education. The first, and most overt, method is through the formal curriculum. The second is more subtle. Since schools are communities, they also have the potential to provide their students with practical experience as members of that community, preparing them for membership in other, larger communities.[2] It is the first of these, the impact of the formal curriculum, that has been the subject of most empirical scrutiny. In the first wave of this research in the 1960s and early 1970s, scholars had high hopes for the empirical study of civics instruction. Since one's level of educational attainment had long been shown to be an important factor contributing to civic orientations, it seemed logical to turn to research to determine the means through which schools have their effect. However, in the first wave of research into the effects of civic education, little evidence was uncovered that civics instruction has any bearing on civic attitudes and/or behavior in either the short *or* long term. In summarizing this literature, Richard Niemi and Jane Junn remark that "the accepted wisdom in the political science profession is that civics classes have little or no effect on the vast majority of students" (1998, 16). The conventional wisdom to which they refer arises largely from the work of Kenneth Langton and M. Kent Jennings in the 1960s (1968), who drew upon the first wave of what has come to be known as the Youth-Parent Socialization Study (YPSS) to conclude that civics courses had no impact on the civic orientations of most American high school students. The YPSS is a unique study of influences upon the civic and political development of adolescents. It began in 1965, when interviews were conducted with a representative sample of high school seniors and their parents, the component of the study from which Langton and Jennings drew their conclusion that civics classes have little or no measurable effect on the civic development of young people. In addition to the 1965 wave of the study, students and parents were then re-interviewed in 1973 and 1982. Later on in this chapter, I will draw on the longitudinal aspect of this study to revisit the question of whether schools shape the public engagement of their students over their life span.

Scholars have offered numerous reasons for the absence of a link between civics courses and civic attitudes (and civic behavior for that matter). For one, by its very nature civics instruction is not confined to a single course, or to school at all, in a way that is unique among academic subjects. Unlike politics, you are not going to learn much algebra or chemistry from reading the newspaper or watching television. Students, however, can absorb a lot of political information that is just floating in the ether around them, making classroom instruction redundant. Furthermore, politically relevant material is covered in the course of studying subjects other than what was once called civics (and is more commonly known today as social studies). Pamela Conover and Donald Searing (2000) have found that this is especially true in literature classes. Also, Paul Beck and M. Kent Jennings (1982) suggest that civics instruction is more or less constant across different schools, making it difficult to uncover its effect on variables like political knowledge or efficacy.

As political scientists' attention began to turn away from adolescent socialization to other topics, little new research on the impact of classroom civics instruction was conducted. And so the conventional wisdom remained that classroom civics instruction had little or no impact on civic outcomes. Recently, scholarly attention has again turned to civic education, with research that questions the conventional wisdom. Civics classes, it turns out, appear to have an effect on civic education after all. However, this new evidence only underscores the dramatically diminished expectations within the research community for the impact of civics instruction. Richard Niemi and Jane Junn (1998) have analyzed the 1988 National Assessment of Educational Progress (NAEP) civics exam and found that classroom instruction in civics (that is, social studies courses) does correlate with a higher score on the test, even when controlling for students' demographic characteristics known to affect academic performance. Niemi and Junn's conclusion that civics courses boost performance on a civics exam is inarguably intuitive, but it is also indicative of the lowered expectations for the study of civic education within the research community. Originally, scholars examining the role of high school curricula sought to uncover how it nurtures such abstract ideals as political tolerance and efficacy, and expected to find that it has an impact well beyond high school. Decades after those first studies bore little fruit, the best research on the subject can merely conclude that taking a course with a civics component leads to a higher score on a civics exam. Furthermore, the score is not even that much higher. "[N]et of all the other influences, having had a civics or American government course in twelfth grade gives a student a 2 percentage-point edge over someone whose last course was earlier, and an additional 2 points over students who have had no civics courses." Niemi and Junn make the case that these are significant gains. They describe their results as "uncommonly meaningful," leading to an "altogether different conclusion from one of the enduring findings in the field of political socialization," and then stress that the observed gains are "anything but trivial" (121, 122). Jay Greene (2000), however, has reanalyzed the same data and argues that of the classroom factors in Niemi and Junn's analysis, the only one that really matters is whether the student was enrolled in a civics class at the time of the exam. In other words, it would appear that we can have confidence in the conclusion that a high school student's grade on a civics test increases by, at most, four percentage points. But two of those points result from being enrolled in a course with civics content at the time that the student takes the test. It seems fair to say that civics courses do appear to have an impact, but it is modest at best. For comparison's sake, it is hard to believe that we would make much of finding that scores on a chemistry exam increased by two percentage points when a student is enrolled in a chemistry course. Rather than trumpet this as evidence that chemistry classes are effective, we would probably wonder why the gain in test scores is so slight.

I want to be clear that I have no quibble with either the substance or methodology of Niemi and Junn's research. The problem is not that they were looking for the effects of high school on someone's preparation for public engagement. I am certainly sitting in the choir seats when they preach that adolescent experiences affect civic development. Nor is there a problem with how they studied the impact of formal civics instruction. Theirs is a very thorough study using high-quality data and the appropriate methodology. Rather, the reality is that when it comes to civic education the action does not appear to be in the formal curriculum.

Given the central importance of school in the life of the typical adolescent, and the historic mandate for schools to prepare their students for a lifetime of active and engaged citizenship, the onus would seem to be on those who argue that school experiences have no effect on students' civic preparation. Yet we have seen that the existing evidence is underwhelming, to say the least. Since there seems to be little empirical traction to the study of the formal curriculum, perhaps our attention should be directed toward the second way in which schools potentially affect civic development—the experience they provide of being part of a community.

To understand how membership in a small, tightly defined community like a school might affect the development of civic inclinations, we are informed by what we have already learned about how larger, more amorphous communities foster civic norms. In preceding chapters, we have seen evidence that communities characterized by strong civic norms facilitate civically motivated collective action, including voter turnout. If a school is a community, then we should expect that schools characterized by strong civic norms also foster civically motivated behavior.

Indeed, social capital theory would suggest that schools are precisely the sort of social environment governed by norms. Members of a school community spend a lot of time in close proximity to one another, behavioral expectations are often clearly established, and sanctions (social and otherwise) are imposed to encourage behavior that conforms to those expectations. In the words of a landmark report on civic education by the Carnegie Corporation and the Center for Information and Research on Civic Learning and Engagement, *The Civic Mission of Schools,*

> Schools are communities in which young people learn to interact, argue, and work together with others, an important condition for future citizenship. Schools have the capacity to bring together a heterogeneous population of young people—with different backgrounds, perspectives, and vocational ambitions—to instruct them in common lessons and values. They can also bring young people into significant relationships with adult role models. (Carnegie Corporation of New York and Center for Information and Research on Civic Learning and Engagement 2003, 12)

YOUTH-PARENT SOCIALIZATION STUDY

Studying how the high school you attend as an adolescent might affect your public engagement as an adult presents a number of challenges. The data employed in such an analysis must simultaneously meet two criteria. First, the study must be *contextual.* We require measures not only of individuals' attitudes, behavior, and characteristics but also of the characteristics of their social environment. These environmental measures parallel the contextual characteristics of counties and metropolitan areas that have been used in the preceding chapters. Second, the data must be *longitudinal.* Adolescents interviewed in high school must be tracked into adulthood, with follow-up interviews to determine their level of civic and political engagement. The combination of both elements in a single data set requires a considerable investment of resources (not to mention a fair degree of patience). Fortunately, the Youth-Parent Socialization Study meets both criteria. As mentioned above, the YPSS is a panel study and thus has a longitudinal component to it. It also has a contextual component, as it is possible to construct measures describing the social environment of the adolescent panel members.

The evolution of the YPSS is itself an interesting statement on how political scientists have become increasingly concerned with the state of public engagement in America. The publications based on the YPSS provide a window into the changing priorities of political scientists from the 1960s to the present (Jennings and Niemi 1968, 1974, 1975, 1981; Jennings

1971, 1979, 1987; Jennings and Markus 1977, 1984, 1988; Beck and Jennings 1979, 1982, 1991; Jennings and Stoker 2004). Betraying its origins as a project emanating from the University of Michigan, the progenitor of much research on how party identification affects the vote, many early publications based on the YPSS dealt with how and when people begin to develop a partisan identification, and the persistence of that identity across time. Only later did the study's principal investigator, M. Kent Jennings, and his coauthors set their sights on understanding the precursors to civic and political participation. Jennings himself has noted that when the project began, "the topic of political participation assumed a relatively minor role. As the project expanded over time, participation came to occupy a more prominent role in study design, instrument content, and analysis. Indeed, in many respects we are just beginning to realize fully the fruits of the design with respect to participation" (2000, 1). Not coincidentally, this increased attention to participation coincided with the decline in public engagement within the body politic, especially among young people.

One aspect of the YPSS's design that has not been the subject of much research is the fact that in addition to interviews with adolescent panel members and their parents in 1965, Jennings and his colleagues gathered data from a survey administered to the entire senior class of each youth's high school (consequently, I will refer to it as the high school sample). For every question asked of the individual students, it is thus possible to construct school-level measures for each high school, analogous to the community, county, and metropolitan-area measures employed in previous chapters.[3]

The YPSS is an ideal source of data to examine the impact of adolescents' social environments on their long-term public engagement. Perhaps the study's greatest virtue is that it permits the *direct* measurement of the degree to which voting is seen as a civic obligation within each high school. Recall that in the preceding chapters, the degree to which civic norms facilitate behavior within communities has been approximated by their degree of social consensus, which in turn has been operationalized with a measure of political heterogeneity. Civic norms, it has been hypothesized, are stronger where people hold values (or preferences) in common. By necessity, therefore, our attention has been focused on political heterogeneity, *but only as a means of inferring the strength of civic norms within that community*. Ideally, we would have a direct measure of the civic norms in every community, but for the communities studied in the previous chapters, those data do not exist. With the YPSS, though, we can measure the degree to which voting is seen as a civic obligation within each high school, and so we need not rely on political homogeneity as a proxy. Since it is possible to measure political heterogeneity as well as the prevalence of a norm encouraging voting within each high school, it is possible to test the fundamental assumption underlying this entire analysis: whether political heterogeneity is actually related to the strength of civic norms within a community. Is it really the case that homogeneous communities, in this case high schools, foster a sense of civic obligation?

Having a measure of both political heterogeneity and civic norms also permits testing the impact of each simultaneously to see whether the degree of heterogeneity affects public engagement above and beyond any effect it has on the development of civic norms. Is political heterogeneity merely a facilitating condition for the development of civic norms, or does it shape public engagement independent of any impact on the normative climate within a social environment? As chapter 8 discusses in greater detail, the answer speaks to the policy implications that can be drawn from this analysis. But any mention of normative conclusions stemming from empirical analysis is premature in the absence of the empirical analysis. The remainder of this chapter will thus be occupied with that analysis, leaving the normative discussion for chapter 8. The analysis that follows is guided by two questions. First, is there evidence for the hypothesized link between a community's political heterogeneity and the strength of civic norms within that community? Second, what impact do those civic norms have on public engagement in the years following high school?

IMPACT OF POLITICAL HETEROGENEITY ON CIVIC NORMS

We begin with a test that is the linchpin linking the analysis in the preceding chapters to that which follows. Are civic norms actually related to political heterogeneity? The first step is to define how it is that the prevalence of a norm encouraging voting, or what I will refer to as "civic climate," has been measured. Within each high school in the YPSS, students were asked, "What three things about a person are most important in showing that he is a good citizen?" and then shown a list of possibilities. The choices are designed to capture different dimensions of citizenship, and include religious involvement, adherence to the law, and a sense of privatism (or minding one's own business). For our purposes, one of the choices relates directly to public engagement: "He votes in elections."

The beauty of this measure is its simplicity. Also, since it relies on the students' initiative to identify voting as a component of good citizenship, it largely avoids the problem of having everyone reflexively endorse voting as a normative expectation, as happens when respondents are simply asked whether they think voting is important. As a result, there is a considerable amount of variation in the percentage of students in each high school who endorse voting as a component of good citizenship, ranging from 46 to 85 percent across the seventy-seven schools from which students were sampled (with a mean of 70 percent).[4]

The next step is to specify how political heterogeneity has been measured within the environment of a high school. Of course, it is not possible to use election returns, since none of these students would have been eligible to vote (in 1965, the voting age was still twenty-one in all but two states). Instead, I draw on the partisan identification of students in the school, with political heterogeneity measured in the same manner as ethnic and racial heterogeneity in earlier chapters. Student respondents were asked to identify their partisan affiliation as Republican, Democrat, or Independent.[5] By identifying each respondent as falling into one of these three categories, aggregate political heterogeneity can be calculated using a Herfindahl Index, where a higher number represents a greater degree of political heterogeneity.[6] This measure of political heterogeneity within the school correlates highly, but not perfectly, with the level of political competition in the 1964 presidential election (the most recent) within the county in which the school is located ($r = .53$, $p < 0.001$).

It is important to remember that the working assumption is not that party identification is a topic of much interest to most adolescents. That is, it is not likely that young people spend a lot of time discussing their political views with one another. Rather, as with adults, party identification is actually a social identity (Green, Palmquist, and Shickler 2002) that in turn is related to a bundle of opinion, preferences, and values. So while high school students are unlikely to identify each other by partisan labels, they are likely to differentiate among their peers on the basis of other criteria—economic class, career path, religious affiliation, and so forth—which *are* related to partisanship.

Table 7.1 displays a model that tests whether political heterogeneity is, as hypothesized, related to the civic climate of a high school. In this case, the unit of analysis is the school, so the dependent variable is the percentage of students in the school who endorse voting as a component of good citizenship, while the independent variables are also measured at the school level. In addition to the degree of political heterogeneity within the school, the model also tests whether two other dimensions of heterogeneity, religion and race, have any impact on the prevalence of a norm encouraging voting.[7] The model also accounts for other factors that we would expect to impact a school's civic climate. Perhaps most important, the model includes the mean level of education attained by students' parents, which serves to account for the general socioeconomic status of the school's population.[8] The model further accounts for the

TABLE 7.1
Political Heterogeneity and School Civic Climate

	% *"Good Citizen Votes"*
Heterogeneity	
Political heterogeneity	−0.100** (0.045)
Religious heterogeneity	0.053 (0.040)
Racial heterogeneity	−0.029 (0.044)
Other contextual demographics	
Mean parents' education	0.143** (0.055)
Mean years lived in community	−0.074* (0.043)
Constant	0.739*** (0.051)
Observations	77
Adjusted R²	0.13

Source: Youth-Parent Socialization Study.

Note: Results from linear regression. Standard errors in parenthesis. Independent variables standardized on 0–1 scale. Weighted data.

 * significant at .10   ** significant at .05   *** significant at .01

average length of time that students have lived in their community, as it is likely that civic norms are more likely to be inculcated in places where people have deep roots (Coleman 1990, 1988).[9] All variables are coded on a 0–1 scale, allowing a rough comparison of their magnitudes (that is, we can compare the impact of each independent variable on the dependent variable as it varies across its entire range).

As hypothesized, the more politically homogeneous the environment within a high school, the stronger the norm linking voting with being a good citizen. We also see that the substantive magnitude of political heterogeneity's impact is the second largest in the model, following only parents' education. Of course, education, coupled with the status it confers, has long been recognized as a major facilitator of social norms generally, and civic engagement especially.[10] Once again, we find that it is political heterogeneity that has an impact on the civic character of a community; neither religious nor racial heterogeneity reaches statistical significance.

Thus, at the aggregate level we see that political heterogeneity has the hypothesized effect on civic climate—greater heterogeneity is accompanied by a weaker sense that voting is a necessary element of citizenship. Given that the link between political heterogeneity and civic norms underpins the entire analysis, it is important to underscore that this finding should strengthen our confidence in the theoretical structure that has been assembled as we have moved through the preceding chapters.

Nonetheless, perhaps doubts linger about inferring an individual-level process exclusively from data that are not actually at the individual level. For that reason, I have also modeled the relationship between political heterogeneity and the endorsement of voting as a civic norm using individual-level data. For this model, the dependent variable is simply whether the respondent selected voting as a component of good citizenship. The hierarchical nature of the data—students sampled within schools—once again means that a hierarchical model is appropriate, as in chapters 3 and 5. In this case, hierarchical estimation is used to model a binary, rather than linear, outcome: whether the student identifies voting as a component of good citizenship or not. The resulting parameters, therefore, are interpreted as logistic regression coefficients.[11]

As we turn to the analysis of individual-level data, note that our focus will be on white students only. The reader is reminded that the baseline data for the Youth-Parent Socialization Study were collected in 1965, when America was still in the throes of the civil rights movement. At the time, many American secondary schools were racially segregated, even though *Brown v. Board of Education* had been on the books for a decade (Rosenberg 1991). The distribution of nonwhites—for the most part, blacks—in the student bodies of the schools included in the high school sample vividly reflects this fact.[12] As would be expected in racially segregated schools, the distribution is sharply bimodal. Either a school has very few nonwhites, or it has a lot. Twenty percent of schools have not a single nonwhite student, and almost 40 percent have a student body that is over 90 percent white. At the other end of the distribution, 8 percent of the schools have a nonwhite population of at least 80 percent; one school is 100 percent nonwhite. That school, not surprisingly, is in a southern state (North Carolina). Reinforcing the point, the sample includes another school found in the very same city which is 98 percent white.[13]

Not only were many schools racially segregated in 1965, in a number of states African Americans still lived with the lingering effects of Jim Crow. This lamentable fact means that a question about voting as a civic duty most certainly had a very different meaning to whites, who could vote, and blacks, many of whom could not. Undoubtedly, there is much to be learned about the effects of growing up during the peak of the civil rights on the political socialization of African Americans. That important research question is regrettably beyond the scope of this particular study, as it deserves at least a book-length treatment of its own. To avoid conflating the very different experiences of white and black adolescents, the analysis in this chapter focuses only on the white members of the YPSS panel. Note, however, that only 8 percent of the YPSS student panel is classified as "nonwhite," so relatively few cases are lost.

TABLE 7.2
Political Heterogeneity and Voting as a Civic Norm

	"Good Citizen Votes"
Political heterogeneity	−0.369** (0.168)
Level-1 effects	
Anticipated education	0.375*** (0.037)
Parents' education	0.181*** (0.064)
Years lived in community	0.106* (0.064)
Female	0.178*** (0.033)
Level-2 effects	
Mean parents' education	0.184 (0.249)
Mean years lived in community	−0.569*** (0.202)
Constant	0.816*** (0.039)
Number of level-1 units	16,625
Number of level-2 units	76
Individual-level variance explained	0.01

Source: Youth-Parent Socialization Study.

Note: Results from hierarchical generalized linear model (population-average model). Robust standard errors in parenthesis. Independent variables standardized on 0–1 scale. Weighted data. Identity link function is logit. Bernoulli distribution of the dependent variable assumed.

* significant at .10   ** significant at .05   *** significant at .01

Table 7.2 displays the results of the individual-level model, including the lineup of "usual suspects" as control variables. We see from Table 7.2 that political heterogeneity is indeed negatively related to the endorsement of voting as a civic obligation when the unit of analysis is the individual, as it is when the unit is the school.

The models displayed in Tables 7.1 and 7.2 parallel the results we saw in chapter 3, when voters were asked why they turned out at the polls. There, we saw that as communities become more politically heterogeneous, voters were less likely to report that they cast their ballots out of a sense of civic obligation. Here, we have seen that as high school environments become more politically heterogeneous, their students are less likely to endorse voting as a necessary component of good citizenship. As noted, this finding is important evidence for the theoretically foundational claim that political uniformity fosters strong norms. Interpreting the impact of political heterogeneity on civic climate is a mixed bag, depending on which aspect of the models reported in Tables 7.1 and 7.2 is in focus. As noted, relative to the other factors included in the models, political heterogeneity's impact is, substantively, one of the largest. However, it is also important to note that the variation in civic climate explained by the models in Tables 7.1 and 7.2 is relatively modest, suggesting that the degree of political heterogeneity is a weak signal amid a fair amount of noise.

In short, political heterogeneity is *a* factor contributing to the civic climate within a school environment, but by no means can it simply be equated with civic climate. Since our interest is really in the impact of civic norms rather than political heterogeneity, from here on civic climate will move from the left- to the righthand side of the equation. In other words, rather than testing what shapes civic climate we will now see the impact of civic climate on public engagement, both in the present and the future.

ANTICIPATED PARTICIPATION

Throughout, I have referred to the dual motivations theory. Now, I focus on the civic dimension of public engagement and so will instead refer to the *civic motivation model*. By this I simply mean the idea that civic norms imprinted in adolescence can lead people to engage in civically oriented participation even beyond their teenage years. With a direct measure of the norms within each school community, it is possible to test multiple implications of the civic motivation model. I begin with what is perhaps the most straightforward. If there is anything to the claim that an adolescent's social environment affects the development of normative attitudes about civic engagement, we should expect that the stronger a norm encouraging voting within a community, the more likely its teenage residents are to *anticipate* their participation later in life. In other words, young people in a civic climate that fosters engagement as a civic duty should be more likely to envision themselves as active participants in their communities upon reaching adulthood. A question that asks about young people's anticipated participation is an interesting window into what they see as normative, and is just as much a guide to their *present* state of mind as it is a precise prediction of their future behavior. It is likely that, to an adolescent, a question that essentially asks, "Will you be publicly engaged in the future?" is really asking, "Do you think people *should* be publicly engaged?" Or, perhaps more accurately, "Do you think people *like you* should be publicly engaged?" Anticipated participation has been measured straightforwardly, as respondents in the high school sample were asked, "Looking ahead to the time when you are on your own, what about actual participation in public affairs and politics? How active do you think you will be in these matters?" In

TABLE 7.3
School Civic Climate and Anticipated Participation

	"How Active Will You Be?"
Civic climate	0.171*** (0.067)
Level-1 effects	
Good citizen votes	0.072*** (0.010)
Anticipated education	0.185*** (0.012)
Parents' education	0.216*** (0.023)
Years lived in community	−0.006 (0.026)
Female	−0.033*** (0.010)
Level-2 effects	
Political heterogeneity	−0.025 (0.059)
Mean parents' education	−0.270** (0.071)
Mean years lived in community	0.060 (0.061)
Constant	1.78*** (0.019)
Number of level-1 units	16,629
Number of level-2 units	76
Individual-level variance explained	0.02

Source: Youth-Parent Socialization Study.

Note: Results from hierarchical linear model. Robust standard errors in parentheses. Independent variables standardized on 0–1 scale. Weighted data.

* significant at .10   ** significant at .05   *** significant at .01

response, they had three choices: not very active, somewhat active, very active.[14]

When the school is the unit of analysis, the relationship between anticipated participation and the civic climate (along with the usual control variables) is positive and well past the threshold for statistical significance ($p > 0.05$). Table 7.3 replicates the same analysis at the individual level, again using a hierarchical model. Critically, in addition to the standard set of control variables, the model in Table 7.3 also accounts for whether the individual student believes that citizenship obligates voting. In other words, the model isolates the impact of being surrounded by others who hold that voting is a norm by controlling for the individual's own sense of civic duty. As expected, adolescents who report that good citizens exercise their right to vote also report that they anticipate being publicly engaged upon reaching adulthood. We can also see, however, that there is an effect of being immersed in a civic duty–rich environment *over and above the individual's own sense of civic obligation*. It is also important to stress that, when the civic climate is accounted for, the level of political heterogeneity within the school does not have an effect.

LOOKING FORWARD AND BACKWARD

We have seen that being surrounded by peers who share the belief that voting is a social norm leads adolescents to anticipate that they will participate in public affairs when they reach adulthood. To the extent that social norms have an impact on behavior in the here and now, this is to be expected—especially if adolescents' reports of what they will do in the future reflect their current perception of that activity's normative value. As discussed at length in chapter 6, adolescence is an especially significant period of the life span for the internalization of social norms. That is, the adoption of norms in adolescence affects not only the present but also the future. If a norm encouraging public engagement, namely voting, is internalized in adolescence, we should see the civic climate of a high school reaching into adulthood to affect public engagement.

While these results suggest a link between norms then and public engagement now, the evidence is hardly definitive. For one, we do not know whether adolescents' stated expectation that they will be publicly engaged at some unspecified point in the future actually translates into engagement in adulthood. Also, the wording of the question leaves some ambiguity regarding whether the engagement students envision is better characterized as civic or political—or both—in nature. The civic motivation model, however, leads to a specific expectation: civic climate in adolescence fosters the development of *civic* norms, which subsequently translates into civically motivated behavior rather than sparking the desire to engage in politically motivated activity.

Consider the model of anticipated participation, therefore, to be only a warm-up for the headline act: determining whether the anticipation of engagement in adolescence corresponds to actual behavior in adulthood. Specifically, does the civic climate of your high school affect your likelihood of turning out to vote in the years following high school? Our inquiry will center on the second wave of follow-up interviews, conducted in 1982, which asked the study's participants to report on whether they turned out in the 1980 presidential election, fifteen years following the panel members' graduation from high school. Three central questions will guide the analysis. First, at the individual level, do norms internalized in adolescence have any impact on public engagement in adulthood? Second, does the degree of political heterogeneity within an adolescent's social environment have an impact? Third, do the social norms in an adolescent's community affect engagement as an adult?

We turn first to the question of whether an adolescent's sense of voting as a civic obligation affects adult behavior at all. After all, it might very well be that changes across the life span are so great that normative beliefs in adolescence turn out to be largely irrelevant as time passes. In chapter 6, we saw that civic-oriented behavior in adolescence increases the likelihood of voting and volunteering in the decade or so following high school, which was hypothesized to result from the internalization of a norm encouraging civically motivated activity. That norm is adopted in adolescence and continues to shape behavior as someone ages. With these data we can conduct a similar test, only now we have a direct measure of whether voting is viewed as an obligation of good citizenship in adolescence. The key independent variable, therefore, is whether or not a participant in the YPSS said that voting is a component of being a good citizen. Note that members of the YPSS panel received a slightly different, and thus more detailed, questionnaire than the respondents in the larger high school sample. Whereas students in the high school sample were asked to identify the elements of good citizenship from a predetermined list, panel members were free to offer any response they wished in an open-ended format. The resulting answers have been combined into a set of discrete categories, one of which includes such responses as "voting" and "exercising your right to vote."[15] The advantage of this approach is that it captures what is on the "top of one's head," and thus undoubtedly better reflects what adolescents consider to be normative than a set of responses provided to them on a questionnaire. To ensure that the model reflects what is held to be most important in a student's self-definition of good citizenship, the variable records the students' first response to the question (they could identify up to four). Using this stringent measure of voting-as-a-norm, roughly 16 percent of students put voting on the top of their list as essential for being a good citizen.

As shown in Table 7.4, the belief that voting is an obligation of citizenship in adolescence has a long reach into adulthood. The table displays a model of its impact on voting in the 1980 presidential election, while controlling for an array of other factors known to influence voting (education, residential stability, and so forth). That an attitude developed in adolescence would continue to guide behavior well over a decade past high school is remarkable, given all the changes that occur during this period of life. It is perhaps even more remarkable in light of the other factors that have been accounted for in this model. As discussed at length in chapter 5, the political socialization literature has long recognized the home as a critical factor affecting an individual's civic development. It could be the case, therefore, that the manifestation of a civic norm merely reflects the engagement level of students' parents. That is, students with participatory parents might be inclined to report that such engagement is an indication of good citizenship, and so three parental measures have been added. The first records whether the parent

TABLE 7.4
Civic Norm in Adolescence, Voter Turnout in Adulthood

	Voted in 1980?
"Good citizen votes" (1965)	0.789** (0.341)
Female	0.410* (0.213)
Residential mobility	1.297*** (0.382)
Married	1.256*** (0.226)
Education	2.008*** (0.349)
Parent was a voter	0.022 (0.296)
Parents' electoral activism index	1.541*** (0.582)
Parents' Community Voluntarism	0.216 (0.239)
Constant	−1.522*** (0.375)
Observations	658
Pseudo-R^2	0.13

Source: Youth-Parent Socialization Study.
Note: Results from logistic regression. Standard errors in parentheses. Independent variables standardized on 0–1 scale. Weighted data.
* significant at .10   ** significant at .05   *** significant at .01

who participated in the study was a voter, or at least whether the parent voted in the most recent (1964) presidential election. Second is an index of the parents' level of political activism.[16] The third has a more civic flavor, and records whether the parent has taken an "active part" in "local or community affairs" or "anything of that kind" (coded as yes/no).

When the logit coefficients in Table 7.4 are converted to relative impacts on the probability of voting, identifying voting as a component of good citizenship in adolescence translates into a 9 percentage-point gain in the probability of turning out to vote fifteen years later. While certainly non-negligible, this is nonetheless a modest effect relative to the factors in the model. By way of comparison, the impact of having adopted voting as a civic obligation in 1965 is smaller than that of parents' electoral activism, which boots turnout by about 18 percentage points (when it moves from its minimum to maximum value). Interestingly, note that whether the participating parent had recently turned out to vote has no impact on whether his or her child ends up a voter a decade and a half later. This is likely because, in 1964, voter turnout was quite common, and so being in a home with parents who turned out to vote was not much of a stimulus. (Parents in the YPSS reported turning out at a rate of 82 percent in the 1964 election, a high but not implausible rate.)

To find that having adopted the belief that voting is an important obligation of citizenship affects voter turnout a decade and a half following high school is in and of itself a notable result. We might say that what you do now depends on what you believed then. Remember, though, that our primary interest is in whether what you do now depends on where you *were* then or, more specifically, what your social environment was like then. The next step, therefore, is to see whether the nature of one's adolescent social environment has a long-term impact on one's public engagement as an adult. Our attention is centered on whether the civic climate of an adolescent's social environment has a measurable impact on voter turnout. Specifically, what is the impact of having attended a high school where voting is widely thought to be a component of good citizenship? Of interest also, however, is the degree of political heterogeneity within an adolescent's community. Echoing the earlier models, at the individual level the equation accounts for parents' education, as well as residential stability, gender, and whether the individual indicated that voting is a mark of a good citizen. School-level controls include the mean level of parents' education, residential mobility, and the aggregate level of anticipated participation. Once more, the parents' level of participation is added to the mix, to account for influences in the home. The dependent variable is binary—either the respondent voted in 1980 or not—and so the model employs logistic regression adapted for hierarchical estimation.

As displayed in Table 7.5, the degree of political heterogeneity within the high school environment has no apparent impact on voting fifteen years later. Because so much of the focus throughout this book has been on the effects of political heterogeneity I wish to emphasize that, across time, *political heterogeneity in and of itself does not have a bearing on voter turnout*. This is not to say, however, that turnout in adulthood is unaffected by experiences in adolescence. As in the previous model, exposure to politics at home through the activism of one's parents has a significant impact.

The main question deriving from the civic motivation model is whether attending a high school where voting is widely recognized as a social norm has a positive impact on voter turnout fifteen years following high school. It does, as shown in Table 7.5. Significantly, an individual's own belief that voting characterizes good citizenship as an adolescent ceases to have a statistically significant impact when the civic climate is taken into account. The fact that it is the civic climate that boosts turnout, rather than an individual's own reported sense of civic obligation, is intriguing. It suggests that norms are largely the product of one's social environment, thus underscoring the importance of considering contextual influences on our public engagement. And because we have seen the impact of adolescents' environments, it bolsters the evidence that socialization matters; an exclusive focus on contemporaneous factors to explain political behavior misses an important part of the story.

TABLE 7.5
High School Civic Climate and Voter Turnout in 1980

	(1)	With 1980 community heterogeneity
Civic climate (1965)	1.033** (0.466)	0.882** (0.437)
Political heterogeneity (1965)	−0.091 (0.251)	
"Good Citizen Votes" (1965)	0.152 (0.229)	
Community political heterogeneity (1980)		
Political homogeneity (mean to minimum)		0.634* (0.346)
Political heterogeneity (mean to maximum)		−0.771 (0.883)
Level-1 effects		
Education level	1.041*** (0.252)	0.995*** (0.282)
Married	0.699*** (0.219)	0.788*** (0.234)
Female	−0.020 (0.154)	
Years lived in community	0.829*** (0.256)	0.827*** (0.269)
Parental participation (also level 1)		
Electoral activism index (1965)	0.744** (0.303)	0.947*** (0.305)
Community voluntarism (1965)	0.135 (0.134)	
Parents were voters	0.241 (0.231)	
Level-2 effects		
Mean parents' education	0.527 (0.539)	
Mean years lived in community	1.135*** (0.405)	1.193*** (0.370)
Mean anticipated participation	−0.937* (0.518)	−0.362 0.471
Constant	0.469* (0.256)	0.758*** 0.192
Number of level-1 units	567	567
Number of level-2 units	70	70
Individual-level variance explained	0.17	0.16

Source: Youth-Parent Socialization Study.
Note: Results from hierarchical generalized linear models (population-average model). Robust standard errors in parentheses. Independent variables standardized on 0–1 scale. Weighted data.
    * significant at .10   ** significant at .05   *** significant at .01

In a nutshell, we have seen evidence that a norm *then* continues to have an impact on voter turnout *now*. But how does it stack up against a civic norm *now*? Ideally, we would weigh the civic climate in the past against that in the present with directly comparable measures. Unfortunately, however, it is not possible to make a direct comparison since we do not have a ready measure of civic norms within each respondent's community. It is possible, however, to use the indirect measure of civic norms employed in previous chapters—the degree of political heterogeneity within a community—for an approximate evaluation of their relative degrees of influence. To that end, the second column of Table 7.5 displays the results of a model that accounts for the political composition of each respondent's metropolitan area, averaged from 1960 to 1980.[17] As has been done previously, the political composition of one's community has been divided into measures of homogeneity and heterogeneity that indicate whether a community falls above or below the mean level of political heterogeneity.[18] Political homogeneity is interpreted, therefore, as a rough indicator of the extent to which voter turnout is driven by civic motivations, whereas political heterogeneity gauges political motivations.[19]

An equation of this sort asks a lot of the software required to estimate hierarchical models, which are intensively computational. To ensure that the computer is able to arrive at a solution, the model is therefore relatively lean. In order to economize, I have only included as controls variables that achieved a significance level of $p < 0.10$ in the previous specification, namely the individual's education level in 1982, marital status in 1982, residential stability in 1982, and parental electoral activism in 1965. The contextual variables include the high school's mean level of residential mobility and the degree of anticipated public engagement within the high school community.

We see that both civic climate in 1965 and political homogeneity in 1982 are positive and statistically significant, while political heterogeneity does not clear the bar for statistical significance (and, interestingly, is negative). Figure 7.1 displays the substantive impact of five variables, civic climate in the past, political homogeneity in the present, one's education level in the present, parental activism in the past, and marital status (in the present). The impact for each variable has been calculated as it varies from its lowest to highest value. Because voter turnout is relatively high among this sample and thus bumps up against the natural ceiling of 1 when calculating the probability of voting in 1980, the impact of each variable on the probability of turning out is muted. For example, the impact of shifting education across its entire range is roughly 13 percentage points (in models of public engagement, the effect of education is generally much higher). Having attended a high school where

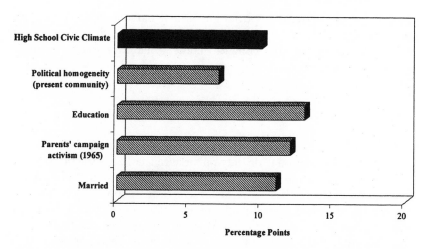

Figure 7.1. Impacts on the probability of voting in 1980. All control variables set to their means. Youth-Parent Socialization Study.

the norm encouraging voting is strongest rather than weakest is right in the same neighborhood, bumping up the likelihood of turning out to vote by 10 percentage points. This is slightly higher than the rise in turnout as one moves from a community with the mean to the highest level of political homogeneity, which is 7 points.

Numerous elements of Table 7.5 are worth highlighting. While the substantive impact of the high school civic climate is relatively modest, it is nonetheless noteworthy that a norm within an adolescent's social context has *any* impact on voter turnout fifteen years later, especially in light of the litany of factors that have no effect over the long haul. Furthermore, the size of the impact is of the same order of magnitude as factors that have long been known to affect political participation, like education and parental political involvement. Among these factors is the degree of political heterogeneity within one's current community, which was earlier shown to approximate the strength of that community's norms encouraging civic-oriented activity. It is tempting to compare high school civic climate and community political homogeneity and declare that norms *then* matter more than norms *now*. Because the two measures constitute an apple and an orange, however, we must be more cautious. The political complexion of a community is only an approximation—and an imperfect one at that—of the strength of civic norms within it. Indeed, because this is such a noisy measure of civic norms, it is reasonable to assume that a more precise gauge would show an even greater effect. When weighing the effects of environmental influences in the past and the present, therefore, the bottom line is that barring an apple-to-apple comparison, all we can say is that we have enough evidence to say that they both matter, but not enough to make a definitive statement about which matters more.

CIVIC VERSUS POLITICAL

A theory, like a building, is only as sturdy as its foundation. This study rests on the foundational distinction between collective action that is civically motivated and that which is politically motivated. As I have defined them, the latter has as its raison d'être the expression of political preferences in order to affect public policy, while the former is driven by adherence to a civic norm. One important influence on the civic side of voter turnout, I am suggesting, is the strength of civic norms in one's adolescent environment. The theoretical importance of this conclusion compels that it be confirmed with collateral evidence. Just how solid is the theory's foundation? If civic motivations are really the link between then and now, two complementary hypotheses should be supported. First, civic norms in adolescence should have a measurably positive impact on civic behavior in adulthood, like volunteering. Second, they should not be significantly related to adult participation that is primarily political in motivation. The catch here is that the question used in the norms measure deals with voting specifically, leaving it unclear whether it taps into a generally civic orientation. Only if it is general in nature should we expect it to have an impact on other forms of civically oriented activity. In other words, if the question about whether voting is a civic obligation is actually an indicator of a broader norm encouraging civically oriented activity, then we should expect the strength of this norm to lead to other forms of civic participation. If, however, it is only an indicator of a norm narrowly focused on voting per se, then it should not have an impact on behavior other than voting. With the YPSS, it is possible to test whether the measure of civic climate has a narrow or broad impact and, if the latter, whether it affects civic and/or political participation in adulthood. In the 1982 wave, respondents were asked about their participation in community voluntarism.[20] They were also asked about their participation in an array of political acts since they were last interviewed in 1973, which have been combined into two additive indices, one for electoral activism and the other for the expression of political voice.[21]

Table 7.6 displays three hierarchical models with our group of "usual suspects" as control variables. Since volunteer service is measured dichotomously—either you are a volunteer or you are not—and the two

TABLE 7.6
High School Civic Climate and Public Engagement in 1980

	Volunteering (HGLM) (1)	Electoral activism (HLM) (2)	Political voice (HLM) (3)
School civic climate (1965)	1.162**(0.590)	−0.003 (0.399)	0.041 (0.195)
School political heterogeneity (1965)	−0.068 (0.347)	−0.023 (0.363)	−0.032 (0.122)
Level-1 effects			
Education level	0.894**(0.358)	0.754***(0.215)	0.303**(0.128)
Married	0.890***(0.190)	0.072 (0.132)	−0.006 (0.073)
Female	0.194 (0.176)	−0.211 (0.139)	−0.127**(0.063)
Years lived in community	−0.524 (0.331)	−0.305 (0.246)	−0.006 (0.082)
Parental participation (also level 1)			
Electoral activism index (1965)		0.884***(0.284)	0.294**(0.144)
Community voluntarism (1965)	−0.149 (0.218)		
Level-2 effects			
Mean parents' education	−0.401 (0.638)	0.111 (0.437)	0.673***(0.193)
Mean years lived in community	0.088 (0.423)	−0.022 (0.345)	−0.167 (0.169)
Mean anticipated participation	−0.656 (0.838)	0.335 (0.406)	−0.101 (0.214)
Constant	−1.255***(0.220)	1.281***(0.148)	0.631***(0.070)
Number of level-1 units	70	70	70
Number of level-2 units	535	535	535
Individual-level variance explained	0.10	0.11	0.32

Source: Youth-Parent Socialization Study.

Note: Results from hierarchical models (population-average model). Robust standard errors in parentheses. Independent variables standardized on 0–1 scale. Weighted data.

  * significant at .10   ** significant at .05   *** significant at .01

indices of political activity are ordinal, the estimators differ slightly, but the specification is identical.[22] The expectations are unambiguous. If the civic climate in high school engenders turnout motivated by a general civic orientation, then the norm should be *positively* related to voluntarism but have *no* relationship to either electoral activism or political voice.

These expectations are met. The coefficient for high school civic climate in the volunteering model looks a lot like its coefficient in the voter turnout model—positive, statistically significant, and even of a similar magnitude. By contrast, in both the electoral activism and political voice models, the magnitude of its coefficient is swamped by the corresponding standard error. We can thus see that the long arm of civic norms in adolescence reaches voluntarism, a form of civically motivated participation, but not politically motivated participation like working on a political campaign or the expression of political voice outside of the electoral arena. This is entirely consistent with the inference that civic norms *then* have an impact on voter turnout *now* by eliciting a civic motivation for voting.

THE SLEEPER EFFECT

We have seen that the civic climate in one's adolescent years reaches at least fifteen years into the future. It does not, however, predict voting at an earlier stage of life. This is known as the *sleeper effect*, an impact that is time delayed. In statistical terms, a sleeper effect manifests itself with a coefficient for civic climate that does not start out as a positive and statistically significant predictor of voter turnout, but becomes so over time. This is precisely what is observed between the two follow-up waves of the YPSS. In 1973, when respondents were asked whether they turned out in the 1972 presidential election, the civic climate in their high school had no significant impact on whether they voted. As we have seen, however, by the 1980 election the endorsement of voting as a norm in their high school had become a predictor of voter turnout. What changed between 1972 and 1980? By 1980, for the most part participants in the YPSS had passed through the early years of what Benjamin Highton and Raymond Wolfinger call the most critical period in the "political life cycle" (2001)—the stretch of time that is often punctuated by such life-defining events as college attendance, the beginnings of a career, marriage, homeownership, children, and so on. In 1972, however, YPSS participants were at the tail end of the highly mobile, socially disruptive years of post-adolescence. While the fifteen-year mark following high school is somewhat arbitrary, it is long enough that most people have passed through the life transitions that follow adolescence. By this point in their lives, most Americans have settled down into their "adult" lives—owning homes, raising kids, and so on. This is roughly the point in time, therefore, when we should expect an internalized civic norm to have an impact on the decision to vote.

The evidence for a sleeper effect adds to our understanding of how adolescent experiences can come to affect an adult's public engagement, as sleeper effects have largely been the subject of more speculation than evidence. In the words of M. Kent Jennings and Laura Stoker:

> Manifestations of sleeper, or delayed, effects have been hard to come by in the socialization literature. . . . The seeds planted during the high school years germinate and only gradually bear fruit. As people move into the life situations of middle age that evoke or require civic engagement, they draw on the predispositions and skills set in place at an earlier time. Pre-adult experiences do eventually matter. (2004, 363)

The process observed for the impact of civic climate in one's adolescence appears to unfold as Jennings and Stoker describe. Civic norms incubate, serving to motivate behavior only when an individual's situation in life otherwise facilitates it. We have just seen evidence that suggests a focus on the present means we miss the importance of the past, in contrast to the bulk of the political behavior literature, which looks almost exclusively at the present and pays little attention to the past. The study of participation, not to mention other areas of political behavior research, would benefit from more attention to the long-term influences of youthful experiences. If nothing else, the YPSS stands as an example of the insights to be gained from carefully designed longitudinal research.

SUMMARY OF FINDINGS

This chapter is rife with statistical models, the presentation of which always runs the risk of obscuring the theoretical importance of the results. Because I have covered a lot of material, perhaps it is useful to take a panoramic view in order to see the theory at work as a whole. Most important, we have seen that the civic climate of one's high school has an impact on voter turnout at least fifteen years following high school. However, the pithiness of this statement does not do justice to its significance.

First, we have seen that it is the *civic* climate of the school community that has a robust impact on participation in adulthood, not the degree to which an adolescent's peers see themselves as active in public affairs. What matters is that an adolescent's environment is populated with a high percentage of peers who express that voting is an indicator of good citizenship—that it is a civic duty. A high school context characterized by adolescents who are politically engaged, and anticipate being so in the future, has no similar effect.

Second, we have seen that it is the norms within the adolescent's *community*, defined in this case as the high school, that matter. Once we account for environmental factors, an individual's own belief that voting is a civic duty does not have an impact on voting as an adult. We are thus reminded that individual-level factors are only part of the story explaining participation, and political behavior more generally. While political scientists, for the most part, recognize the hazards of inferring individual-level behavior from aggregate data, it can also be the case that inferring individual-level behavior without information about individuals' social contexts is equally fallacious (Huckfeldt and Sprague 1993). Individuals do not act, nor are they acted upon, in isolation. Rather, norms are inculcated within collectivities, such as the family, the neighborhood, and the school.

Third, strong civic norms within a school community reach into the *future*. While we have seen that what you do *now* depends on where you are *now*—one's current social context has an impact on behavior—it is also the case that where you were *then* affects what you do *now*. This blend of both a contextual and longitudinal effect is the apex of the theoretical structure built in support of the civic motivation model.

BACK TO TRACI

With all these statistical models can we explain why Traci Hodgson bothered to vote in an election about which she knew nothing? From the newspaper article detailing her solitary trip to the polls, we know three things about Traci. One, she comes from a community where we would expect civic norms to be strong. Two, she commented that she cast her vote because she felt it was her duty. Three, she "did her duty" even though she had moved out of her hometown to attend college in the heart of a major urban center. We have seen how an adolescent social environment with strong civic norms leads to civic engagement later in life, even when people leave that environment. Being immersed in an environment where norms are strong leads to those norms being internalized, and thus continue to shape behavior beyond adolescence. The fact that her civic environment manifested its effect early into her post-adolescent years, rather than years later (as suggested by the evidence of the sleeper effect), suggests that her particular adolescent community had especially strong civic norms.

WHAT'S NEXT

This study has shown it is plausible that social contexts matter for public engagement, even over the long haul, but it is hardly the final word on the subject of contextual, longitudinal, and/or both types of effects. Hopefully it is the beginning of a scholarly conversation that further explores the long-term implications of contextual influences on participation, building on these rudimentary results. Perhaps this study has raised more questions than it has answered. For example, more research is needed to understand the effects of moving from one community to another. How long does one have to live in a new place before acting in accordance with the prevailing civic climate? What happens when the norms of one's adolescence conflict with the norms of the community to which one has moved? Similarly, does age affect the rate at which a newcomer absorbs a community's norms? What about other factors, like the difference between being a member of a majority versus minority group? Furthermore, this study has only examined the imprint left on individuals during their adolescence. While this is undoubtedly a critically formative period, presumably norms are absorbed during childhood and early adulthood, too, and perhaps continuously across the entire life span. In particular, it would be interesting to examine whether one's college environment has an impact comparable to that of the high school community. In short, there is much to be learned about what effects are found for which communities at what ages, and for how long.

Finally, we are left with the question of whether a school has any control over its civic climate. Do the civic norms inside a school simply reflect the norms in the community outside the school? Are there efforts schools can take to enhance the sense of civic commitment among their students? The answer has important policy implications for anyone who wishes to enhance the civic commitment of the nation's young people. If schools can enhance the civic dimension of public engagement in America, it is worth finding out how. The next, and final, chapter considers some of the ways this might be done and explains why fostering civic norms within schools has the potential to stem the decline in voter turnout among America's youth.

APPENDIX

Other Norms

The analysis in chapter 7 centers on only one norm within a high school community, specifically the degree to which students consider voting as an obligation of citizenship. The theoretical significance of this particular norm is underscored when we examine other contextual measures of what high school students perceive as the components of good citizenship. Are any of them related to partisan heterogeneity and, if so, how? Moving to the other side of the equation, do any of them share the same relationships to civic and political participation as the measure of whether voting is a civic obligation?

When students in the YPSS were asked about what makes for a good citizen, "voting regularly" was one option among many.[23] The others were:

He goes to church.
He obeys the laws.
He is proud of his country.
He minds his own business.
He doesn't think he is better than people of other races, nationalities, or religions.

Not surprisingly, given that this question's objective is to identify what adolescents see as the obligations of citizenship, these measures all arguably have a civic dimension, although they each tap into a different conception of what it means to be "civic." Represented among them are fairly minimal obligations that center around oneself or family, like going to church and minding your own business. Another is patriotism, while yet another is a sense of egalitarianism. Of this array of norms, obeying the law and being proud of one's country top the list as the most widely endorsed sentiments, as on average 74 and 73 percent of students, respectively, reported that they characterize what it means to be a good citizen. Voting is just behind, at 70 percent, followed closely by not thinking that one is better than others (64 percent). On average, only 11 percent of high school students see attending church as part of being a good citizen and even fewer (5 percent) characterize minding your own business as a component of citizenship.

Table 7.A1 regresses the percentage of students endorsing each norm on political, religious, and racial heterogeneity, as well as the level of parents' education and residential mobility. Of these five norms, only "minding one's business" is significantly related to political heterogeneity, but in a different direction than the voting norm: positive rather than negative. Greater religious heterogeneity means fewer students endorse "going to church" as part of being a good citizen, but it is not significantly related to any of the other norms. Racial heterogeneity is negatively related to the belief that good citizens are proud of their country, and positively related to minding one's own business. It has no effect on any of the other norms.

TABLE 7.A1
Factors Shaping "Good Citizen" Norms

	(1)	(2)	(3)	(4)	(5)
	Goes to church	Obeys the law	Is proud of his country	Does not think he is better than others	Minds his own business
Political heterogeneity	0.049 (0.033)	−0.048 (0.036)	−0.031 (0.042)	0.064 (0.068)	0.042**(0.017)
Religious heterogeneity	−0.061**(0.029)	−0.025 (0.031)	0.007 (0.037)	0.046 (0.060)	−0.016 (0.015)
Racial heterogeneity	−0.043 (0.032)	0.056 (0.035)	−0.216***(0.041)	0.083 (0.066)	0.061***(0.017)
Mean parents' education	−0.159***(0.040)	0.182***(0.044)	−0.174***(0.052)	0.026 (0.084)	−0.021 (0.021)
Years lived in community	0.042 (0.031)	−0.032 (0.034)	−0.052 (0.040)	0.114* (0.065)	0.007 (0.016)
Constant	0.152*** (0.037)	0.743***(0.040)	0.865***(0.048)	0.461***(0.077)	0.025 (0.019)
Observations	77	77	77	77	77
R^2	0.26	0.26	0.37	0.09	0.22

Source: Youth-Parent Socialization Study.

Note: Results from linear regression. Standard errors in parentheses. Independent variables standardized on 0–1 scale. Weighted data.
* significant at .10   ** significant at .05   *** significant at .01

TABLE 7.A2
School Norms and Public Engagement in 1980

	Voting (HGLM)	Volunteering (HGLM)	Electoral activism (HLM)	Political Voice (HLM)
	(1)	(2)	(3)	(4)
School norms (1965)				
Votes	0.744*(0.412)	0.818**(0.406)	−0.092(0.386)	−0.005(0.162)
Goes to church	−0.617(0.913)	−1.146(1.253)	0.200(0.690)	−0.790***(0.282)
Obeys the law	−1.483(1.111)	3.013**(1.197)	0.611(0.885)	0.802**(0.309)
Is proud of his country	−2.948**(1.450)	−3.758**(1.585)	−2.141**(0.869)	−1.677**(0.454)
Does not think he is better than others	3.978***(1.189)	−0.275(1.384)	0.327(0.907)	0.867**(0.434)
Minds his own business	1.985**(0.766)	2.624**(1.121)	1.266(0.806)	0.648*(0.346)
Level-1 effects				
Education level	0.966***(0.329)	0.635*(0.381)	0.698***(0.231)	0.337**(0.132)
Married	0.889***(0.234)	0.950***(0.192)	0.088(0.140)	−0.002(0.073)
Years lived in community	0.809***(0.288)	−0.437(0.345)	−0.371(0.248)	−0.008(0.080)
Parental participation (also level 1)				
Electoral activism index (1965)	1.293***(0.325)	0.664(0.467)	0.897***(0.279)	0.299**(0.145)
Community voluntarism (1965)		−0.251(0.218)		
Level-2 effects				
Mean years lived in community	0.802(0.486)	0.645(0.391)	0.062(0.371)	−0.207(0.160)
Constant	0.758***(0.194)	−1.115***(0.183)	1.162***(0.124)	0.570***(0.056)
Number of level-1 units	535	535	535	535
Number of level-2 units	70	70	70	70
Individual-level variance explained	0.22	0.11	0.11	0.26

Source: Youth-Parent Socialization Study.

Note: Results from hierarchical models (population-average model). Robust standard errors in parentheses. Independent variables standardized on 0–1 scale. Weighted data.

* significant at .10   ** significant at .05   *** significant at .01

Next, we examine whether any of these norms have the same effect on civic and political participation as the voting norm. The difficulty in setting up such an analysis is that many of these norms are highly correlated with one another, clouding any interpretation of their effects. In order to adjust for the fact that these norms are all highly correlated with one another, each norm (as measured at the school level) has been regressed on the other norms. By saving the residuals from each of these regressions, we have a measure of each norm that has been "purged" of its correlation with the others. Each of these corrected measures of social norms within a school has been entered into models predicting the four forms of participation (in the 1980s) that have been highlighted already: voter turnout, voluntarism, electoral activism, and political voice.

Table 7.A2 contains a hodgepodge of results that, frankly, are difficult to interpret. For example, the prevalence of linking pride in one's country to good citizenship has a negative impact on all four forms of engagement, whereas a belief that good citizens should obey the laws of the nation is a positive predictor of volunteering and voice. Perhaps most intriguing is the belief that being a good citizen means minding one's own business, since it has a positive, statistically significant impact in three of the four models. Other than the norm connecting good citizenship and voting, this is the only one related to political heterogeneity. The more heterogeneous the environment, the more adolescents endorse a view of citizenship that is focused on the individual, perhaps suggesting that political heterogeneity leads to a diminishment of concern for the public good. I hesitate to make too much of this admittedly tenuous hypothesis, however, since a very small percentage of students endorse this vision of citizenship in any given school. Like Rorschach inkblots, it is possible to come up with a story for the patterns we see, but in the absence of theory such an effort is almost entirely speculation. The bottom line is that none of the other norms behaves in accordance with the theory of dual motivations. A participatory norm—that is, one encouraging voting out of civic obligation—is unique in its effect.

CHAPTER EIGHT

Conclusion: Implications for Theory and Policy

AT ITS CORE, THIS IS a book about a theory meant to explain why people vote—more specifically why some people do and some people don't. At the foundation of the theory is the simple claim that an internalized sense of civic duty is an important factor motivating people to cast a ballot. However, shining a light on civic duty as a motivation for voting has also served to illuminate a number of other relevant findings, which bear on both the study of political science and the practice of public policy. For one, we have examined the consequences for public engagement of community heterogeneity or, more colloquially, diversity. And so this concluding chapter will discuss the implications for American civil society of the connections between diversity and public engagement.

From there the chapter will turn to discussing the one form of engagement that has been our primary concern: voter turnout. Turnout is low across the board, but especially so for our youngest voters. While there have been a number of reforms, both proposed and implemented, to boost turnout among Americans (and young Americans especially), none has made much difference. The reason, I suggest, is that reformers have ignored the one factor with the potential to have the biggest impact, namely adherence to a norm of voting out of civic duty. I then discuss the implications of an electorate with an enhanced sense of civic obligation. Finally, I consider ways in which civic duty might be enhanced, with a particular eye toward schools as a policy lever with which to strengthen the civic responsibility of America's young people.

POLITICAL DIVERSITY

Recent years have seen the embrace of diversity become a defining characteristic of contemporary American society. In the American public creed, it is now placed firmly beside other bedrock values like liberty and equality. While diversity perhaps does not have the longevity of these other ideals—the word did not roll off the lips of the Framers—it has quickly made up for lost time. Legal scholar Peter Schuck begins his book *Diversity in America* by noting, "In the pantheon of unquestioned goods, diversity is right up there with progress, motherhood, and apple pie" (2003, 12).

The rising attention to diversity has led to research on its consequences, including the question of whether public engagement rises or falls as a community's level of diversity rises. The answer is "yes." Or, it depends. Community heterogeneity and public engagement share a nuanced connection, as it is not as simple as asking whether engagement rises or falls as heterogeneity rises. The answer depends on the type of engagement in question. Civically motivated participation is more common in politically homogeneous communities, while people are more likely to engage in politically motivated activity in politically heterogeneous communities. Political diversity pulls civic involvement down while pushing political involvement up.

Because diversity and its consequences has increasingly become a popular topic of study across numerous academic disciplines, it has come to be defined in different ways. Yet among the various types of diversity that have been the subject of scholarly scrutiny, one that rarely comes up is political heterogeneity, even though there is a solid theoretical rationale for the expectation that political diversity and public engagement are related. As detailed in chapter 2, the prevailing explanation for the decline in civic involvement in communities that are racially, ethnically, and economically heterogeneous rests on the assumption that people favor associating with people who are "like them," and thus share their preferences, opinions, and values. There are many ways in which people can be alike, including their political views. Indeed, in our politically polarized times there is good reason to think that shared political preferences represent an especially significant piece of common ground. The empirical results have borne this out; political heterogeneity has an impact on public engagement in ways that ethnic, racial, and economic heterogeneity do not. It should not be surprising that short shrift is made of political diversity within the current literature. After all, partisanship and ideology are generally thought to be more malleable than social identities like race, ethnicity, and class, although it turns out that political preferences—especially partisanship—remain largely fixed over the average person's life span (Green, Palmquist, and Shickler 2002).[1]

I hope the discussion and analysis in the preceding chapters has successfully made the point that our understanding of diversity's consequences is the poorer for the omission of political heterogeneity, particularly when it comes to the study of public engagement. As the literature on diversity expands, social scientists will be well served by paying at least as much attention to the effects of heterogeneity defined by political preferences as we do race, ethnicity, and income. It is also important that we in the social science community be mindful of *all* diversity's consequences, whatever we may think of their normative implications. When I have presented my research, I sometimes encounter people who assume that because my research demonstrates a positive link between political homogeneity and civic participation—activity that by definition for most people has a positive normative gloss—I am therefore implicitly endorsing politically homogeneous communities as a policy objective. This is not the case. Rather, I am simply interested in understanding the implications of community heterogeneity for public engagement, and the inherent trade-offs that accompany a diverse society. For the foreseeable future there will continue to be much discussion of diversity, much of it from a Panglossian perspective. Americans' abiding interest in—and celebration of—diversity is noble, deeply rooted in our history as a pluralist nation. But we should never forget that there is no free lunch. Increased diversity, particularly in a political context, appears to mean a trade-off between one type of public engagement and another, with normatively ambiguous consequences. To put our thumb on the purely civic side of the scale is to withdraw from the public decision making that is integral to a pluralist democracy, thus impoverishing our politics. Too much politics and too little civic involvement, however, runs the risk that contention will supplant community. I suspect that most of us would not want to live in a place constantly riven with political discord.

Owing to its immigrant roots, America has always been a nation distinguished by its diversity. In recent decades America has exceeded its historical baseline for social heterogeneity, already high by global standards, as ethnic and racial diversity have accelerated and the level of income inequality has grown. Yet while it is clearly the case that America is becoming more diverse along other dimensions, it is not so clear that we are becoming much more politically diverse. At first blush, this may seem to be a strange observation to make given that ours is a nation closely divided along partisan lines, as recent presidential elections have put into sharp relief for all the world to see. Remember, however, that turnout is shaped more by local than national forces. With all the talk of America being divided between red and blue states, it may seem obvious that Americans increasingly live in ideologically insular enclaves. The real story, however, is more complicated and the source of some dispute. In an innovative and provocative series of articles for the *American-Statesman* of Austin, Texas, journalist Bill Bishop claims that "Today, most Americans live in communities that are becoming more politically homogeneous and, in effect, diminish dissenting views" (2004c). Political scientist Philip Klinkner, however, has taken Bishop to task for making much ado about nothing: "By historical standards, political diversity and integration are alive and well, and the average American lives in an area with a great degree of exposure to members of the opposing party" (2004b, 1). Sorting through the exchange between Bishop and Klinkner rests on whether we focus on trends since the 1960s or the 1860s.

Klinkner stresses that, *over the long arc of American history*, today's counties do not have an unusually high degree of political heterogeneity. Bishop, on the other hand, emphasizes the trend in the last three to four decades, in which there does appear to have been a modest increase in the degree of political segregation.[2] In other words, while much of the discussion among political pundits about the cultural chasm between red and blue America is hyperbolic to say the least (Fiorina, Abrams, and Pope 2005), there is a nugget of truth to the claim that Americans tend to cluster among political fellow travelers and have done so increasingly over the last political generation (Brooks 2001; White 2003). A judicious assessment of the debate between Bishop and Klinkner would seem to be while there is more community-level political heterogeneity today than a few decades ago, there is less than at other points in American history. Hopefully, the foregoing work will help inform our expectations for levels of public engagement as we watch trends in America's political demography unfold. Contrary to the dire statements regarding the destruction to America's civic infrastructure wrought by political homogeneity, it is important to remember that there is a complex relationship between political uniformity and public engagement.

Voter Turnout

While along our journey we have learned much about community heterogeneity, this has not been our final destination. This book is *really* about why we vote (or not). Focusing on community heterogeneity has highlighted that people come to the polls for different reasons, and that those reasons differ according to the type of communities in which we live. Voter turnout can have a civic—publicly spirited, duty-driven—motivation, or it can be motivated by political considerations—the advancement or protection of one's interests. Voting is more likely to have a civic flavor in places characterized by political consensus, while conflict triggers turnout seasoned with a political motivation.

Understandably, political scientists have long been interested in who votes. That interest has increased in recent years, however, as evidence has accumulated that there has been a decline in voter turnout during the post–World War II era. In the 1956 presidential election, when popular incumbent Dwight Eisenhower faced Adlai Stevenson during a time of peace and economic prosperity, turnout was just over 60 percent. In 2000, the closest election in modern history saw a turnout level of 54 percent. The election of 2004 again brought us a highly competitive race, and while turnout did rise from 2000 it was still lower than, to take a telling example, 1960—when the race between John F. Kennedy and Richard

Nixon similarly came down to the wire. In that contest, 64 percent of eligible voters came to the polls, versus roughly 60 percent in 2004.[3]

The fact that turnout dropped over this period is notable. It is all the more notable, however, because there is every reason to think that there should have been a massive increase in voting rates over the last fifty years or so. For one thing, the average American has a much higher level of education now than in the 1950s and 1960s. Since more education correlates with a greater likelihood of turning out, it is all the more puzzling that turnout did not rise (Brody 1978). This period also saw the demise of the Jim Crow South, and thus the full incorporation of African Americans into the electorate, another reason we would have expected turnout to climb. In fact, when we separate voting trends in the Southern states versus the rest of the nation, we see a big difference. The states of the former Confederacy have actually seen turnout rise slightly over the last few decades, while in the Northern states, it has fallen (McDonald and Popkin 2001; Wattenberg 2002). Further heightening our expectation that turnout would have risen, voter registration has become much easier. A lot of research has suggested that barriers to registration were a significant impediment for many potential voters (Fenster 1994; Knack 2001; Mitchell and Wlezien 1995; Rhine 1995, 1996; Teixeira 1992; Wolfinger and Rosenstone 1980). With the passage of the Motor Voter Act in 1993, in most states one can register to vote at the same time that one registers for a driver's license or for other government services. Six states[4] even allow voters to register on election day (not including North Dakota, which has no voter registration), while Oregon conducts its elections entirely by mail—eliminating the need to leave one's home to vote at all. Every one of these demographic and legal changes is a force pushing turnout upward, and yet it still declined.

It is difficult to get political scientists to agree on anything, and so it is remarkable that independent streams of research have converged on the conclusion that the decline in turnout is concentrated largely among the youngest Americans eligible to vote (Miller and Shanks 1996; Putnam 2000; Levine and Lopez 2002; Wattenberg 2002). It is not only that young people vote less than their elders—owing to a life-cycle effect, that has always been true—it is that young people today vote at lower rates than young people in the past. In 1964, the turnout rate of voters eighteen to twenty-four was 16 points lower than voters age sixty-five and over. In 2000, that gap widened to over 35 points, a change attributed entirely to a drop among the young (U.S. Department of Commerce, Census Bureau 2002). In their exhaustive analysis of trends in voter turnout, Warren Miller and Merrill Shanks (1996) confirm the eyeball inference suggested by the census figures. They identify the abnormally low voting rates of the youngest cohort of voters as the primary cause of the aggregate decline in turnout, a point reinforced independently by Robert Putnam (2000) and researchers at the Center for Information and Research on Civic Learning and Engagement (Levine and Lopez 2002). The more the electorate is composed of people who came of age in the 1960s and later, the lower turnout falls.

The early analysis of the 2004 election only underscores the decline in young people's turnout. Given that young people voted at a higher rate in 2004 than 2000, that may seem to be a strange claim for me to make. It is true that turnout among eighteen- to twenty-four-olds rose. According to the University of Maryland's Center for Information and Research on Civic Learning and Engagement, the increase was roughly six percentage points—certainly, a sizable gain (2004). However, turnout among the young increased only to the same extent as turnout in the general population, as evidenced by the fact that young people's share of the voting public was the same as in 2000. In other words, turnout among young people did not rise disproportionately, even though there was a disproportionate amount of effort expended on getting out the youth vote. Significantly, even with all the attention paid to young people in 2004, their turnout was still lower than in 1992, when by comparison far less attention seemed to be paid to mobilizing young voters.[5]

We should not be surprised that turnout rose in 2004, as no one has claimed that the decline in turnout is inexorable. The 2004 contest was one of the most intensive election campaigns in recent years, and consequently throughout the campaign season, interest in the election was higher than in recent contests.[6] Similarly, turnout also rose in 1992, a boost commonly attributed to third-party candidate Ross Perot, who attracted new voters to the polls. In other words, from election to election, voters respond to their political environment. But over the last few decades the general trend has been downward, especially when we focus our attention on young people. Perhaps the jump up in 2004 will be the start of a new era for voter participation. But judging from past experience, that seems unlikely. It seems more likely that 2004 will be like 1992, an upward blip on a downward-sloping line. As young people occupy an ever-increasing share of the population, we can only expect the overall level of turnout to fall.

WHO CARES WHO VOTES?

In the midst of the minutiae of trends in voter turnout, it is easy to get caught up in technical matters and miss the larger significance of why anyone should care about the level and distribution of voting rates. Does it really matter how many people turn out to vote? Or, more specifically, does low voter participation among young people matter? From a purely self-interested perspective, it does if you are one of those young people. As Ruy Teixeira has put it, with low voter turnout, "in the long run the policy agenda may only poorly represent the segments of the population that vote the least" (1992, 3). More memorable are the words of Walter Dean Burnham: "[I]f you don't vote, you don't count" (1987, 99). Elected officials have demonstrated that they are acutely sensitive to groups within the electorate who vote in large numbers. America's senior citizens are the quintessential example. Why has Social Security come to be known as the "third rail of American politics," because if you touch it you die? Seniors are a highly engaged group, and consequently policy-makers are highly responsive to seniors' policy preferences, particularly when it comes to Social Security (A. Campbell 2003). By voting in such low numbers, young people make it less likely that lawmakers will take their preferences into account when formulating policy.

In the literature on voter turnout, the rationale for advocating an increase is typically framed in the language of "making your voice heard." But there is an irony, even a tension, within this body of research. The prevailing school of thought holds that increasing the number of voters would not actually change who gets elected. In their seminal book *Who Votes?*, Ray Wolfinger and Stephen Rosenstone simulate what would happen if voter registration were made substantially easier:

> The number of voters would increase, but there would be virtually no change in their demographic, partisan, or ideological characteristics. They would be more numerous, but not different. (1980, 88)

Their conclusion has subsequently been affirmed by a small army of political scientists who have conducted similar studies (Teixeira 1992; Mitchell and Wlezien 1995; Franklin and Grier 1997; Highton 1997; Knack and White 1998, 2000; Martinez and Hill 1999; Citrin, Schickler, and Sides 2003).

The conventional wisdom that high turnout would make little or no difference puts advocates of higher voter turnout in a peculiar position. Why bother to boost turnout if it is not going to make a difference? The current system is far more efficient than one in which more people turn out to vote. After all, under the status quo half the voters are able to represent the whole electorate. Two for the price of one is a pretty good deal. In fact, if the only reason to vote is to advance your own interests, then it would make more sense to figure out how *low* turnout can go and still adequately represent the electorate.

One response to this line of reasoning is to argue that higher turnout would make a difference after all, a point made in a few recent studies that fly in the face of the conventional wisdom (Hajnal and Trounstine 2005; Wattenberg 2002). The problem, of course, is that resting the argument for higher turnout on an empirical foundation runs the risk that contrary evidence will arise, rendering the point moot. And in this case, we have already seen that there is plenty of evidence suggesting that higher turnout would have no partisan impact.

I have a different perspective. I submit that boosting turnout would be worth it even if not a single election outcome would change. This is because voting is not just about "who gets what"—the aggregation of individuals' preferences. I have detailed, at some length, that voting has both political and civic motivations. Similarly, voting also has both political and civic *consequences*. On the political side, *who votes* affects the public policy our elected officials enact. On the civic side, *how many vote* reflect the nation's collective level of commitment to the responsibilities of citizenship in a participatory democracy. Voting has a communal dimension to it, thus triggering a concern that voter apathy impacts a whole that is greater than the sum of individuals' interests. The level of voter participation is an important indicator of our electoral system's legitimacy. As turnout falls, that legitimacy is threatened.

Far from being an abstraction, the link between turnout and democratic legitimacy was thrown into sharp relief in the run-up to Iraq's first free election since the American-led invasion and subsequent occupation. The world held its breath as election day approached, as we all waited to see how many Iraqis would turn out to vote. Had turnout been too low, the Iraqi electoral process would have been deemed illegitimate. Given the threats of violence against those who went to the polls to vote, there was every reason to think that few Iraqis would venture to do so. But vote they did. While turnout was not even across the country, and many Sunni Iraqis boycotted the election, enough voters turned out that in the court of world opinion the election was judged legitimate.

My point is not that all is well in Iraq because turnout in one election beat expectations. I will leave that for others to debate. I simply want to note that the well-placed concern about the number of Iraqis who would show up to vote underscored that voter turnout is related to democratic legitimacy. Granted, low turnout matters more when the election has high stakes. Low turnout in any single American election is not going to threaten the legitimacy of our electoral system. But perhaps a decline in voter participation means a slow ebbing away of America's collective sense of commitment to the nation's future.

Turning Turnout Around

So what is to be done? How can we boost voter turnout? To answer that, it is helpful to return to the calculus of voting (COV), introduced in chapter 2, as a lens through which to understand why people vote (Riker and Ordeshook 1968). As a brief reminder, this simple equation consists of:

$$Vote = pB + D > C$$

where

p is the probability of casting the deciding vote
B is the perceived benefit from a victory by the preferred candidate
C represents all of the costs associated with voting
D is one's sense of civic duty

When applied to the study of turnout in the aggregate it has stood up rather well, as voters have been shown to respond as expected in the wake of changes in the components of the equation. Take, for example, the fact that turnout rises when and where elections are competitive. This is precisely what the COV predicts. As p—the probability of swaying an election, however infinitesimal—increases, so does turnout. (It just does not increase by much.)

If we want to increase turnout, then, it makes sense to look at ways to change the components of the COV. The p term is one place to start, although as a strategy to increase turnout, it is difficult to see what could be done to make our elections more competitive, given the photo finishes of our recent presidential elections. Perhaps presidential elections could be made more competitive at the state level by eliminating the electoral college (Edwards 2004; Dahl 2001) and moving to a purely proportional electoral system, although to say that this change is currently infeasible is to risk a gross understatement. Slightly more feasible would be the adoption of a system in which states allocate their electoral votes by congressional district, which might also make a few more states competitive in presidential elections. However, Maine and Nebraska already do this, and it is not at all clear that it has made much, if any, difference in presidential turnout. We should not be terribly surprised that tinkering with the process of selecting electoral college delegates, what we might call an indirect route to enhancing the p term, has had little effect on turnout. After all, the existing evidence suggests that even living in a place where the election is competitive—presumably the most direct means of boosting p—has a negligible impact on turnout. It does not appear, therefore, that reforms to affect p hold much promise for increasing turnout. Abolishing the electoral college would likely have an effect (although no doubt accompanied by other unintended consequences), but is a quixotic cause to say the least. Tinkering with the electoral college from within the existing parameters is more feasible, but experience suggests it is unlikely to have much of an impact.

An increase in B also appears to increase voter participation, as evidenced by the apparent rise in turnout when credible third-party candidates enter a race. Third-party candidates give voice to new issues in a campaign, thus engaging some voters whose preferences are not represented by the Democrats or Republicans. In 1992 we saw an uptick in turnout when Ross Perot earned a significant share of the presidential vote. This is arguably because he attracted voters who did not see their interests represented by the two major-party candidates. Jesse Ventura's independent candidacy appears to have had a similar effect in the 1998 Minnesota gubernatorial election, as turnout rose by seven percentage points from the previous election in 1994.[7] One way to boost turnout, then, might be to make it easier for third-party candidates to run. Perhaps credible—admittedly a contentiously ambiguous term—third-party candidates could have an easier time getting on every state's ballot, greater access to public campaign financing, and regularly invitations to participate in televised debates among presidential candidates. Given the duopoly that the Republicans and Democrats have in the current political system, however, reforms to advantage third-party competitors are unlikely. In fact, closer analysis suggests that it may not be worth the trouble after all. Even though there was a detectable rise in turnout during 1992 in the wake of Ross Perot's high-profile bid for the presidency, scholars do not agree that Perot was actually the cause of the upswing, calling into question whether viable third-party candidates equal more voters (Knack 1997; Rosenstone, Behr, and Lazarus 1996).

There is also considerable evidence that C, the costs of voting, also affect turnout. It is no coincidence that the United States consistently ranks near the bottom in global comparisons of turnout rates and also imposes the high cost of making it unusually difficult to register as a voter (Powell 1986). Within the borders of the United States we find a similar pattern. States that make it easier for their residents to vote find that more of them do so (Wolfinger and Rosenstone 1980). In recent years, policymakers have taken numerous steps to lower the costs associated with voting, most notably through the adoption of the National Voter Registration Act (NVRA), more popularly known as the Motor Voter Act. Its moniker derives from the fact that the NVRA requires states to link voter registration with the renewal of drivers' licenses.[8] While this is the law's best-known provision, it also includes other substantial changes to how voters are registered. States must also allow voter registration at various public agencies beyond the department of motor vehicles, including welfare and unemployment offices, as well as military recruitment centers. In addition, the NVRA introduced universal mail registration and restrictions on removing voters from the registration rolls for not having voted (known as purging). As vindication of the COV, the implementation of the NVRA does appear to have increased voter turnout, even if not by much. It is likely that Motor Voter was a force pushing upward against other forces pulling downward, but clearly it has had no more than a limited effect. A number of studies have examined the impact of Motor Voter on turnout, and each has arrived at the same conclusion: making voter registration easier lifts turnout a little. But only a little. The consistency across these studies is as rhetorical as it is statistical. By far, the most common word used to describe the magnitude of electoral reforms is "modest."[9] Similarly, other efforts to make voting easier—same-day voter registration and voting by mail—have had only small effects (Karp and Banducci 2000, 2001; Stein 1998; Stein and Garcia-Monet 1997; Oliver 1996; Magleby 1987; Berinsky, Burns, and Traugott 2001; Knack 1995; Rhine 1995, 1996; Franklin and Grier 1997; Highton 1997; Highton and Wolfinger 1998; Martinez and Hill 1999).

Even though many of the studies just referred to do not explicitly invoke the COV, when taken as a group they offer it considerable support. Whether explicitly acknowledged or not, the above studies all confirm elements of the calculus of voting. Note, however, that they have centered on p, B, and C. Within the expansive literature on voter turnout there has been little discussion of D, a sense of civic duty. One notable exception is the work of Stephen Knack, as he has underscored the importance of civic duty when seeking to understand why people turn out to vote in an American context (1992). Knack and his coauthor, Martha Kropf, find, for example, that people who live in communities with strong civic norms—evidenced by their high response rates to the U.S. Census—are more likely to vote (1998). In another paper, Knack finds that the old saw about rain on election day helping the Republicans should be revised, as rain only depresses turnout among people who have a low sense of civic duty (1994). That is, the people most likely to pay the costs of voting in inclement weather are those who have a strong sense of civic duty—D trumps C. In a similar vein as Knack's work (and discussed more fully in chapter 3), Sidney Verba, Kay Schlozman, and Henry Brady have found that when asked why they vote, Americans widely report that they do so out of civic obligation (1995; Schlozman, Verba, and Brady 1995). Andre Blais weighs in as well, demonstrating that civic duty applies not only in the United States but is also a major factor leading Canadians to the polls (2000).

The fact that within the library of research on voter turnout so few studies highlight the significance of duty suggests that they are the exceptions to prove the rule, namely that a sense of civic obligation has been largely ignored as a subject of serious research. This omission is ironic, given that duty has long been recognized as an important motivation for the vote, even before William Riker and Peter Ordeshook published their seminal article on the calculus of voting (1968). As far back as 1954, the original Michigan School team of Angus Campbell and his colleagues empirically demonstrated that many people vote because they feel it is their duty to do so (1954). Gabriel Almond and Sidney Verba (1989 [1963]) similarly reported that Americans have a strong sense of civic duty in *The Civic Culture*.

In the wake of these seminal works, one might have thought that questions relating to the study of civic duty would have become a flourishing body of scholarship. After all, these studies merely demonstrate that when explaining voter participation, duty matters. That blunt conclusion is certainly important, but only prompts second-order questions, like where a sense of civic duty comes from and why some people have more of it than others. Rather than a starting point for further research, however, the early consensus regarding the importance of civic duty seems to have closed it off. Having recognized that people vote out of a sense of duty, political scientists moved on to other explanations for why people vote. There has been a litany of books and articles on voter turnout, but within them civic duty warrants only a passing mention at most (Miller and Shanks 1996; Rosenstone and Hansen 1993; Teixeira 1992), and sometimes no mention at all (Patterson 2002; Wattenberg 2002). When it is mentioned, it is often dismissed as tautological. As Stephen Rosenstone and Mark Hansen put it, "The connection between belief in a duty to participate and participation itself is distressingly close" (1993, 20 n. 23), suggesting that we gain little purchase on voting by asking people whether it is their obligation to vote. Of course, the fact that far fewer people vote than say it is their duty to do so suggests that, pace Rosenstone and Hansen, perhaps a verbal commitment to civic duty and public engagement are separable after all.[10]

Whatever the reasons, the fact remains that political science has largely left civic duty alone as a subject of sustained research. As a result, the recent work on civic duty thus simply brings us full circle to the initial conclusions on the subject from fifty years ago—duty mattered then, and it continues to matter now. The present study has been intended to push our understanding a little further. We have thus seen that civic duty is stronger in some communities than others, and that political homogeneity strengthens the norm that voting is an obligation of citizenship. Furthermore, the strength of civic norms in one's adolescent social environment shapes participatory patterns for years to come. Clearly, this only scratches the surface of what can be learned about civic duty, but at the least it demonstrates that a sense of duty is not a hopelessly "squishy" or circular concept but worthy of rigorous empirical study.

It hardly seems coincidental that over the same period that turnout has declined, at least among young people, there is evidence that civic duty has also declined, at least among young people. Data on the self-perceived sense of civic duty among young people is spotty, at least over the long haul. Fortunately, the 1973 replication of the 1965 high school sample of the YPSS repeated the very same question about civic duty asked eight years before. Just in the years between 1965 and 1973, there was a decline in the percentage of high school seniors who reported that voting is a component of good citizenship. In 1965, 70 percent of adolescents indicated that someone who "votes in elections" is a good citizen. By 1973, that had dropped to 58 percent. By 1999, it appears to have dropped even lower, although because the wording of the question changed we cannot make a direct comparison. In that year, as part of the international Civic Education Study, almost 3,000 American ninth-graders (in 124 schools) were asked their opinion regarding the requirements for an adult to be considered a good citizen. Only 36 percent indicated that it is very important for a citizen to vote in every election. Contrast that with a similar study done in 1971, when only 11 percent disagreed with the statement that a good citizen votes in every election (International Association for the Evaluation of Educational Achievement 1977). Qualitative evidence tells a similar story. William Damon, director of the Center on Adolescence at Stanford University, reports that in 1999 researchers conducted interviews with American youth about their role in society. He notes that in the course of these interviews, young people "showed little interest in people outside their immediate circles of friends and relatives (other than fictional media characters and entertainment or sports figures); little awareness of current events; and virtually no expressions of social concern, political opinion, *civic duty*, patriotic emotion, or sense of citizenship in any form" (2001, 124, emphasis added). In sum, while we have no smoking gun we do nonetheless have a preponderance of evidence that the link between voting and civic duty has diminished among America's youth.

Among the reforms—both proposed or implemented—to the p, B, and C terms of the calculus of voting, there is an unmistakable pattern. The policy reforms that appear most likely to affect turnout are the least likely to be implemented. On the other hand, the reforms that do seem within the realm of possibility, including those that have already been adopted, do not seem to make much difference at all. Having run through p, B, and C as options for reform, only D, adherence to a civic norm, remains. It is time for political scientists and policymakers alike to consider seriously the possible gains in turnout from enhancing Americans' civic motivations for voting.

CONSEQUENCES

Before moving on to a discussion of how civic duty might be enhanced, it is worth considering what the potential consequences of such a reform would be. Assume for a moment that we knew of a way to increase voter turnout by somehow boosting Americans' sense of civic duty. What would be the result? Taken to an extreme, this is an example of having to be careful what we ask for. To see what I mean, think back to Traci Hodgson. When she first made her appearance, I stressed that she had voted out a sense of civic obligation. But recall that she also admitted that she knew nothing about the candidates on the ballot. I for one would be uncomfortable with an electorate of Tracis—dutiful but uninformed.

However, I would be just as uncomfortable with an electorate composed of people who voted only when they felt their own narrow interests were threatened. Imagine two electorates, one in which voting was motivated solely by duty, the other where its only motivation was self-interest. Neither would be very appealing. In the former, voters would be ignorant automatons, but in the latter voters would have to be convinced that their own interests were under threat before heading to the polls, a condition that would no doubt be spurred by fear-mongering campaigns.

Of course, the two electorates described are merely hypothetical ideal types, as we have seen that voting shares the twin motivations of both duty and interest. For analytical purposes, I have separated them from one another, although in practice they exist in tandem. The apparent decline in civic responsibility suggests that, more often than not, interest trumps duty. Fostering a greater sense of duty would only bring the two closer to equilibrium.

What we want is an electorate in which, because of voters' sense of civic obligation, turning out to vote is the default option. Rather than deciding to vote only when they see an overt threat to their interests, voters would make voting a habit. Knowing they were coming to the polls would then lead them to weigh their options carefully, as there is no reason that dutiful voters cannot also be informed. Interest-driven voters ask themselves: Do I need to vote in this election to defend my interests? Instead, we would hope that duty-driven voters ask: Given that I am going to vote in this election, which candidate best represents my preferences? In the interest-driven case, the electorate is composed only of people who care enough about a particular issue (or issues) to get off their couches and vote. Under this condition, voters will be out of step with the mainstream almost by definition, because people who care deeply about an issue typically have extreme views. There are not many passionate moderates. A duty-driven electorate, on the other hand, will have more voters from the moderate middle, since their primary motivation for coming to the polls is a sense of duty, not a passionate opinion. Duty-driven voters, in other words, serve as a moderating influence in the political environment. And our politics could use a little more moderation.

To this point the reader has seen that civic norms are *meaningful*—far from simply being tautological, adherence to a norm encouraging collective action has traction for explaining turnout, and is thus a logical place to direct efforts at increasing turnout. Also, we have seen that civic norms are *measurable*. It is possible to find theoretically derived and analytically tractable indicators of civic norms within a community. The question now is whether they are *manipulable*—is it possible to take steps to shape the civic character of a community?

What Schools Can Do

In chapter 7, we saw that the civic norms within a high school have a long-term impact on voting. Therefore, it is natural to turn to America's schools as the institutions through which we can enhance the level of voter participation. Just as Archimedes said that if he was given a place to stand he could move the world, schools represent a promising place to stand if we wish to move the level of turnout.

Others before me have also identified the nation's schools as a means to catalyze civic engagement. While political scientists have long identified schools as critical to civic development (Merriam 1934), more recently political theorists like Amy Gutmann (1999, 2000) and Stephen Macedo (2000) have written eloquently of the essential role schools play in preparing young people for a lifetime of civic involvement. Reform-minded empirical researchers like Ruy Teixeira (1992) have also advocated schools as potential sources of civic renewal. The difficulty, however, in reforming schools to accomplish civic ends is that little research has been conducted to test what it is about schools that makes a difference. This study can hopefully offer some guidance on how schools can help their students gain a foothold in the civic realm. While far from definitive, my findings can offer an informed guide to school-level factors that appear likely to have a participatory payoff in the long run. As we have seen, the civic norms reinforced within the nation's high schools hold promise as a means to enhance civic engagement in America.

Homogeneity Is Not the Answer

If we proceed by assuming (a) the norm that voting is a civic duty has weakened among American adolescents, and (b) civic norms can be taught and internalized in secondary schools, a course of action presents itself. Schools need to become seedbeds for civic norms. The question, of course, is how that can be done. At this point I can offer no definitive answers but can suggest some avenues worth exploring.

Let me begin stressing what I am *not* advocating. A glance at the foregoing chapters might suggest that homogeneity is the solution to our civic ills—conservatives should be shunted off to their communities and schools, and liberals to theirs. However, a closer reading of both the empirical results and the supporting theoretical apparatus clarifies why we will not pull out of our participatory tailspin by segregating our schools along ideological or any other lines. Even though I have used measures of communities' partisan and ideological heterogeneity as proxies for the presence of civic norms, we need not conclude that the strength of norms is inevitably a function of a community's political composition. Nor is their strength necessarily determined by religious, ethnic, racial, or income heterogeneity, nor any similar form of demographic profile. The civic motivation model merely offers an explanation for why commonality breeds civic norms; it does not specify the criteria by which people consider themselves as being "in common" with others.

The perception of what we have in common is entirely a malleable social construction. Today, partisan preferences unite us (and, consequently, also divide us). Tomorrow, other factors could overshadow partisanship as glue bonding people together. Indeed, the reaction to September 11, 2001, has offered a glimpse of how easily our conception of commonality can change. In the wake of the terrorist attacks on the United States, there was a palpable feeling throughout the nation that we all share more unum than pluribus with our fellow citizens, a conclusion supported by more than sentimental anecdotes. Using survey data from a panel of Americans interviewed before and after September 11, Robert Putnam reports,

> More Americans now express confidence that people in their community would cooperate . . . with voluntary conservation measures in an energy or water shortage. In fact, in the wake of the terrorist attacks, more Americans reported having cooperated with their neighbors to resolve common problems. (2002)

Furthermore, this upsurge in civic attitudes was not directed only at members of one's own community. People in Manhattan, Kansas, stood as one with people in Manhattan, New York; more concretely, Putnam finds that generalized trust almost uniformly increased following September 11. In his State of the Union address a few months following the terrorist attacks, President George W. Bush spoke eloquently of the need for Americans to increase their civic involvement: "[A]fter America was attacked, it was as if our entire country looked into a mirror and saw our better selves. We were reminded that we are citizens, with obligations to each other, to our country, and to history. We began to think less of the goods we can accumulate, and more about the good we can do" (Bush 2002).

In the antiseptic language of social science, September 11 was an "exogeneous shock" to the nation. More colloquially, it showed us that things change. The nation's collective response to September 11 has demonstrated that there *is* a latent sense of collectivity within the body politic, all the more remarkable given the rancorous environment of contemporary politics. However, September 11 has also taught us that a sense of collectivity in and of itself is not enough to foster long-term civic commitment; although civic activity spiked just after September 11, it has declined since. Perhaps we should not be surprised that the unity forged in the immediate aftermath of September 11 quickly dissipated. There is no better example of how we, as a nation, find it difficult to speak of communal obligations and even sacrifice than what Americans were asked by their leaders, especially the president, to do after September 11. While the president, and others, called for more civic commitment, Americans also heard their elected leaders tell them that it was their duty to go shopping and attend Broadway shows (Kowalczyk 2001). While the price of a Broadway show may seem like a sacrifice, somehow it does not seem to be a step toward increasing the strength of the citizenry's civic bonds.

It is too easy, however, to lay the blame for the impoverishment of civic responsibility entirely at the feet of our political leaders. Certainly they deserve some criticism, as historically one way citizens' civic commitment has been strengthened is in response to sustained calls for greater civic involvement from the top. Bush's remarks in the State of the Union were a good start, but there was little follow-up. At the end of the day, though, the rhetoric emanating from the president, or any other political leader, is far less important than the real work of strengthening civic norms. This work will be done from the bottom up through local institutions, especially our schools. The challenge, therefore, is to build that sense of "we" within our schools *in order to nurture civic norms, including the encouragement of voting as a civic obligation.* It is the norms that are critical. In other words, while a sense of communality— that we are all in this together—may be necessary to facilitate civic norms, it is not sufficient.

Taking Civics Seriously

Having explained what the schools should not do, we are in a better position to explore more affirmative options. However, it would be premature to advocate a single silver bullet as the way to strengthen the civic commitment of today's youth, as we know surprisingly little about the process of civic development among adolescents. Therefore, the first order of business must be recognition among legislators, educators, parents, and the public alike that the civic dimension of our educational system deserves more than lip service, but should be subject to the same scrutiny as other educational outcomes. In an era when high-stakes testing has become a national obsession, we have largely forgotten our schools' civic mission. Certainly, little effort is expended in evaluating whether they are accomplishing that mission. I fear that our preoccupation with testing means that schools are evaluated solely in terms of scholarship, with no attention paid to citizenship, objectives that should not be competitors but complements. I echo Stephen Macedo's lament: "Given the centrality of civic purposes to public schools it is ironic that studies of 'effective schools' pay so little attention to civic ends" (2000, 235). We need to learn what works, and then make it possible for our schools to do it. In addition to the systematic research of scholars, the impetus for schools to take civic education seriously is for policymakers and parents to pay attention to the civic experiences provided by their schools as closely as they currently monitor academic performance.

Learning from the Social Norms Approach to Substance Abuse

Although at first blush it probably seems far afield from the subject of civic participation, we can learn useful lessons about strengthening civic norms from a growing literature within the field of public health. After decades of minimal success using scare tactics to discourage substance abuse, a few pioneering public health experts have increasingly studied and adopted a method of combating binge drinking, smoking, and similarly destructive behaviors among young people that relies on social norms (Perkins 2003). At the core of the social norms approach, as it has come to be called, is the fact that many young people mistakenly assume there is more drinking and smoking among their peers than is actually the case, which matters because perceptions of, say, how much drinking is "normal" affects how much people drink. The greater you think others' alcohol consumption to be, the more you imbibe. The fundamental insight of the social norms approach, therefore, is that reducing substance abuse among young people requires changing their perceptions of what is normal. A sizable body of evidence has accumulated demonstrating that public information campaigns which promote an accurate perception of social norms regarding drinking and smoking lead to a drop in the incidence of substance abuse. Practitioners of the social norms approach have found their method to be successful in a variety of settings, including both college and high school campuses (Baer et al. 1992; Baer, Stacy, and Larimer 1991; Graham, Marks, and Hansen 1991; Haines and Spear 1996; Marks, Graham, and Hansen 1992; Perkins and Berkowitz 1986; Perkins and Wechsler 1996; Prentice and Miller 1993; Thombs, Wolcott, and Farkash 1997).

Obviously, preventing substance abuse is not the same as promoting a sense of civic commitment; discouraging vice is one thing while encouraging virtue is quite another. Nonetheless, the power of social norms is the common thread that weaves them together. Most important, the effectiveness of the social norms approach to substance abuse demonstrates that it is possible to change young people's perceptions of what is normative and thus change their behavior. Armed with that insight, an entire research agenda opens up to study what leads to stronger civic norms. For example, what are the relative benefits of a public information campaign versus classroom instruction for enhancing the sense of civic commitment among young people? A good model for the study of interventions designed to affect the civic climate within a school community can be found in the work of Alan Gerber and Donald Green, who have used a wide array of randomized experiments to demonstrate the effectiveness (or not, as the case may be) of various voter mobilization techniques (Green and Gerber 2004). Similar experiments can easily be designed to gauge efforts taken to strengthen civic norms within a school environment.

Is it really possible to expect today's schools, beleaguered as many of them are, to add the promotion of civic duty to their long list of responsibilities? A model can be found in the way that contemporary schools have come to embrace tolerance for diversity as a preeminent value. Arthur Powell, Eleanor Farrar, and David Cohen make this point well in *The Shopping Mall High School*. I thus quote them at length.

> The one theme that schools can rally around is *tolerating* differences. . . . In school after school, all members of the community spoke with pride and feeling about the growth of tolerance. . . . [D]iscussions of tolerance most frequently concerned racial harmony. Several schools had recently undergone traumas of actual or potential racial discord and had expended considerable emotional and financial resources on that issue. For many teachers the struggle had been the high point of their careers. They were proud of the results: "Here we give kids a really beautiful social education. No one can beat us at that."

When racial or ethnic slurs occurred within classrooms, teachers virtually never ignored them. They pounced on them as educational opportunities. . . .

In a curiously American, wholly noble, and completely exhausting way, the tolerance of diversity has become the basis for community within high schools. It is not easy to build community on the basis of differences rather than similarities; it goes against the expected grain. . . . But the schools settle for the absence of conflict as the definition of community. Community means an attitude of "Live and let live" rather than of people working together. (1985, 57–58)

I am particularly struck by the way Powell and his colleagues describe the spontaneous way that teachers stress tolerance when derogatory comments are made in their classrooms. It seems clear that this respect for differences has not come about through a particular class that students take, nor is it restricted to a select few who participate in a specific program. Nor is it the subject of a standardized evaluation. It has become part of the modern public school's culture, quietly and consistently reinforced by teachers and administrators. It has, in other words, become a norm.

Since so much attention is often paid to what our schools do wrong, it is worth noting that teaching tolerance is something that our schools do right. This is no small accomplishment, given that political theorists identify toleration for differences as a bedrock principle of a democratic education. Just as our schools have come to embody tolerance, I see no reason why they cannot become equally effective at fostering a norm of civic engagement.

In short, our schools have excelled at promoting pluribus. Now they must do the same for unum. In this regard, we can draw a useful parallel to Putnam's distinction between bonding and bridging social capital. Recall that social capital refers to the presence of norms, taught and enforced within social networks. The bonding variety consists of relationships among people among whom you have much in common, whereas bridging social capital is characterized by connections across social cleavages. Putnam stresses that both types of social capital are essential to a healthy civil society. Our schools have come to excel at building bridges; they should now focus on forging bonds, for the sake of the nation's civic health.

Schools need to become more cohesive communities, which admittedly runs the risk that cohesiveness breeds insularity. Civic invigoration in the schools will only succeed if students are taught to look outward rather than inward. By learning the obligations that come with being part of a school community, students can develop an appreciation for the duties accompanying membership in the community beyond the school's walls. To that end, I echo a recommendation of the National Commission on Civic Renewal:

> Schools should reorganize their internal life to reinforce basic civic virtues such as personal and social responsibility, by giving students far more responsibility for maintaining cleanliness and discipline in classrooms and on school grounds. (1998, 14)

There are myriad other possibilities. And while such efforts should begin with the school, they should not end there. Students must come to see themselves as part of their neighborhood, municipality, state, and nation. Perhaps students need experience with meaningful decision making on school policies; perhaps service learning will prove to be an effective means of promoting civic obligation. These and many other ideas should be implemented—and evaluated. Some ideas will work, some will not. It is worth finding out which is which.

INVESTMENT STRATEGY

I conclude this book with an experience I had just as I was beginning my work on the question of why we vote. The setting was a panel discussion on the subject of voter turnout at the annual meeting of the National Association of Secretaries of States. As the elected officials charged with overseeing the electoral machinery in each state, secretaries of state have more than a passing interest in the level of turnout within their respective jurisdictions. This is a group genuinely concerned with America's civic health and in a position to do something about it. After hearing a series of presentations on trends in participation, one particularly earnest secretary of state pointedly asked the panel members, of which I was one, "What can I do *tomorrow* to get more people to vote in my state?"

At the time, I did not have an answer. Now I do. We need to strengthen civic norms among our young people. But it is important to realize that while we can start tomorrow, the effects of our efforts will not become apparent for years to come. We have made the easy fixes to increase turnout by marginally reducing the costs associated with voting and have been able to detect marginal turnout gains as a result. It is time to consider the more difficult task of increasing the civic gratification that accompanies voting. I readily concede that fostering civic norms among adolescents will not have an immediate participatory payoff. But it *is* an investment that has the potential to pay large dividends over the long term. It is time that we made it.

Data Sources

CITIZEN PARTICIPATION STUDY

Sidney Verba, Kay Lehman Schlozman, Henry E. Brady, and Norman Nie. *American Citizen Participation Study, 1990* [computer file]. ICPSR version. Chicago: University of Chicago, National Opinion Research Center (NORC) [producer], 1995. Ann Arbor: Inter-university Consortium for Political and Social Research [distributor], 1995. ICPSR #6635.

I obtained geographic identifiers for this file not publicly available from J. Eric Oliver of the University of Chicago.

CURRENT POPULATION SURVEYS

U.S. Dept. of Commerce, Bureau of the Census. *Current Population Survey, May 1989: Multiple Job Holding, Flextime, and Volunteer Work* [computer file]. ICPSR version. Washington, DC: U.S. Dept. of Commerce, Bureau of the Census [producer], 1990. Ann Arbor: Inter-university Consortium for Political and Social Research [distributor], 1991. ICPSR #9472.

U.S. Dept. of Commerce, Bureau of the Census. *Current Population Survey: Voter Supplement File, 1992* [computer file]. ICPSR version. Washington, DC: U.S. Dept. of Commerce, Bureau of the Census [producer], 1992. Ann Arbor: Inter-university Consortium for Political and Social Research [distributor], 1997. ICPSR #6365.

U.S. Dept. of Commerce, Bureau of the Census. *Current Population Survey: Voter Supplement File, 1996* [computer file]. ICPSR version. Washington, DC: U.S. Dept. of Commerce, Bureau of the Census [producer], 1997. Ann Arbor: Inter-university Consortium for Political and Social Research [distributor], 1997. ICPSR #2205.

GENERAL SOCIAL SURVEY

James A. Davis, Tom W. Smith, and Peter V. Marsden. General Social Survey, 1972–2000 [computer file]. ICPSR version. Chicago: University of Chicago, National Opinion Research Center (NORC) [producer], 2001. Ann Arbor, MI: Inter-university Consortium for Political and Social Research [distributor], 2001. ICPSR #3197.

I obtained geographic identifiers for this file through personal correspondence with Tom Smith.

IEA Civic Education Study

U.S. Dept. of Education, National Center for Education Statistics. *IEA Civic Education Study* [computer file]. Washington, DC: U.S. Dept. of Education, Office of Educational Research and Improvement [producer], 2002.

I obtained geographic identifiers for this file with a restricted data license from the National Center for Education Statistics.

Monitoring the Future

Lloyd D. Johnston, Patrick M. O'Malley, and Jerald G. Bachman. *Monitoring the Future: National Survey Results on Drug Use, 1975–2000* [computer file]. Bethesda, MD: University of Michigan, Institute for Social Research and the National Institute on Drug Abuse [producers]. Ann Arbor, MI: Monitoring the Future Program [distributor], 2001.

I obtained a subset of the panel component of the Monitoring the Future study through a restricted data license from the Institute for Social Research at the University of Michigan.

National Election Study

Steven J. Rosenstone, Donald R. Kinder, Warren E. Miller, and the National Election Studies. *American National Election Study, 1996*: Pre- and Post-Election Survey [computer file]. 4th release. Ann Arbor: University of Michigan, Center for Political Studies [producer], 1999. Ann Arbor, MI: Inter-university Consortium for Political and Social Research [distributor], 1999. ICPSR #6896.

National Household Education Survey

U.S. Dept. of Education, National Center for Education Statistics. *National Household Education Survey, 1996* [computer file]. ICPSR version.

Washington, DC: U.S. Dept. of Education, Office of Educational Research and Improvement [producer], 1997. Ann Arbor, MI: Inter-university Consortium for Political and Social Research [distributor], 1998. ICPSR #2149.

I obtained geographic identifiers for this file with a restricted data license from the National Center for Education Statistics.

SOCIAL CAPITAL COMMUNITY BENCHMARK SURVEY

Saguaro Seminar: Civic Engagement in America. John F. Kennedy School of Government, Harvard University. *Social Capital Community Benchmark Survey, 2000*. Cambridge, MA: Saguaro Seminar [producer], 2001. Storrs, CT: Roper Center for Public Opinion Research [distributor], 2001.

I obtained geographic identifiers for this file with a restricted data license from the Roper Center.

U.S. COUNTIES

This file is a compilation of data from different sources. The data are primarily derived from the Census Bureau's *County and City Data Book* (1994), with additional data from the election statistics compiled by David Leip's *Atlas of U.S. Presidential Elections*. Data from Congressional Quarterly's *America Votes 1996* were entered manually. Robert Putnam originally compiled the core of the data set; I am grateful that he was willing to make it available to me.

YOUTH-PARENT SOCIALIZATION STUDY

M. Kent Jennings, Gregory B. Markus, and Richard G. Niemi. *Youth-Parent Socialization Panel Study, 1965–1982: Three Waves Combined* [computer file]. Ann Arbor: University of Michigan, Center for Political Studies/Survey Research Center [producers], 1983. Ann Arbor, MI: Inter-university Consortium for Political and Social Research [distributor], 1991. ICPSR #9553.

M. Kent Jennings. *High School Seniors Cohort Study, 1965* [computer file]. Ann Arbor: University of Michigan, Institute for Social Research [producer], 1979. Ann Arbor, MI: Inter-university Consortium for Political and Social Research [distributor], 1980. ICPSR #7575.

I obtained geographic identifiers for this file through a restricted data license from ICPSR, under the direction of M. Kent Jennings.

Questions from the 1996 National Election Study Used in Table 2.1 and Figure 2.4

Government Spending

Some people think the government should provide fewer services even in areas such as health and education in order to reduce spending. Suppose these people are at one end of a scale, at point 1. Other people feel it is important for the government to provide many more services even if it means an increase in spending. Suppose these people are at the other end, at point 7. And, of course, some other people have opinions somewhere in between, at points 2, 3, 4, 5, or 6. Where would you place yourself on this scale, or haven't you thought much about this?

Environment

Some people think it is important to protect the environment even if it costs some jobs or otherwise reduces our standard of living. (Suppose these people are at one end of the scale, at point number 1.) Other people think that protecting the environment is not as important as maintaining jobs and our standard of living. (Suppose these people are at the other end of the scale, at point number 7.) And, of course, some other people have opinions somewhere in between, at points 2, 3, 4, 5, or 6. Where would you place yourself on this scale, or haven't you thought much about this?

Gay Rights

Do you favor or oppose laws to protect homosexuals against job discrimination [if respondent favors laws to protect homosexuals against job discrimination / if respondent opposes laws to protect homosexuals against job discrimination]?
    Do you favor such laws strongly or not strongly?
    Do you oppose such laws strongly or not strongly?

Health Care

There is much concern about the rapid rise in medical and hospital costs. Some people feel there should be a government insurance plan which would cover all medical and hospital expenses for everyone. (Suppose these people are at one end of a scale, at point 1.) Others feel that all medical expenses should be paid by individuals and through private insurance plans like Blue Cross or some other company-paid plans. (Suppose these people are at the other end, at point 7.) And, of course, some other people have opinions somewhere in between at points 2, 3, 4, 5, or 6. Where would you place yourself on this scale, or haven't you thought much about this?

Moral Traditionalism

Now I am going to read several statements. After each one, I would like you to tell me whether you agree strongly, agree somewhat, neither agree nor disagree, disagree somewhat, or disagree strongly with this statement. The first statement is. . . .

The newer lifestyles are contributing to the breakdown of our society.

The world is always changing and we should adjust our view of moral behavior to those changes.

This country would have many fewer problems if there were more emphasis on traditional family ties.

We should be more tolerant of people who choose to live according to their own moral standards, even if they are very different from our own.

[From these questions, an additive scale was created so that a higher score represents greater moral traditionalism. This requires reversing the responses for the second and fourth items in the scale.]

Government Assistance for African Americans

Some people feel that the government in Washington should make every effort to improve the social and economic position of blacks. (Suppose these people are at one end of a scale, at point 1.) Others feel that the government should not make any special effort to help blacks because they should help themselves. (Suppose these people are at the other end, at point 7.) And, of course, some other people have opinions somewhere in between, at points 2, 3, 4, 5, or 6. Where would you place yourself on this scale, or haven't you thought much about this?

Defense Spending

Some people believe that we should spend much less money for defense. (Suppose these people are at one end of a scale, at point 1.) Others feel that defense spending should be greatly increased. (Suppose these people are at the other end, at point 7.) And, of course, some other people have opinions somewhere in between at points 2, 3, 4, 5, or 6. Where would you place yourself on this scale, or haven't you thought much about this?

Death Penalty

Do you favor or oppose the death penalty for persons convicted of murder [if respondent favors the death penalty for persons convicted of murder / if respondent opposes the death penalty for persons convicted of murder]?

Do you favor the death penalty for persons convicted of murder strongly or not strongly?

Do you oppose the death penalty for persons convicted of murder strongly or not strongly?

Abortion

There has been some discussion about abortion during recent years. Which one of the opinions on this page best agrees with your view? You can just tell me the number of the opinion you choose.

1. By law, abortion should never be permitted.
2. The law should permit abortion ONLY in case of rape, incest, or when the woman's life is in danger.
3. The law should permit abortion for reasons OTHER THAN rape, incest, or danger to the woman's life, but only after the need for the abortion has been clearly established.
4. By law, a woman should always been able to obtain an abortion as a matter of personal choice.

Working Mothers

Recently there has been a lot of talk about women's rights. Some people feel that women should have an equal role with men in running business, industry, and government. (Suppose these people are at one end of a scale, at point 1.) Others feel that a woman's place is in the home. (Suppose these people are at the other end, at point 7.) And, of course, some other people have opinions somewhere in between, at points 2, 3, 4, 5, or 6. Where would you place yourself on this scale, or haven't you thought much about this?

Crime

Some people say that the best way to reduce crime is to address the social problems that cause crime, like bad schools, poverty, and joblessness.

(Suppose these people are at one end of a scale, at point 1.) Other people say the best way to reduce crime is to make sure that criminals are caught, convicted, and punished. (Suppose these people are at the other end, at point 7.) And, of course, some other people have opinions somewhere in between at points 2, 3, 4, 5, or 6. Where would you place yourself on this scale, or haven't you thought much about this?

Full Results of Models Discussed in the Text

FOR THE LINEAR, LOGISTIC, and ordered logistic regression models presented in the pages that follow, I simply report the results in tabular form. Because the hierarchical models are less conventional, I present their complete equations in addition to the results. It is important to note that the models allow the level-1 effects to vary randomly for each level-2 unit—which simply means that the impact of each individual-level independent variable is not assumed to be constant across all the contextual units in the data. Note that none of the results reported here is dependent on specifying the level-1 effects as random or fixed.

I also present a measure of fit, the "individual-level variance explained" by each hierarchical model. Following the guidance of Raudenbush and Bryk (2002), this has been calculated by comparing the individual-level variance in a model with no independent variables (a one-way random ANOVA, or Model 1) with the variance in the model as fully specified (Model 2). More technically:

$$\frac{\sigma^2 (\text{Model 1}) - \sigma^2 (\text{Model 2})}{\sigma^2 (\text{Model 1})}$$

EQUATIONS FOR HIERARCHICAL MODELS IN TABLE C4

This is the basic model for each of the three equations displayed in Table C4, with slight variations in the specifications as discussed in the text. (The models in Tables C5 and C6 are as described in the text.)

LEVEL-1 MODEL

$Y_{ij} = \beta_{0j} + \beta_{1j} Education_{ij} + \beta_{2j} Age_{ij} + \beta_{3j} Married_{ij} + \beta_{4j} African$ American$_{ij} + \beta_{5j} Female_{ij} + \beta_{6j} Years$ in Community$_{ij} + \beta_{7j} Central$ City$_{ij} + \beta_{8j} Importance$ of Religion$_{ij} + r_{ij}$

LEVEL-2 MODEL

$\beta_{0j} = \gamma_{00} + \gamma_{01} Ideological Heterogeneity + \gamma_{02} Mean Education Level + \gamma_{03}$ Community Stability $+ \gamma_{04} Income$ Heterogeneity $+ \gamma_{05} Racial$ Heterogeneity $+ u_{0j}$

$\beta_{1j} = \gamma_{10} + u_{1j}$ $\qquad \beta_{3j} = \gamma_{30} + u_{3j}$ $\qquad \beta_{5j} = \gamma_{50} + u_{5j}$ $\qquad \beta_{7j} = \gamma_{70} + u_{7j}$

$\beta_{2j} = \gamma_{20} + u_{2j}$ $\qquad \beta_{4j} = \gamma_{40} + u_{4j}$ $\qquad \beta_{6j} = \gamma_{60} + u_{6j}$ $\qquad \beta_{8j} = \gamma_{80} + u_{8j}$

TABLE C1
Community Political Heterogeneity and Motivations for Voting (Figure 3.2)

	(1)	(2)
	"My duty as a citizen"	"Chance to influence government policy"
County partisan composition		
County partisan competition (minimum to maximum)	−0.994** (0.488)	0.907* (0.540)
Individual demographics		
Education level	0.020 (0.100)	0.226*** (0.088)
Family income	−0.006 (0.004)	−0.002 (0.003)
Age	−0.078** (0.039)	0.055* (0.028)
Age squared	0.981** (0.397)	−0.608** (0.283)
Married	0.472** (0.192)	0.211 (0.148)
African American	0.458** (0.195)	0.191 (0.180)
Female	0.836*** (0.158)	−0.064 (0.157)
Years lived in community	0.007* (0.004)	0.000 (0.003)
Political interest	0.149** (0.068)	0.351*** (0.054)
Contextual demographics		
% with college degree	−0.006 (0.017)	−0.013 (0.017)
Mean household income (log)	−0.101 (0.618)	1.528** (0.635)
Urbanicity	0.652 (0.423)	−0.760* (0.410)
Population density	−0.030 (0.020)	0.075*** (0.021)
Residential mobility	−0.014 (0.010)	0.030*** (0.010)
Mean commuting time	0.038 (0.030)	−0.066** (0.030)
Region		
South	0.534*** (0.206)	0.099 (0.218)
Central midwestern state	0.287 (0.397)	0.368 (0.265)
Observations	1,520	1,519
Pseudo-R^2	0.07	0.07

Source: Citizen Participation Study.

Note: Results from ordered logistic regression. Robust standard errors in parentheses (allowing for clustering at the county level). Independent variables standardized on 0–1 scale. Weighted data.

* significant at .10   ** significant at .05   *** significant at .01

TABLE C2
Political Heterogeneity and Volunteering (Table 3.1, Figure 3.4)

	Volunteer at least once in previous year, 2002 (logistic regression)	Hours spent volunteering in previous week, 2002 (ordered logistic regression)	Volunteer at least once in previous year, 1989 (logistic regression)	Hours spent volunteering in previous week, 1989 (ordered logistic regression)
Political context				
Mean political heterogeneity (minimum to maximum)	−0.716*** (0.090)	−0.608*** (0.084)	−0.193** (0.080)	−0.304*** (0.099)
Individual characteristics				
Education level	2.902*** (0.066)	2.912*** (0.064)	3.604*** (0.086)	3.386*** (0.106)
Family income	0.734*** (0.047)	0.702*** (0.046)	0.517*** (0.047)	0.498*** (0.061)
Age	2.392*** (0.303)	2.533*** (0.296)	5.153*** (0.368)	6.625*** (0.473)
Age squared	−1.946*** (0.247)	−2.010*** (0.241)	−4.286*** (0.341)	−5.057*** (0.437)
Married	0.309*** (0.023)	0.253*** (0.022)	0.329*** (0.026)	0.411*** (0.033)
African American	−0.149*** (0.037)	−0.151*** (0.036)	−0.256*** (0.043)	−0.112*** (0.054)
Female	0.500*** (0.020)	0.446*** (0.019)	0.436*** (0.023)	0.403*** (0.029)
Community characteristics				
% with college degree	0.636*** (0.144)	0.645*** (0.139)	0.972*** (0.129)	1.129*** (0.157)
Mean household income (log)	−0.772*** (0.210)	−0.757*** (0.204)	−1.603*** (0.206)	−1.878*** (0.253)
Urbanicity	−0.032 (0.148)	−0.013 (0.142)	0.020 (0.102)	0.102 (0.129)
Population density	−0.712*** (0.114)	−0.657*** (0.111)	−0.350*** (0.133)	−0.470*** (0.166)
Residential mobility	−0.224*** (0.084)	−0.204** (0.081)	−0.157* (0.091)	−0.303*** (0.114)
Mean commuting time	−0.468*** (0.123)	−0.454*** (0.119)	−0.356** (0.144)	−0.134 (0.180)
Racial heterogeneity	−0.548 (1.667)	0.435 (1.618)	0.197* (0.107)	0.204 (0.135)
Ethnic heterogeneity	−0.128 (0.177)	−0.101 (0.173)	−0.597*** (0.177)	−0.439** (0.219)
Income heterogeneity	−7.254*** (0.891)	−7.625*** (0.855)	−0.847*** (0.129)	−1.022*** (0.161)
Region				
Upper midwestern state	0.139*** (0.041)	0.134*** (0.038)	0.100** (0.050)	−0.013 (0.062)
Southern state	−0.033 (0.030)	−0.018 (0.029)	−0.038 (0.032)	−0.113*** (0.040)
Constant	−2.791*** (0.200)		−4.464*** (0.175)	
Observations	54,466	54,467	58,156	58,156
Pseudo-R²	0.09	0.06	0.08	0.06

Source: Current Population Survey

TABLE C3
Community Political Heterogeneity and Political Participation (Figure 3.5)

	Political Voice (Protesting)	Electoral Activism
Political context		
Mean political heterogeneity (minimum to maximum)	2.267** (1.131)	1.500** (0.655)
Individual demographics		
Education level	0.163 (0.137)	0.489*** (0.114)
Family income	0.007 (0.005)	0.006* (0.003)
Age	−0.036 (0.048)	0.036 (0.033)
Age squared	−0.007 (0.496)	−0.213 (0.333)
Married	−0.293 (0.206)	0.183 (0.165)
African American	0.380 (0.264)	−0.018 (0.146)
Female	0.183 (0.222)	−0.193 (0.145)
Civic skills index	0.126*** (0.030)	0.162*** (0.027)
Political interest	0.474*** (0.090)	0.459*** (0.063)
Contextual demographics		
Years lived in community	0.002 (0.004)	−0.000 (0.002)
% with college degree	−0.050* (0.029)	−0.029 (0.018)
Mean household income (log)	3.706*** (1.350)	1.597* (0.882)
Urbanicity	−1.229 (0.944)	−0.502 (0.510)
Population density	0.117*** (0.027)	−0.001 (0.020)
Residential mobility	0.046* (0.024)	−0.000 (0.012)
Mean commuting time	−0.087** (0.038)	−0.014 (0.028)
Ethnic heterogeneity	3.961* (2.280)	−0.525 (1.084)
Racial heterogeneity	−1.128 (1.700)	0.398 (0.770)
Income inequality	6.811 (6.494)	8.186* (4.471)
Region		
South	0.039 (0.355)	0.251 (0.213)
Upper midwestern state	0.319 (0.355)	0.057 (0.275)
Constant	−23.507*** (7.537)	−15.860*** (4.157)
Observations	2,121	
Pseudo-R^2	0.17	0.20

Source: Citizen Participation Study.

Note: Results from logistic regression. Standard errors in parentheses. Independent variables standardized on 0–1 scale. Weighted data.

* significant at .10   ** significant at .05   *** significant at .01

TABLE C4
Impact of Ideological Heterogeneity (Figures 3.7 and 3.8)

	(1)	(2)	(3)
	# of times volunteering (poisson model)	Political voice index	Trust in neighbors
Ideological Heterogeneity			
Standard deviation of ideology (level 2)	-0.255** (0.102)	0.220*** (0.071)	-0.148*** (0.057)
Level-1 effects			
Education level	0.746191*** (0.050)	0.693*** (0.040)	0.508*** (0.034)
Age	-0.133 (0.095)	-0.498*** (0.067)	0.881*** (0.048)
Married	0.125*** (0.031)	0.018 (0.020)	0.190*** (0.015)
African American	-0.162* (0.092)	0.071** (0.028)	-0.411*** (0.027)
Female	0.302*** (0.029)	-0.016 (0.015)	0.037*** (0.013)
Years lived in the community	0.281*** (0.056)	0.157*** (0.035)	0.245*** (0.022)
Live in central city	-0.014 (0.037)	0.051*** (0.014)	-0.125*** (0.018)
Religion is important	0.547*** (0.065)		
Political Interest		1.047*** (0.040)	
Ideology		0.400*** (0.046)	0.039 (0.025)
Ideological difference (from mean of community)			-0.079*** (0.023)

Level-2 effects			
Mean level of education	−0.038(0.106)	−0.034 (0.084)	0.171*** (0.053)
Community stability	0.030 (0.125)	−0.119 (0.102)	0.011 (0.066)
Income heterogeneity	0.070 (0.173)	−0.328** (0.127)	−0.052 (0.07)
Racial heterogeneity	−0.054 (0.151)	−0.127 (0.089)	−0.235*** (0.054)
Constant	2.000*** (0.041)	0.968 (0.029)	2.279*** (0.017)
Number of level-1 units	41	41	41
Number of level-2 units	18,278	18,278	18,278
Individual-level variance explained	n/a	0.16	0.17

Source: Social Capital Community Benchmark Survey.

Note: Results from hierarchical models. Robust standard errors in parentheses. Independent variables standardized on 0–1 scale. Weighted data.

* significant at .10   ** significant at .05   *** significant at .01

TABLE C5
Social Network Homogeneity and Public Engagement (Figure 4.1)

	(1) Logistic regression	(2) Ordered logistic regression	(3) Ordered logistic regress
	Voted in presidential election	Frequency of voting in local elections	Electoral activi
Social network homogeneity	0.748*** (0.252)	0.382** (0.190)	0.209 (0.197)
Number of discussion partners	0.261 (0.418)	−0.254 (0.292)	−0.249 (0.340)
Knowledge of network members' partisanship	−0.575* (0.305)	−0.293 (0.221)	0.246 (0.208)
Frequency of political conversation	1.260*** (0.455)	0.931*** (0.313)	1.017*** (0.3
Partisan identifier	0.859*** (0.211)	0.717*** (0.210)	0.774*** (0.2(
Interest in politics	1.944*** (0.394)	2.249*** (0.320)	2.736*** (0.3
Individual demographics			
Education level	4.054*** (0.678)	1.815*** (0.410)	3.009*** (0.4
Family income	1.029*** (0.358)	0.733*** (0.276)	0.491 (0.301)
Age	5.088*** (0.595)	4.506*** (0.404)	1.531*** (0.3
Married	0.300* (0.168)	0.104 (0.118)	−0.085 (0.111)
Black	0.121 (0.188)	0.028 (0.157)	0.219 (0.150)
Female	0.365** (0.146)	0.098 (0.102)	−0.031 (0.105)
Constant	−7.593*** (0.642)		
Observations	1,497	1,594	1,599
Pseudo-R^2	0.22	0.12	0.10

Source: 1987 General Social Survey.

Note: Robust standard errors in parentheses. Independent variables standardized on 0–1 scale. Weigh
data.

* significant at .10   ** significant at .05   *** significant at .01

TABLE C6
Community Political Heterogeneity and Political Makeup of Social Networks
(Figure 4.2)

	Social network homogeneity
Political context	
Mean political heterogeneity (minimum to maximum)	−0.469** (0.199)
Individual characteristics	
Education level	0.135 (0.375)
Family income	−0.072 (0.290)
Age	0.704** (0.309)
Married	0.198* (0.119)
Black	0.990*** (0.151)
Female	−0.016 (0.118)
Community characteristics	
% with college degree	−0.695* (0.393)
Mean household income (log)	−7.200** (3.232)
Urbanicity	0.905*** (0.298)
Population density	−0.376** (0.147)
Residential mobility	−0.388 (0.352)
Number of discussion partners	2.327*** (0.223)
Observations	1,622
Pseudo-R^2	0.04

Source: 1987 General Social Survey.
Note: Results from ordered logistic regression. Robust standard errors in parentheses.
Independent variables standardized on 0–1 scale. Weighted data.
* significant at .10   ** significant at .05   *** significant at .01

EQUATIONS FOR HIERARCHICAL MODELS IN TABLE 5.1

The specifications for the models of civic activity, political voice, and electoral activism are identical.

LEVEL-1 MODEL

$Y_{ij} = \beta_{0j} + \beta_{1j}$ *Anticipated Education* $_{ij} + \beta_{2j}$ *African American* $_{ij} + \beta_{3j}$ *Female* $_{ij} + r_{ij}$

LEVEL-2 MODEL

$\beta_{0j} = \gamma_{00} + \gamma_{01}$ *Political Heterogeneity* $+ \gamma_{02}$ *Mean Education Level* $+ \gamma_{03}$ *Mean Household Income (log)* $+ \gamma_{04}$ *Urbanicity* $+ \gamma_{05}$ *Population Density* $+ \gamma_{06}$ *Residential Mobility* $+ \gamma_{07}$ *Mean Commuting Time* $+ \gamma_{08}$ *Ethnic Heterogeneity* $+ \gamma_{09}$ *Racial Heterogeneity* $+ \gamma_{10}$ *Income Inequality* $+ u_{0j}$

$\beta_{1j} = \gamma_{10} + u_{1j}$
$\beta_{2j} = \gamma_{20} + u_{2j}$
$\beta_{3j} = \gamma_{30} + u_{3j}$

EQUATIONS FOR HIERARCHICAL MODELS IN CHAPTER 7

Table 7.2. Political Heterogeneity and Voting as a Civic Norm

LEVEL-1 MODEL

$\text{Prob}(Y = 1 | \beta) = \varphi$
$\text{Log}[\varphi / (1 - \varphi)] = \eta$
$\eta = \beta_{0j} + \beta_{1j}$ *Anticipated Education* $_{ij} + \beta_{2j}$ *Parents' Education* $_{ij} + \beta_{3j}$ *Years Lived in Community* $_{ij} + \beta_{4j}$ *Female* $_{ij}$

LEVEL-2 MODEL

$\beta_{0j} = \gamma_{00} + \gamma_{01}$ *Political Heterogeneity* $+ \gamma_{02}$ *Mean Parents' Education* $+ \gamma_{03}$ *Mean Years Lived in Community* $+ u_{0j}$

$\beta_{1j} = \gamma_{10} + u_{1j}$
$\beta_{2j} = \gamma_{20} + u_{2j}$
$\beta_{3j} = \gamma_{30} + u_{3j}$
$\beta_{4j} = \gamma_{40} + u_{4j}$

TABLE C7
Community Political Heterogeneity and Volunteering (Table 5.2, Figures 3.4, 5.1 and 5.2)

	Youth (1)	Parents (2)
Political Context		
Mean political heterogeneity (minimum to maximum)	−0.712** (0.283)	−1.005*** (0.258)
Individual Demographics		
Parent volunteers	0.725*** (0.077)	
Parent's education	0.494*** (0.183)	1.361*** (0.174)
Family income	0.015 (0.173)	0.969*** (0.162)
Two-parent household	−0.018 (0.096)	0.128 (0.087)
Academic performance	1.536*** (0.243)	
Educational expectations	0.263* (0.135)	
African American	−0.204 (0.126)	0.524*** (0.124)
Female	0.184** (0.075)	
Age	0.351* (0.194)	
Catholic school	0.758*** (0.225)	0.789*** (0.233)
Other religious school	0.536** (0.254)	1.071*** (0.275)
Private secular school	0.079 (0.272)	−0.155 (0.255)
Racial composition of school	0.026 (0.053)	
Size of school	0.023 (0.042)	
School arranges service	1.000*** (0.101)	
Contextual Demographics		
% with college degree	−1.020** (0.467)	−0.642 (0.449)
Mean household income (log)	1.089 (0.704)	0.697 (0.651)
Urbanicity	−0.103 (0.221)	−0.505** (0.217)
Population density	−0.042 (0.499)	−0.606 (0.541)
Residential mobility	−0.491 (0.316)	−0.645** (0.316)
Mean commuting time	−0.695** (0.344)	−0.217 (0.340)
Ethnic heterogeneity	0.325 (0.391)	−0.333 (0.365)
Income inequality	0.575 (0.567)	0.065 (0.533)
Racial heterogeneity	−0.280 (0.335)	1.068*** (0.307)
Region		
South	−0.068 (0.097)	−0.113 (0.092)
Upper midwestern state	0.092 (0.143)	−0.393*** (0.130)
Constant	−2.913*** (0.597)	−0.427 (0.472)
Observations	5,057	5,740
Pseudo-R^2	0.08	0.06

Source: 1996 National Household Education Survey.

Note: Results from logistic regression. Robust standard errors in parentheses. Independent variables standardized on 0–1 scale. Weighted data.

* significant at .10   ** significant at .05   *** significant at .01

TABLE C8
Community Political Heterogeneity and "Order" (Table 5.3, Figure 5.3)

	Discipline at school (parents) (1)	Discipline at home (youth) (2)
Political context		
Mean political heterogeneity (minimum to maximum)	−0.523** (0.249)	−1.137*** (0.246)
Individual demographics		
Parent's education	−0.319* (0.172)	0.163 (0.162)
Family income	0.081 (0.172)	−0.430*** (0.153)
Two-parent household	0.125 (0.090)	0.286*** (0.083)
Academic performance	1.206*** (0.242)	−0.127 (0.217)
Educational expectations	0.295** (0.120)	0.010 (0.119)
African American	0.130 (0.137)	0.220* (0.117)
Female	−0.142** (0.070)	−0.026 (0.066)
Age (of student)	−0.763*** (0.184)	−4.106*** (0.177)
Racial composition of school	0.038 (0.048)	0.040 (0.047)
Size of school	−0.035 (0.039)	0.054 (0.038)
Contextual demographics		
% with college degree	−0.783** (0.393)	−1.806*** (0.459)
Mean household income (log)	0.756 (0.653)	1.841*** (0.642)
Urbanicity	0.140 (0.205)	0.170 (0.202)
Population density	0.975** (0.489)	−0.492 (0.501)
Residential mobility	−0.506* (0.278)	−0.836*** (0.320)
Mean commuting time	−0.263 (0.327)	−0.565* (0.313)
Ethnic heterogeneity	−0.135 (0.349)	0.700** (0.342)
Income inequality	−0.375 (0.513)	0.432 (0.509)
Racial heterogeneity	−0.077 (0.284)	0.066 (0.282)
Region		
South	−0.021 (0.090)	0.044 (0.084)
Upper midwestern state	0.238** (0.121)	−0.213 (0.132)
Observations	4,708	4,708
Pseudo-R^2	0.01	0.07

Source: 1996 National Household Education Survey.
Note: Results from ordered logistic regression. Robust standard errors in parentheses. Independent variables standardized on 0–1 scale. Weighted data.
* significant at .10   ** significant at .05   *** significant at .01

TABLE C9
Community Political Heterogeneity and "Voice" (Table 5.4, Figure 5.4)

	Students' voice at school (youth) (1)	Parents' voice at school (parents) (2)	Students' voice at home (youth) (3)
Political context			
Mean political heterogeneity (minimum to maximum)	-0.598** (0.238)	-0.560** (0.258)	-0.548** (0.258)
Individual demographics			
Parent's education	-0.306* (0.164)	-0.182 (0.161)	0.494*** (0.161)
Family income	-0.081 (0.158)	0.252 (0.158)	0.317** (0.160)
Two-parent household	0.073 (0.088)	-0.012 (0.084)	-0.462*** (0.084)
Academic performance	0.928*** (0.221)	1.130*** (0.227)	1.187*** (0.226)
Educational expectations	0.210 (0.128)	0.324*** (0.118)	0.112 (0.116)
African American	-0.174 (0.129)	0.176 (0.126)	-0.431*** (0.111)
Female	-0.141** (0.069)	-0.121* (0.068)	0.067 (0.067)
Age	-2.128*** (0.194)	-0.473*** (0.176)	0.689*** (0.172)
Racial composition of school	0.090* (0.047)	0.120** (0.049)	0.015 (0.046)
Size of school	0.022 (0.038)	-0.070 (0.038)	0.101*** (0.035)
Contextual demographics			
% with college degree	-0.937** (0.389)	-0.621 (0.383)	-0.926** (0.399)
Mean household income (log)	1.189* (0.628)	0.072 (0.630)	0.333 (0.595)
Urbanicity	-0.127 (0.201)	0.190 (0.205)	0.113 (0.203)
Population density	0.598 (0.489)	1.016** (0.448)	-0.167 (0.544)
Residential mobility	-0.020 (0.280)	-0.350 (0.283)	-0.139 (0.276)

(continued)

TABLE C9
(*continued*)

	Students' voice at school (youth) (1)	Parents' voice at school (parents) (2)	Students' voice at home (youth) (3)
Mean commuting time	−0.468 (0.327)	−0.266 (0.344)	−0.695** (0.319)
Ethnic heterogeneity	0.098 (0.350)	−0.291 (0.333)	0.151 (0.330)
Income inequality	0.249 (0.525)	−0.645 (0.514)	−0.646 (0.486)
Racial heterogeneity	−0.270 (0.265)	0.044 (0.259)	−0.150 (0.249)
Region			
South	0.031 (0.088)	−0.036 (0.085)	−0.064 (0.083)
Upper midwestern state	0.181 (0.130)	0.192 (0.124)	−0.240* (0.130)
Observations	4,708	4,708	4,708
Pseudo-R^2	0.03	0.01	0.02

Source: 1996 National Household Education Survey.
Note: Results from ordered logistic regression. Robust standard errors in parentheses. Independent variables standardized on 0–1 scale. Weighted data.

* significant at .10 ** significant at .05 *** significant at .01

TABLE C10

Community Political Heterogeneity and Political Tolerance, Efficacy (Table 5.5, Figure 5.5)

	Political efficacy (youth) (1)	Political tolerance (youth) (2)
Political context		
Mean political heterogeneity (minimum to maximum)	0.995*** (0.358)	0.568* (0.343)
Individual demographics		
Parent's political tolerance	0.309*** (0.055)	0.402*** (0.072)
Parent's education	0.875*** (0.220)	0.617*** (0.224)
Family income	0.424** (0.206)	0.341 (0.223)
Two-parent household	−0.055 (0.111)	−0.138 (0.115)
Academic performance	1.014*** (0.263)	0.056 (0.311)
Educational expectations	0.389*** (0.142)	0.104 (0.141)
African American	0.247* (0.148)	0.010 (0.147)
Female	−0.240*** (0.087)	−0.079 (0.091)
Age	1.149*** (0.341)	1.645*** (0.381)
Racial composition of school	0.016 (0.059)	−0.002 (0.064)
Size of school	−0.064 (0.044)	0.056 (0.051)
School arranges service		−0.049 (0.133)
Catholic school		0.168 (0.200)
Other religious school		−0.588* (0.308)
Private secular school		1.064*** (0.393)
Contextual demographics		
% with college degree	0.271 (0.507)	0.443 (0.592)
Mean household income (log)	−0.991 (0.801)	−0.187 (0.848)
Urbanicity	0.329 (0.268)	−0.001 (0.275)
Population density	0.095 (0.622)	0.027 (0.788)
Residential mobility	−0.002 (0.410)	0.462 (0.424)
Mean commuting time	0.307 (0.406)	−0.021 (0.443)
Ethnic heterogeneity	0.259 (0.420)	−0.061 (0.470)
Income inequality	−0.830 (0.618)	−0.620 (0.674)
Racial heterogeneity	−0.245 (0.346)	−0.355 (0.351)
Region		
South	−0.112 (0.107)	−0.292** (0.115)
Upper midwestern state	−0.163 (0.178)	−0.078 (0.183)
Observations	3,161	3,161
Pseudo-R^2	0.04	0.04

Source: 1996 National Household Education Survey.

Note: Results from ordered logistic regression. Robust standard errors in parentheses. Independent variables standardized on 0–1 scale. Weighted data.

* significant at .10   ** significant at .05   *** significant at .01

Table 7.3. School Civic Climate and Anticipated Participation

LEVEL-1 MODEL

$Y_{ij} = \beta_{0j} + \beta_{1j}$ *Good Citizen Votes* $_{ij} + \beta_{2j}$ *Anticipated Education* $_{ij} + \beta_{3j}$ *Parents' Education* $_{ij} + \beta_{4j}$ *Years Lived in Community* $_{ij} + \beta_{5j}$ *Female* $_{ij} + r_{ij}$

LEVEL-2 MODEL

$\beta_{0j} = \gamma_{00} + \gamma_{01}$ *Civic Climate* $+ \gamma_{02}$ *Political Heterogeneity* $+ \gamma_{03}$ *Mean Parents' Education* $+ \gamma_{04}$ *Years Lived in Community* $+ u_{0j}$

$\beta_{1j} = \gamma_{10} + u_{1j}$
$\beta_{2j} = \gamma_{20} + u_{2j}$
$\beta_{3j} = \gamma_{30} + u_{3j}$
$\beta_{4j} = \gamma_{40} + u_{4j}$
$\beta_{5j} = \gamma_{50} + u_{5j}$

Table 7.5 High School Civic Climate and Voter Turnout in 1980

Table 7.6 High School Civic Climate and Public Engagement in 1980

This is the basic model for each of the three equations displayed in Tables 7.5 and 7.6, with slight variations in the specifications as discussed in the text.

LEVEL-1 MODEL

$\text{Prob}(Y = 1 | \beta) = \varphi$
$\text{Log}[\varphi / (1 - \varphi)] = \eta$
$\eta = \beta_{0j} + \beta_{1j}$ *"Good Citizen Votes"* $_{ij} + \beta_{2j}$ *Education* $_{ij} + \beta_{3j}$ *Married* $_{ij} + \beta_{4j}$ *Female* $_{ij} + \beta_{5j}$ *Years Lived in Community* $_{ij} + \beta_{6j}$ *Parental Electoral Activism* $_{ij} + \beta_{7j}$ *Parental Community Voluntarism* $_{ij} + \beta_{8j}$ *Parents Were Voters* $_{ij}$

LEVEL-2 MODEL

$\beta_{0j} = \gamma_{00} + \gamma_{01}$ *Civic Climate* $+ \gamma_{02}$ *Political Heterogeneity* $+ \gamma_{03}$ *Mean Parents' Education* $+ \gamma_{04}$ *Years Lived in Community* $+ \gamma_{05}$ *Years Lived in Community* $+ u_{0j}$

$\beta_{1j} = \gamma_{10} + u_{1j}$
$\beta_{2j} = \gamma_{20} + u_{2j}$
$\beta_{3j} = \gamma_{30} + u_{3j}$
$\beta_{4j} = \gamma_{40} + u_{4j}$
$\beta_{5j} = \gamma_{50} + u_{5j}$

Notes

1. http://skyways.lib.ks.us/towns/LittleRiver/index.html.
2. To be more precise, these turnout figures are for Rice County, Kansas, and Suffolk County, Massachusetts, respectively.
3. Full citations to these data sets can be found appendix A.

1. Conceptually, it does not include contacting elected officials for the benefit of an individual (e.g., traditional constituency service like asking a member of Congress for help obtaining a passport or correcting a problem with one's Social Security payments).
2. More specifically, they find that in an area of general Democratic dominance (the Baltimore-Washington metropolitan area), Republican and Independent students have higher levels of efficacy where the local community is, relatively speaking, more politically diverse.
3. These turnout figures are derived from the estimates of Michael McDonald and Samuel Popkin (2001), who have done political science a valuable service by pointing out that accurate turnout figures require an accurate count of the population eligible to vote. While the verdict is still out on the utility of their adjusted figures (Freeman 2001), as their calculations of the voting eligible population are estimates at best, at the very least we can say that they are an improvement over using the voting-age population, which includes people who are not eligible to vote (e.g., ex-felons in some states, noncitizens in all states). See also http://elections. gmu.edu/voter_turnout.htm (accessed April 28, 2005).
4. See http://elections.gmu.edu (accessed September 22, 2005).
5. Voter turnout is measured as the number of votes cast in a presidential election divided by the voting-age population (VAP) for each of the roughly 3,000 counties in the continental United States. The alternative method of calculating turnout is to use the percentage of registered voters who cast a ballot, which for the purposes at hand is an inferior measure. To leave the unregistered out of the equation is only to beg the question of what factors lead to voter registration. Furthermore, it is impossible to arrive at reliable voter registration statistics across the states. VAP, however, does have its weaknesses. As noted by McDonald and Popkin (2001), the population count is inflated, since the tally includes noncitizens and others not eligible to vote (in some states, ex-felons). In order for this overcount to affect the substantive interpretation of our results, however, it would have to be systematically related to the independent variable, which seems unlikely. Regardless, the McDonald-Popkin adjustments cannot be made at the

county level. To assuage concern over the use of the VAP in estimating turnout, in the next section I replicate the aggregate-level analysis with individual-level data from the Current Population Survey (CPS), which screens out respondents ineligible to vote. Alaska and Hawaii are excluded only because they do not have counties. In Louisiana, parishes are substituted for counties.

6. More technically, ethnic and racial heterogeneity have been measured by calculating a Herfindahl Index for each.

$$Ethnic\ Heterogeneity\ Index = 1 - \sum_e h_{ec}^2$$

where e represents the six ethnic groups and c represents each county. The term h_{ec}, therefore, is the proportion of each ethnic group in each county. The ethnic groups are:

Anglo-American: English, Canadian, Irish, Scotch-Irish, Scottish, Welsh, and American

Western European: Austrian, Belgian, Dutch, French (except Basque), French Canadian, German, Swiss

Scandinavian: Finnish, Norwegian, Swedish

Latino/Hispanic: Hispanic ethnicity as identified in the census ethnicity item

Mediterranean: Italian, Portuguese

Eastern European/Balkan: Czech, Greek, Hungarian, Polish, Romanian, Russian, Slovak, Ukrainian, Yugoslavian

West Indian: West Indian (excluding Hispanic origin groups)

Racial heterogeneity is calculated in essentially the same way, only with the standard Census Bureau racial categories substituting for ethnic groups, namely: (1) White; (2) Black; (3) American Indian, Eskimo, Aleutian; (4) Asian, Pacific Islander. Intuitively, a Herfindahl Index calculates the probability that two randomly chosen members of the population will be from different groups.

7. While these figures show bivariate comparisons, these negative relationships hold up under multivariate scrutiny, controlling for a wide array of factors (the same array, in fact, used in the county-level models of turnout). The year 2000 has been chosen as an illustrative example. The same negative relationships are found in other election years as well.

8. Cited in Schudson 2001.

9. See appendix B for details regarding how each item is worded.

10. In order to simplify comparisons between these groups, only blacks and whites are included in the analysis. Likewise, it only includes respondents who identify as either a Republican or Democrat (not including partisan "leaners"). Restricting the model in this way has been done to maximize the interpretability of the coefficients. The substantive results do not change when all cases are included.

11. Note that subtracting from 100 is not the same as using the vote total of the losing candidate, since third-party candidates often win a non-negligible share of the vote in a given county.

12. Note that the same pattern occurs with more complex methods of calculating the average level of competition from 1980 to 2000, like using a weighted average, which places more weight on earlier than later elections.

13. The exception that proves the rule is 1992. Voter turnout rose by 5 points from 1988 to 1992, a jump generally attributed to Ross Perot's bid for the presidency. This increase in turnout, which was not sustained in 1996, generated a lot of discussion.

14. These data are taken from the 1990 U.S. Census.

15. Education has long been identified as a primary predictor of voter turnout (Wolfinger and Rosenstone 1980). Income, while not as consistent a predictor as education, is nonetheless widely recognized as a factor facilitating political participation (Verba and Nie 1972). Urban areas generally have lower voter turnout than rural communities. The hypothesized sign on the coefficient for population density is not so clear. On the one hand, highly dense areas might facilitate the anonymity of urban living, and thus lead to lower turnout. But on the other hand, political mobilization might be easier where people live close together, leading to higher turnout. Regardless, we would expect population density to be related to voter turnout, and so it is accounted for in the model. Residential mobility is known to deflate turnout (Squire, Wolfinger, and Glass 1987). Participation has long been lower in the South, and higher in the Upper Midwest, so these are the regional controls in the model. Robust standard errors have been calculated using the Huber/White correction for heteroskedasticity, as we might expect that counties are not totally independent observations.

16. Results are substantively identical when an index of mean state political competition from 1980 to the year in question is substituted.

17. I would like to thank John Collins of Harvard University's Government Documents Library for his assistance in working with the CPS data.

18. For those metropolitan statistical areas (MSAs) that cover more than one county, the contextual measures have been averaged over all of the relevant counties, weighted by their population. In 1996 and 2000, respondents in larger counties had their county identified. Where the county is known, data from it have been used in lieu of the MSA.

19. These include education and family income, which, as explained above, have long been known to affect voter turnout. Additionally, there is a measure for the respondent's age, owing to the longstanding observation that participation increases over the life cycle. A term for age squared is also included, because previous research has found that elderly people become less likely to vote (that is, we would expect the coefficient for age to be positive and for age squared to be negative). The model includes a control for marital status, since prior studies have found that married people are more likely to vote than those who are unmarried. Other controls are for gender and whether a respondent is African American, as the literature suggests that these are also factors potentially affecting voter turnout (Burns, Schlozman, and Verba 2001; Tate 1994).

The model also includes two relevant measures of the political context within a respondent's state. First is the ease of voter registration, an important factor affecting voter turnout. This is operationalized as the presence of a closing date for voter registration, one of the few remaining restrictions on registration. Previous studies have coded this variable as the number of days between the closing date and the election. I have chosen to code it dichotomously, however, as there is little variation among the states that have a closing date. Furthermore, Highton and Wolfinger (1998) demonstrate that election-day registration has a qualitatively different effect on turnout than simply moving the closing date by one day. That is, "the difference in turnout between a state with election-day registration and one with a registration deadline one day before the election is greater than the difference between turnout in states where the closing dates are a single day apart" (86–87). Again, a measure of state-level political competition is included in the model.

20. Once more, the standard errors correct for heteroskedasticity.

21. Again, the mean is calculated for every presidential election from 1980 to that particular year.

22. The objective of this figure is only to provide a sense of comparable magnitude of these independent variables. Thus, I do not display the impact of education as it varies from its lowest to its highest level, which is considerably greater than the impact of moving from a high school diploma to attending some college.

CHAPTER 3: FURTHER IMPLICATIONS OF THE DUAL MOTIVATIONS THEORY

1. The Citizen Participation Study consists of two stages. In the first, 15,000 randomly selected respondents completed a twenty-minute telephone interview about their civic and political engagement. In the second stage, 2,517 of the original group of respondents were selected for a longer, face-to-face interview. In this second group political activists were oversampled, as well as African Americans and Latinos. The results reported here are derived from this second set of interviews, with the appropriate weights applied to the data to account for the oversampling.

2. Three control variables have been added to the array used in chapter 2. One is the number of years that the respondent has lived in his or her community (city, town, etc.). The social capital literature, particularly Coleman's work, highlights the importance of residential stability for an individual to become enmeshed in networks of reciprocity. The second is the mean commuting time in a respondent's county. Putnam presents evidence that "increased commuting time among the residents of a community lowers average levels of civic involvement even among noncommuters" (2000, 213). Norm enforcement requires face-to-face interaction, the frequency of which is a function of propinquity. The more time commuters spend out of their communities, the fewer opportunities they will have to be both enforcers and enforcees of social norms. The other additional control is for an individual's political interest, owing to the concern that either the duty or policy motivation is a function of general engagement in politics.

3. The level of political heterogeneity within a county is calculated as the mean level of competitiveness of presidential elections from 1980 to 1988. Ordered logistic regression is the estimator, since the dependent variable consists of

three ordered categories. Again robust standard errors are calculated, specifically accounting for clustering of the sample at the county level. This simply means that the standard errors are calculated based on the assumption that observations are independent across counties, but not within them.

4. The full results are found in Table C1, appendix C.

5. See Schlozman, Verba, and Brady (1995) for a discussion of this dispute within the psychology literature.

6. Forty-nine percent of campaign workers said that duty was a very important reason for getting involved, while 60 percent of protestors said the same. Note that these results differ from those reported by Verba, Schlozman, and Brady themselves in *Voice and Equality*. In the book, they refer to "civic gratifications," and present a table (Table 4.1) that shows little variation in the percentage of respondents who reported that civic gratifications are a very important reason for activities that range from voting to contributing money. However, what they label as civic gratifications actually includes three motivations: (1) doing one's duty; (2) being the kind of person who does his or her share; and (3) making the community or nation a better place to live. It is not obvious that (3) is civic in the sense that I have defined it, since partisans likely believe that their preferred policies will make for a better community or nation. In support of my contention, factor analysis reveals that (3) has the lowest loading of the three across all the activities about which these questions were asked. While I have only reported the percentage choosing (1) specifically as a motivation, the results are essentially identical when (1) and (2) are combined.

7. These results come from the author's own analysis of the 1995 Giving and Volunteering Survey.

8. Classifications taken from the codebook for the 1995 Giving and Volunteering Survey. It is impossible to disaggregate political volunteering further, as this is the way the interviewers themselves coded the respondents' answers.

9. In addition to volunteering, activities included within this category include working in a group to solve a community problem, being an active member of a formally organized group, and raising money for charity.

10. Electoral activities include displaying a campaign button, donating money to a campaign, trying to convince someone else to vote a certain way, volunteering for a candidate or political group, and being a regular voter. Voice activities include protesting, boycotting, signing a paper petition, calling a talk show, contacting a public official, contacting the media, and canvassing on behalf of a political cause.

11. Respondents were asked, "This month, we are interested in volunteer activities, that is activities for which people are not paid, except perhaps expenses. We only want you to include volunteer activities that you did through or for an organization, even if you only did them once in a while. Since September 1 of last year, have you done any volunteer activities through or for an organization?" Respondents were then asked a second question, which was not included in 1989, the last time the CPS included questions about voluntarism. "Sometimes people don't think of activities they do infrequently or activities they do for children's schools or youth organizations as volunteer activities. Since September 1 of last year, have you done any of these types of volunteer activities?" The results

reported here use the combined responses to both of these questions, although the results are substantively unchanged when only the response to the first prompt is used. Note that the CPS uses proxy respondents to report on the behavior of other household members where necessary.

12. The 2002 CPS does not identify the geographic location of all its respondents, only those who live in a metropolitan statistical area. As with the analysis of voter turnout, county-level measures were aggregated to the MSA. To maximize comparability between 1989 and 2002, MSA is the only measure of community used in these models (2002 also identifies the county of some respondents, which was not done in 1989). The models are restricted to respondents over age eighteen.

13. For the reasons explained above, the model includes a measure of the mean commuting time in each community. Also, since the survey was administered in 2002, the measure of political heterogeneity averages presidential election returns from 1980 to 2000. Again, robust standard errors have been calculated and logit is the estimator.

14. The full results are found in Table C2, appendix C.

15. For ease of presentation, and because it most closely resembles a measure of voter turnout, I have focused here on the binary measure of whether one has volunteered in the last year. As shown in Table 3.1, the same negative relationship is observed between political heterogeneity and a question that asks how much time one spent volunteering in the previous week.

16. The specific question about volunteering is worded: "Do you participate in any ongoing community service activity, for example, volunteering at a school, coaching a sports team, or working with a church or neighborhood association? [Yes/No.]" The NHES data are weighted, using a methodology known as replicate weights, to ensure that its sample is representative of the national population. All analyses using the NHES employ these weights (FYWT for youth, FPWT for parents). For details, see the NHES codebook (Collins et al. 1997). Respondents' geographic information is not included in the public release version of the NHES file. It was made available to me through a restricted data license granted by the National Center for Education Statistics. I am grateful to Paul E. Peterson and Alan Altshuler, both of Harvard University's Taubman Center for State and Local Government, for their assistance in obtaining these data. Note that the geographic unit identified within the NHES is a respondent's zip code, which I then converted to the county's FIPS (Federal Information Processing System) code. Some zip codes cover more than one county, requiring some discretion on my part. My coding rule was simply to assume that a respondent is located in the county that overlaps most with a particular zip code.

17. Note also that since this survey was administered in 1996, county partisan composition is averaged from 1980 to 1996.

18. Electoral activism:

Contributed money: "Since January 1988, did you contribute money—to an individual candidate, a party group, a political action committee, or any other organization that supported candidates?"

Contributed time: "Since January 1988, the start of the last national election year, have you worked as a volunteer—that is, for no pay at all or for only a token amount—for a candidate running for national, state, or local office?" Cronbach's alpha = 0.53

Political voice:

Protest: "In the past two years, since [current month 1988], have you taken part in a protest, march, or demonstration on some national or local issue (other than a strike against your employer)?" Follow-up: "Was this in the last twelve months?"

19. In their analysis of data from the Citizen Participation Study, Verba, Schlozman, and Brady (1995) make a convincing case for the importance of what they call "civic skills" as a facilitator of political participation. By civic skills they mean the "communication and organizational abilities that allow citizens to use time and money effectively in political life" (304). As they demonstrate, the more such skills—experience running meetings, writing letters, giving speeches, etc.—an individual possesses, the more likely she is to be engaged in politics. An index of each respondent's civic skills, replicating that used by Verba, Schlozman, and Brady, is thus included as a control variable.

20. The full results are found in Table C4, appendix C.

21. In most cases, this is a city or metropolitan area, but in others it consists of a collection of counties, or even a whole state. Therefore, for all of its virtues, the SCCBS does have some peculiarities. In particular, the scope of the geographic areas covered in each of its forty-one community samples varies dramatically. While I have portrayed this as a positive feature of the data, since it eliminates the need to rely on counties as the contextual unit, it does mean that multiple types of communities are treated as conceptually equivalent. For this analysis, I have opted not to exclude portions of the sample (like all statewide samples, for example), for the fear of artificially biasing what is already a relatively small sample of communities.

22. Ideology is measured using a question that asks respondents to classify themselves as a liberal, moderate, or conservative.

23. Furthermore, it eliminates the concern that relying on election results distorts the measure of political heterogeneity by omitting nonvoters. A generation of research has concluded, however, that there are few if any differences in the preferences of voters and nonvoters (Citrin, Schickler, and Sides 2003; Wolfinger and Rosenstone 1980).

24. For a similar analysis that has greatly informed mine, see Rahn and Rudolph (2001).

25. Specifically, Livingston, Macomb, Monroe, St. Clair, Washtenaw, Oakland, and Wayne Counties.

26. If necessary, the interviewer would clarify what counts as volunteering by continuing, "By volunteering, I mean any unpaid work you've done to help those besides your family and friends or people you work with."

27. The scale is not technically ordinal. First, respondents are asked, "How many times in the past month have you volunteered?" Initially, respondents can then provide a number. If they hesitate, the interviewer probes, "Would you say

you never did this, did it once, a few times, about once a month on average, twice a month, about once a week on average, or more often than that?" Then, from this second question the total number of times that the respondent volunteered was estimated. (Answering "a few times" was coded as 3, "two to four times" was coded as 4, and "five to nine times" was coded as 5.) Roughly 55 percent of the sample reported volunteering at least once in the past year. On average, those interviewed for the SCCBS volunteered nine times per year, although that mean has a wide variance (standard deviation of sixteen). Five percent volunteered more than once a week.

28. This index of political voice has a mean of 1, although almost half of the population has not done any of these things. Just under 2 percent report doing all five. Admittedly, some of the activities in the index may be done in the context of a political campaign. Since it is impossible to determine whether, say, a political rally was on behalf of a candidate (which would be electoral) or simply a cause (which would be the expression of political voice), it seems reasonable to combine all of these activities into a single index. This decision is supported empirically, as factor analysis reveals that all of these activities load cleanly on a single dimension. The Cronbach's alpha of the index is 0.61.

29. The variables included in the hierarchical models used in this section parallel the previous models, employing a common set of both individual and aggregate variables with only a few exceptions, one of which is income. In the hierarchical equations I omit the individual's family income, only because of the amount of missing data (roughly 13 percent) for this question. I feel confident omitting income in this case because across the previous models its effect has been inconsistent and has never had a substantive impact on the variables of interest. Furthermore, because there are only forty-one communities represented in the sample, the number of aggregate variables needs to be kept relatively small, and so I have been more selective in that regard here than previously. The model also accounts for two individual-level attributes that have until now only been measured at the aggregate level: time spent commuting and residential stability, or the length of time the respondent has lived in the community.

30. The full results are found in Table C4, appendix C.

31. As has been the case, the independent variables are standardized on a 0–1 scale, allowing us to compare, at least roughly, their relative magnitudes. The full results are found in Table C4, appendix C.

CHAPTER 4: SOCIAL NETWORKS

1. The term "context" peppers the political science literature, with myriad meanings. The specific term "contextual effects," however, generally refers to research that examines how individuals' social environments affect their behavior and/or attitudes. This is how it is used here.

2. This discussion is informed by the analysis of contextual effects in Huckfeldt and Sprague (1993, 1995).

3. A largely unnoticed exception to this statement is the literature linking electoral competition and high turnout, which is reviewed at length in chapter 2. Generally, scholars working in this literature do not identify with, or cite, the

contextual effects literature, even if they use the term "context" in their own work (Caldeira and Patterson 1982). Likewise, contextual effects scholars do not generally identify models linking competition and turnout as falling within the same research literature.

4. Shortly after, Michael Giles and Marilyn Dantico (1982) confirmed the first of these conclusions, but questioned the second.

5. This brief survey only includes contextual research on collective action. A far larger literature examines how social context affects individuals' attitudes and vote choice (see Berelson, Lazarsfeld, and McPhee 1954; Putnam 1966; Wright 1977, 1976; Sprague 1982; Huckfeldt and Sprague 1995; Wald, Owen, and Hill 1988; Huckfeldt, Plutzer, and Sprague 1993; Butler and Stokes 1974).

6. This is not to say that these studies totally ignore factors contributing to political participation. In *The People's Choice*, for instance, Lazarsfeld, Berelson, and Gaudet devote a chapter to voter turnout. The chapter, however, simply makes the point that political interest correlates with turnout.

7. The GSS is a long-running omnibus survey employing a nationally representative sample. It is one of the primary sources of information about Americans' social behavior.

8. This analysis is similar to one done by David Knoke in *Political Networks: The Structural Perspective* (1990). His work is similar to mine, although our analyses (and thus conclusions) differ slightly.

9. As Granovetter (1973) uses the term, "weak tie" refers to an acquaintance unknown to one's other acquaintances. I use the term more loosely, and mean people with whom one has a relatively superficial relationship. Obviously, the two meanings overlap.

10. For ease of presentation, weak and strong partisans are grouped together.

11. While it seems reasonable to assume that, on average, individuals who identify with a given party share common issue positions, it is not clear that this is the case for political independents. As a simple thought experiment, take any issue on the American political agenda and ask yourself the position you would expect an independent to take. It simply is not clear.

12. These totals remain virtually unchanged when we examine Democrats only or Republicans only.

13. An alternative is to include the percentage of respondents with a common partisan affiliation as the dependent variable, which captures essentially the same information. However, I hold that this is an inferior measure because it does not account for the overall size of the network. Someone with three out of three discussion partners sharing the same partisan affiliation receives the same score on the index as someone who has only one discussion partner, but whose partner has the same partisan leanings. Presumably, the first person in this example is enmeshed in a network that is more likely to foster norm-driven behavior. Notwithstanding my objections, results are substantively identical when this variable is substituted in the model.

14. Obviously, there is considerable colinearity between these two variables. As we will see, however, this does not preclude both from achieving statistical significance in some specifications.

15. The political discussion question is worded, "About how often do you talk to ____ about political matters? Almost daily, at least weekly, at least

monthly, at least yearly, or never?" Political interest is gauged with, "How interested are you in politics and national affairs? Are you very interested, somewhat interested, only slightly interested, or not at all interested?" Education is coded as the number of years of school that the respondent has completed. Income is coded on a scale from 1 to 21, ranging from < $1,000 per year (1) to > $60,000 per year (21).

16. The demographic control variables have been omitted from the table. The full results are found in Table C6, appendix C.

17. The percentage of respondents turning out to vote is inflated in the GSS. As is typical with survey data, however, we do not know the cause of the inflation—sampling bias or over-reporting. It is not clear that either of these would be correlated with social network homogeneity, however, thus preserving the interpretation of the trend.

18. The question about the frequency of voting in local elections was asked immediately following a question regarding participation in presidential elections. "What about local elections? Do you always vote in those, do you sometimes miss one, do you rarely vote, or do you never vote?"

19. Displayed is the probability that respondents report "always" voting in local elections or that they "sometimes miss one." When the percentage who always vote is calculated, the overall probability is much lower, but the slope remains essentially the same (it ranges from 30 percent to 38.2 percent).

20. "In the past four years, have you contributed money to a political party or candidate or to any other political cause? Have you done (other) work for one of the parties or candidates in most elections, some elections, only a few, or have you never done such work? In the past three or four years, have you attended any political meetings or rallies?" The index has a Cronbach's alpha of 0.57. I have thus grouped these three items together in order to retain a single index, simplifying the analysis, even though attending a rally could also be considered a means of expressing political voice. The context of the question suggests that most respondents would consider it as referring to a campaign-related rally, given that it immediately follows two questions about involvement in political campaigns. Their intercorrelations are comparable—each is about 0.35.

21. As with the previous measure, political independents are not counted in the tally.

22. Note that some critics of contextual effects research argue that it can never overcome the biases inherent from self-selection (see Achen and Shively 1995). While I do not share Achen and Shively's pessimism, their gloomy assessment reminds us that caution should be exercised when interpreting any contextual model.

23. These geographic identifiers are not included in the public release version of the GSS, and were graciously provided to me by Tom Smith, director of the General Social Survey.

24. Since these data were collected in 1987, the partisan competition measure spans from 1980 to 1984.

25. Because the dependent variable is a count of like-minded discussion partners, ranging from 0 to 3, ordered logistic regression is used to estimate the model. The results are substantively identical when a poisson model is estimated,

which is arguably appropriate because the number of partners is a count, although it only ranges from 0 to 3. The full results are found in Table C6, appendix C.

CHAPTER 5: SOCIAL ENVIRONMENTS AND ADOLESCENTS' PUBLIC ENGAGEMENT

1. Note that Coleman and Hoffer did not coin the term "social capital," as others had used it previously (Portes 1998; Putnam 2000).

2. This study extends beyond the United States, and includes civics evaluations administered to students in twenty-eight nations. For more on the CES, see Torney-Purta et al. (2001). Information about the study is also available at http://www.wam.umd.edu/~iea.

3. The geographic locations of the schools used in the study were released to me through a restricted data license granted by the National Center for Education Statistics.

4. The Cronbach's alpha coefficients for the three indices are 0.71 for the civic index, 0.70 for the political voice items, and 0.58 for the electoral activism scale.

5. That is, the mean level of competition in presidential elections from 1980 to 1996. See chapter 2 for a detailed discussion of this measure.

6. Independent Sector describes its mission as "to promote, strengthen, and advance the nonprofit and philanthropic community to foster private initiative for the public good." The organization's mission statement, as well as other information about it, can be found online at http://www.independentsector.org/about/vision.html.

7. See chapter 3 for a discussion of self-reported motivations.

8. See chapter 2 for a detailed explanation of how this measure has been calculated, as well as a discussion of the pluses and minuses of using counties to approximate "community."

9. For the curious, it turns out that there is a statistically significant relationship between the partisan composition of a community and the likelihood that a school mandates community service. The more heterogeneous the county, the *greater* the probability that a respondent's school has a community service requirement for graduation. This seems consistent with the conclusion that homogeneity leads to voluntarism. In homogeneous communities, teens already volunteer at a relatively high rate, and so perhaps school administrators do not feel that a service requirement is necessary. In places that are more heterogeneous, volunteering is less common, with the potential consequence of spurring schools to mandate community service.

10. School arranges service: "Does your school arrange or offer any service activities that students can participate in?" (0) No; (1) Yes.

11. The NHES only permits the analyst to crudely distinguish between religious schools as Catholic or not. The category of other religious schools thus contains an array of schools, from fundamentalist Christian to Quaker to Jewish. Even if the data did permit finer distinctions among religious schools, the cell sizes would be so small as to render comparisons meaningless.

12. The questions have a four-point Likert scale: strongly agree, agree, disagree, strongly disagree.

13. The index has a Cronbach's alpha coefficient of 0.73.

14. As expected, students in private schools do report high scores on these measures of a respectful school environment.

15. The full results are found in Table C8, appendix C.

16. Cronbach's alpha for home discipline is 0.62 for students asked whether their family had a rule about a bedtime, and 0.60 for students asked if they had to be home by a certain time on school nights.

17. Again displaying the percentage of parents who have the highest or next to highest value on the index, in this case a 3 or 4 on a scale ranging from 0 to 4.

18. Both indices are additive, with Cronbach's alpha scores of 0.57 and 0.79, respectively.

19. For students' voice at school, the figure displays the percentage who scored a 5 or 6 on the 0–6 index. For parents' voice at school, the figure displays the percentage of those scoring 7–9 on the 0–9 index.

20. Cronbach's alpha = 0.58. Figure 5.4 displays the percentage scoring 7 through 9 on the 0–9 scale.

21. This measure consists of the improvement in the log-likelihood of the model over the null (that is, a model without any predictors). It is only roughly analogous to the measure of R^2 in a linear regression context.

22. This is measured with the same question asked of the youth.

23. The NHES also contains a measure of external political efficacy, specifically, "My family doesn't have any say in what the federal government does. Is this true for you?" A model of external efficacy reveals a positive coefficient for community political heterogeneity, but it does not reach statistical significance.

24. An alternative measure of political engagement is an index of political knowledge (Zaller 1992). The NHES contains such a measure, and when used as a dependent variable the coefficient for partisan composition is positive, but only skirts at the edge of conventional statistical significance.

25. The distinction between the two is spelled out in chapter 4. In brief, "network" refers to friends and acquaintances, while "context" refers to the aggregate characteristics of one's community.

26. While authors like Stephen Macedo and Amy Gutmann speak approvingly of how public schools teach tolerance, empirical research suggests that at least some types of private schools may do more to teach respect for civil liberties (D. Campbell 2001b; Wolf et al. 2001). Either way, it is appropriate to account for the type of school a student attends.

27. The parental question is identical to the one asked of their children.

28. The NHES includes a second question related to political tolerance: "If a person wanted to make a speech in your community against churches and religion, should he or she be allowed to speak?" Political heterogeneity is also positively related to responses to this item, but the coefficient does not clear the bar for statistical significance. This is likely because of the limited variation in

responses: 88 percent of adolescents said that the speech should be permitted, compared to 58 percent who said that a book advocating legalizing drugs should be permitted in a public library.

CHAPTER 6: THE LINKS BETWEEN ADOLESCENTS'
AND ADULTS' PUBLIC ENGAGEMENT

1. From the book of Proverbs (22:6).

2. This statement is based on analysis that is not shown.

3. Note that Smith's model uses a four-part index that mixes politically and civically motivated activity. Three of the four index items deal with voting— whether the respondent is registered to vote, whether the respondent has voted in a local election in the previous twelve months, and whether the respondent voted in the 1992 presidential election. The fourth item is whether the individual has worked for a "political club or organization."

4. There have been a few other studies in political science that have employed the MTF data archive (see Rahn and Transue 1998; D. Campbell 2002; Burns, Schlozman, and Verba 2001).

5. Monitoring the Future is administered to respondents in their schools. Schools, both public and private, are selected to produce a nationally representative sample of high school seniors. If a particular school declines to participate, it is replaced with another that matches its profile. In smaller schools the whole senior class participates, while in larger schools a representative sample of up to 350 students is used. There are thus two response rates that apply to these data: the rate of the schools, and the rate of the individual students. The initial response rate of schools has fluctuated from 1977 (the first year for which this figure is reported) to 1996—starting around 60 percent, increasing in the mid-1980s to roughly 70 percent, and dropping to 53 percent in 1996. However, when the response rate is calculated by including the replacement schools, it has never dropped below 95 percent. The principal investigators of the MTF series note that if fluctuating response rates lead to selection bias, the results should also fluctuate erratically over time. They do not. Admittedly, there may be a constant selection bias among schools, but if so the measurement of trends is unaffected. In contrast to other national surveys, the response rate for individual students has increased from the 1970s to the 1990s—from 77 percent in 1976 to 83 percent in 1996. The most common reason that students are missed is simply their absence from school on the day the questionnaire is administered, as less than 1.5 percent of students explicitly refuse to participate (Johnston, O'Malley, and Bachman 2001).

6. While the cross-sectional MTF data are available publicly, the panel data are released only at the discretion of the MTF principal investigators. I was only able to acquire these data with the financial assistance of Harvard University's Center for American Political Studies and the Saguaro Seminar: Civic Engagement in America. I am grateful for the generosity of these two organizations.

7. More precisely, over a two-year period, the whole panel is re-interviewed. Half of the panel is contacted in odd years, half in even. According to the documentation provided by the MTF principal investigators, the retention rates of their panels range from 77 percent in the first wave following high school to 53 percent in the oldest panel (the seventh biennial follow-up, when respondents were about thirty-two years old).

8. MTF consists of interviews with high school students only, thus excluding the roughly 11 percent of this age cohort who drop out of school. Obviously, this constrains the extent to which the sample is fully representative of all American adolescents.

9. On the other hand, it is difficult to compare the MTF estimates of participation in volunteer service with other sources of data because the question is not replicated anywhere else. For example, the 1980 MTF suggests a much higher rate of voluntarism among high school students than the 1996 National Household Education Survey (see chapter 5). But owing to the markedly different questions used to gauge voluntarism, it is impossible to know the extent to which the discrepancy between the two surveys is simply a statistical artifact or represents real change over time. Further complicating any comparisons, the two surveys also differ in their sampling frame, as MTF is a school-based sample, and the NHES uses random-digit dialing. Also, MTF uses a paper and pencil questionnaire, while NHES is a telephone survey. Notably, the NHES asks students whether they participate in volunteer work "at least once a year"—a looser time frame than the NHES question, which asks whether the student has participated in community service within the *current school year*. These differences between the MTF and other sources of data, including but not limited to the NHES, would be especially problematic if my primary objective was to arrive at an estimate of the frequency of volunteering among America's young people. However, our focus is on the *relationship* between volunteering and voting, and there is no reason to think that has been corrupted.

10. With five ordinal categories, ordered logit is an appropriate estimator.

11. This is the mean level of education for both parents. The question is worded, "The next questions ask about your parents. If you were raised mostly by foster parents, stepparents, or others, answer for them. For example, if you have both a stepfather and a natural father, answer for the one that was most important in raising you. What is the highest level of schooling your father/mother completed? Completed grade school or less, some high school, completed high school, some college, completed college, graduate or professional degree after college." Because of confidentiality concerns MTF administrators do not release the education level of each individual parent.

12. Race and gender are binary variables and have been set to their modal categories. Race has been set to "white" and gender to "female."

13. Note that I have corrected for discrepancies in reported turnout from wave to wave. A small percentage of respondents report having voted at one point in time, and then report not ever having voted at the next point. Obviously, given the cumulative nature of the question, this is impossible. I have thus assumed that a respondent's initial report of having voted is accurate. The substantive results are identical whether I make this correction or not.

14. Since the two dependent variables are indices, ordered logit is the estimator. Cronbach's alpha for the political voice index it is 0.55 (at wave 3), while the electoral activism index is .54 (also at wave 3).

Chapter 7: Adolescents' Social Environments and Adults' Public Engagement

1. Obvious exceptions include high school dropouts and youth who are home-schooled. Currently, around 11 percent of 16- to 24-year-olds are high school dropouts (U.S. Department of Commerce 2000), while between 1 and 2 percent of students in grades 9 through 12 are homeschooled (Bielick, Chandler, and Broughman 2001).

2. Note that the experiential education of belonging to a school community is different than what has been called schools' "hidden curriculum." This is defined by Merelman as "a set of common practices which, by teaching quite different behavior and power relationships, supposedly prevents the transmission of democratic values in the school" (1980a, 320). What I am describing are the practices—norms—of community membership. They are "hidden" only in the sense that they are not a formal component of the curriculum. For more on the hidden curriculum, see the 1980 exchange between Merelman and Jennings in the *American Political Science Review* (Jennings 1980; Merelman 1980a, 1980b).

3. I am grateful to M. Kent Jennings for permitting me to obtain the geographic codes for members of the YPSS panel. I am equally grateful that he suggested I use the panel members' schools as measures of their social context in adolescence.

4. Ninety-seven schools were attended by members of the YPSS student panel, meaning that contextual data were collected for about 80 percent of the panel members' schools.

5. Specifically, the question was worded, "Generally speaking, do you usually think of yourself as a Republican, Democrat, or an Independent?"

6. The specific formula for political heterogeneity is as follows:

$$Political\ Heterogeneity = 1 - \sum_{p} h_{ps}^2$$

where p = partisan categories and s = school, and h_{ps} thus represents the degree of heterogeneity in each school.

7. Religious heterogeneity is calculated in a manner comparable to political heterogeneity. Religious categories are (1) Roman Catholic; (2) mainline Protestant (Presbyterian, Lutheran, Episcopalian, and Methodist); (3) conservative Protestant (Baptist, Disciples of Christ, Church of Christ); (4) Mormon; (5) Jewish; (6) Eastern Orthodox; and (7) no religious preference. Racial heterogeneity is simply the percentage of nonwhite students in the school, since the questionnaire only asked students to identify themselves as white or nonwhite, precluding the use of a racial heterogeneity index comparable to the political and religious indices. The questionnaire did not inquire about parents' income, and so income heterogeneity has not been included in this analysis.

8. The high school sample data were collected from students only. They were asked, "How far did your parents go in school?" with six options for each parent: (1) less than high school; (2) some high school (9–11 years); (3) completed high school; (4) some college; (5) completed college; (6) went beyond college. For each student respondent, the mean level of parents' education was calculated by simply averaging the two responses (in the case of single parents, obviously there was no need for an average). The high school sample includes a number of socioeconomic indicators, including the percentage of students who expect to attend college. Their colinearity precludes including more than one. I have chosen parents' education, but essentially identical results are obtained with the others as well.

9. "How many years have you lived in this city (or town or rural area)?" (1) 1 year or less; (2) 2 years; (3) 3 years; (4) 4–5 years; (5) 6–10 years; (6) 11–15 years; (7) 16 or more years, but not all my life; (8) all my life.

10. Surprisingly, the aggregate level of residential mobility is a positive predictor of civic norms.

11. A method of estimation appropriate for data that are both hierarchical and binary must be employed. To accommodate these two demands, I use a hierarchical generalized linear model (HGLM). In its fundamentals, HGLM is an extension of a hierarchical linear model (HLM). It differs in that the level-1 predicted value is transformed so that it falls within a specified interval using what is known as an identity link function. In the case of a dichotomous dependent variable, HGLM employs a binomial sampling model and a logit link function (Raudenbush and Bryk 2002). When employing HGLM, the analyst has a choice of reporting two different types of results: *unit-specific* and *population-average* models. Unit-specific models are appropriate when the research question is centered on the causal processes within each level-2 unit (in this case, schools), while population-average models estimate effects for the population as a whole. The key difference between them is that the unit-specific model estimates a random effect for each unit at level 2. Coefficients in a population-average model are interpreted as the impact averaged over all the units (Raudenbush et al. 2001). In this case, the research question at hand is better addressed with a population-average model, since our interest is not in any particular school. It is also the case that population-average models are less sensitive to model specification, meaning that their results are more robust (although slightly less precise) than unit-specific models. Note that all of the continuous variables at levels 1 and 2 are grand mean-centered. This practice is consistent throughout the chapter.

12. "Nonwhite" is the term used in the study's documentation; unfortunately there is no further differentiation among groups within the nonwhite population.

13. The specific geographic location of the schools in the YPSS sample is not available in the public-release version of the data. These data were made available to me through special arrangement with the Inter-university Consortium for Political and Social Research (ICPSR).

14. The response options were actually listed in the opposite order on the questionnaire. This is the order in which I have coded them.

15. The precise wording of the question is as follows:

People have different ideas about what being a good citizen means. We're interested in what you think. How would you describe a good citizen in this country—that is, what things about a person are most important in showing that one is a good citizen?

Anyone who responded with "voting," "votes," "registers and votes," or "should exercise right to vote" is coded as believing that voting is an element of good citizenship. More precisely, this is category 22 in the codebook for the 1965 portion of the YPSS, which should be consulted for more details (Jennings, Markus, and Niemi 1991).

16. This is an additive index of six acts, based on responses to the following questionnaire item:

I have a list of some of the things that people do that help a party or candidate win an election. I wonder if you could tell me whether you have done these things during any kind of public election involving candidates or issues during the past ten years.

1. Did you talk to any people and try to show them why they should vote one way or another?
2. Did you go to any political meetings, rallies, dinners, or things like that?
3. Did you do any other work for one of the parties, candidates, or issues?
4. Do you belong to any political clubs or organizations?
5. Did you wear a campaign button or put a campaign sticker on your car?
6. Did you give any money or buy any tickets to help a party, candidate, or group pay campaign expenses?

Note that these are primarily electoral in nature. Cronbach's alpha = 0.78.

17. As with the 1965 data, geographic identifiers (specifically, Primary Sampling Units [PSUs]) were made available to me by ICSPR, with the consent of M. Kent Jennings. For virtually every PSU, I was able to determine the MSA. In a few cases, the imprecision of the PSU required me to use an entire state for the contextual measure, rather than an MSA. For example, "New Jersey" is identified as a single PSU and so the aggregate measures were calculated as averages across the entire state.

18. This has been calculated as in chapter 2, where this measure was first introduced. First, the mean level of political competition in each community was calculated by averaging the vote share of the winning party (subtracted from one) from 1960 to 1980. That score is then subtracted from the mean and squared. For the homogeneity measure, each community above the mean receives a score of 0, while for the heterogeneity measure each one below the mean is scored as 0. See chapter 2 for more details.

19. The inclusion of the community variables in 1982 complicates the hierarchical structure of the data, as individuals attending a single high school could end up in any community in 1982. Therefore, the contextual measures of political composition are included in the model as level-1 variables. Consequently, the community-level effects should be interpreted cautiously and considered tentative at best. I have also experimented with a multiple-classification hierarchical model, which permits two nonoverlapping level-2 variables. Using this type of model, the substantive conclusions remain the same.

20. "Apart from any work for which you receive pay, do you do any volunteer work or not? [Yes, No.]" Note that this is slightly different than asking whether the respondent has engaged in volunteer work within the previous year, the measure used in the Current Population Survey and the National Household Education Survey. This question was not asked in previous waves of the YPSS.

21. The electoral activism index includes talking to others in an effort to persuade them to vote one way or the other; attending a political rally or meeting; working for a party or candidate; displaying a campaign button bumper sticker; and giving money to a party, candidate, or cause. Cronbach's alpha = 0.72. The political voice index includes writing a letter to a public official, writing a letter to the editor, and participating in a demonstration or march. Cronbach's alpha = 0.32. This is admittedly an extremely low alpha value, calling into question whether these index items should be combined. The results are the same when each item in the index is modeled separately, and so the index is used to economize on space.

22. Specifically, voluntarism is modeled using binary HGLM, while the campaign participation model employs HLM.

23. Recall that respondents could choose up to three items from the list.

CHAPTER 8: CONCLUSION

1. Note, however, that there is controversy over the extent to which partisanship remains fixed (Erikson, MacKuen, and Stimson 2002).

2. See Bishop's series of articles in the *Austin American-Statesman* on political polarization that triggered Klinkner's rebuttal (Bishop 2004a, 2004b, 2004c, 2004d). The exchange between Klinkner and Bishop was conducted in *The Forum*, an electronic journal (Klinkner 2004a, 2004b; Bishop and Cushing 2004).

3. Turnout figures taken from the estimates of McDonald and Popkin (2001) and http://elections.gmu.edu/voter_turnout.htm (accessed April 28, 2005).

4. Idaho, New Hampshire, and Wyoming all adopted election-day registration prior to the 1994 election, while Maine, Minnesota, Oregon, and Washington enacted it in the 1970s. Oregon subsequently repealed it in the wake of the Rajneesh movement's takeover of the town of Antelope. Rajneesh followers recruited hundreds of homeless people nationwide to vote in local elections in a bid to take over the county government. This happened in 1984; Oregon voters repealed election-day registration in 1985. Ohio flirted with allowing registration on the day of the election in the 1970s, adopting it in the early part of 1977 and then ratifying a constitutional amendment banning it in November of the same year (Knack 2001; Epps 2001).

5. Although I would not want to overstate the case here, as 1992 did see efforts to boost the turnout of young people, including MTV's nonpartisan Rock the Vote campaign and the Clinton-Gore campaign's partisan—obviously— efforts to attract the youth vote. While similar in kind, these efforts were on a smaller scale than what was witnessed in 2004.

6. The fact that voters expressed more interest in the 2004 campaign than in 2000 comes out clearly in the data collected by the Vanishing Voter project at

Harvard University's Kennedy School of Government. See http://www.vanish ingvoter.org (accessed April 28, 2005).

7. Data from the office of Minnesota's Secretary of State, available at http://www.sos.state.mn.us/election/elstat94.pdf (accessed July 8, 2004).

8. States could avoid implementing the NVRA's mandates by adopting election-day registration, which is why Idaho, New Hampshire, and Wyoming did so between 1992 and 1996.

9. "In general, these changes seem to have yielded only modest effects" (Berinsky, Burns, and Traugott 2001, 179); "The data reported here suggest that policies like the National Voter Registration Act of 1993 will modestly increase overall turnout" (Highton 1997, 573); "[T]he duration-based estimates are perhaps disappointingly modest for the more optimistic advocates of registration reform" (Knack 1995, 806); "[T]urnout gains because of the National Voter Registration Act of 1993 are likely, but they will be modest" (Rhine 1995, 409); "The National Voter Registration Act is likely to increase turnout modestly" (Rhine 1996, 181); "Table 1 reports that the effects of NVRA were very modest" (Martinez and Hill 1999, 301).

10. Much skepticism toward the study of civic duty has no doubt been fed by the fact that one of the few sources of relevant data is the battery of questions developed by the early Michigan School researchers to gauge civic duty. Most Americans score very highly on this battery, which includes statements like, "So many other people vote in national elections that it doesn't much matter to me whether I vote or not," and "If a person doesn't care about how an election comes out, he shouldn't vote in it." The highly skewed nature of the original civic duty index is presumably why it was dropped from the National Election Studies in 1980, although the item about voting even when you do not care how an election comes out has occasionally made an appearance since, and the item regarding whether voting in a national election is worthwhile was a late addition to the 2000 NES (Sapiro, Rosenstone, and Studies 2002). The fact that the original civic duty index produces highly skewed results is a problem, since it ends up as virtually a constant rather than a variable—and one cannot explain a variable (like, say, voter turnout) with a constant. It would be a simple matter to re-engineer the index so as to produce greater variation, perhaps by adding more response options. Even this fix, however, would not address my fundamental concern about this scale as a gauge of civic duty, namely that it is only a measure of duty by inference. The questions do not ask people affirmatively whether they feel it is their duty to vote, but only whether they should vote under certain conditions, with the implication that a sense of duty is the motivation leading them to do so. For the purposes of the present study, a better analytical strategy is the one followed by Verba, Schlozman, and Brady (1995). They explicitly ask voters whether they feel it is their duty to vote. Better yet would be to have voters rank-order their motivations for voting to circumvent their inclination to endorse voting out of duty—which is by definition, after all, a norm.

Bibliography

Abramson, Paul R., and William Claggett. 1986. Race-related Differences in Self-Reported and Validated Turnout in 1986. *Journal of Politics* 48 (2):412–22.

———. 1989. Race-related Differences in Self-Reported and Validated Turnout in 1986. *Journal of Politics* 51 (2):397–408.

———. 1991. Race-related Differences in Self-Reported and Validated Turnout in 1986. *Journal of Politics* 53 (1):186–97.

Achen, Christopher, and W. Phillips Shively. 1995. *Cross-Level Inference.* Chicago: University of Chicago Press.

Alesina, Alberto, and Eliana La Ferrara. 2000. Participation in Heterogeneous Communities. *Quarterly Journal of Economics* 115 (August):847–904.

Almond, Gabriel A., and Sidney Verba. 1989 (1963). *The Civic Culture: Political Attitudes and Democracy in Five Nations.* Newbury Park, CA: Sage.

Alt, James. 1992. Race and Voter Registration in the South before and after the Voting Rights Act. In *Controversies in Minority Voting: A Twenty-Five-Year Perspective on the Voting Rights Act of 1965*, edited by Bernard Grofman and Chandler Davidson. Washington, DC: Brookings Institution.

Anderson, Barbara, and Brian D. Silver. 1986. Measurement and Mismeasurement of the Validity of the Self-Reported Vote. *American Journal of Political Science* 30 (4):771–85.

Andrain, Charles F. 1971. *Children and Civic Awareness.* Columbus, OH: Charles E. Merrill.

Baer, John S., Alan Stacy, and Mary Larimer. 1991. Biases in the Perception of Drinking Norms among College Students. *Journal of Studies on Alcohol* 52 (6):580–86.

Baer, John S., G. Alan Marlatt, Daniel R. Kivlan, Kim Fromme, Mary E. Larimer, and Ellen Williams. 1992. An Experimental Test of Three Methods of Alcohol Risk Reduction with Young Adults. *Journal of Consulting and Clinical Psychology* 60 (6):974–79.

Barber, Benjamin R. 1992. *An Aristocracy of Everyone: The Politics of Education and the Future of America.* New York: Ballantine Books.

Bartels, Larry. 2002. A Generational Model of Political Learning. Princeton University, Center for the Study of Democratic Politics.

Barzel, Yoram, and Eugene Silberberg. 1973. Is the Act of Voting Rational? *Public Choice* 16:51–58.

Battistoni, Richard M. 2000. Service Learning and Civic Education. In *Education for Civic Engagement in Democracy: Service Learning and Other Promising Practices*, edited by Sheilah Mann and John J. Patrick. Bloomington, IN: Educational Resources Information Center.

Beck, Paul Allen, and M. Kent Jennings. 1979. Political Periods and Political Participation. *American Political Science Review* 73 (3):737–50.

———. 1982. Pathways to Participation. *American Political Science Review* 76 (1):94–108.

———. 1991. Family Traditions, Political Periods, and the Development of Partisan Orientations. *Journal of Politics* 53:742–63.

Bellah, Robert N., Richard Madsen, William M. Sullivan, and Steven M. Tipton. 1985. *Habits of the Heart: Individualism and Commitment in American Life.* Berkeley: University of California Press.

Berelson, Bernard R., Paul Lazarsfeld, and William N. McPhee. 1954. *Voting: A Study of Opinion Formation in a Presidential Election.* Chicago: University of Chicago Press.

Berinsky, Adam J., Nancy Burns, and Michael W. Traugott. 2001. Who Votes by Mail? A Dynamic Model of the Individual-Level Consequences of Voting-by-Mail Systems. *Public Opinion Quarterly* 65:178–97.

Berry, Jeffrey M., Kent E. Portney, and Ken Thomson. 1993. *The Rebirth of Urban Democracy.* Washington, DC: Brookings Institution Press.

Bielick, Stacey, Kathryn Chandler, and Stephen P. Broughman. 2001. Homeschooling in the United States: 1999. Washington, DC: U.S. Department of Education, National Center for Education Statistics.

Bishop, Bill. 2004a. The Cost of Political Uniformity. *Austin American-Statesman*, April 8.

———. 2004b. Politics 2004: Preach to the Choir. *Austin American-Statesman*, May 2.

———. 2004c. The Schism in U.S. Politics Begins at Home. *Austin American-Statesman*, April 4.

———. 2004d. A Steady Slide toward a More Partisan Union. *Austin American-Statesman*, May 30.

Bishop, Bill, and Robert Cushing. 2004. Response to Philip A. Klinkner's "Red and Blue Scare: The Continuing Diversity of the American Electoral Landscape." *The Forum* 2 (2):1–12. Article 8, available at http://www.bepress.com/forum (accessed September 22, 2005).

Blais, Andre. 2000. *To Vote or Not to Vote? The Merits and Limits of Rational Choice Theory.* Pittsburgh: University of Pittsburgh Press.

Brady, Henry E. 1999. Political Participation. In *Measures of Political Attitudes*, edited by John P. Robinson, Phillip R. Shaver, and Lawrence S. Wrightsman. San Diego: Academic Press.

Brehm, John, and Wendy Rahn. 1997. Individual-Level Evidence for the Causes and Consequences of Social Capital. *American Journal of Political Science* 41 (3):999–1023.

Brody, Richard A. 1978. The Puzzle of Political Participation in America. In *The New American Political System*, edited by Anthony King. Washington, DC: American Enterprise Institute.

Brooks, David. 2001. One Nation, Slightly Divisible. *The Atlantic Monthly* 288 (5):53–65.

Brown v. Board of Education of Topeka, Kansas. 347 (U.S.) 483 (1954).

Bryk, Anthony S., Valerie E. Lee, and Peter B. Holland. 1993. *Catholic Schools and the Common Good.* Cambridge, MA: Harvard University Press.

Burnham, Walter Dean. 1987. The Turnout Problem. In *Elections American Style*, edited by A. James Reichley. Washington, DC: Brookings Institution Press.

Burns, Nancy, Kay Lehman Schlozman, and Sidney Verba. 2001. *The Private Roots of Public Action: Gender, Equality, and Political Participation*. Cambridge, MA: Harvard University Press.

Bush, George W. 2002. State of the Union Address. Available at http://www.whitehouse.gov/news/releases/2002/01/20020129–11.html.

Butler, David, and Donald Stokes. 1974. *Political Change in Britain: The Evolution of Electoral Choice*. New York: St. Martin's Press.

Caldeira, Gregory, and Samuel C. Patterson. 1982. Contextual Influences on Participation in U.S. State Legislative Elections. *Legislative Studies Quarterly* 7 (3):359–81.

Caldeira, Gregory A., Aage R. Clausen, and Samuel C. Patterson. 1990. Partisan Mobilization and Electoral Participation. *Electoral Studies* 9 (3):191–204.

Caldeira, Gregory A., Samuel C. Patterson, and Gregor A. Markko. 1985. The Mobilization of Voters in Congressional Elections. *Journal of Politics* 47 (2):490–509.

Campbell, Andrea Louise. 2003. *How Policies Make Citizens: Senior Political Activism and the American Welfare State*. Princeton: Princeton University Press.

Campbell, Angus, Gerald Gurin, and Warren E. Miller. 1954. *The Voter Decides*. Evanston, IL: Row, Peterson, and Company.

Campbell, Angus, Philip E. Converse, Warren E. Miller, and Donald E. Stokes. 1960. *The American Voter*. New York: John Wiley and Sons.

Campbell, David. 2001a. Civic Education: Readying Massachusetts' Next Generation of Citizens. Boston: Pioneer Institute for Public Policy Research.

———. 2001b. Making Democratic Education Work. In *Charters, Vouchers, and Public Education*, edited by Paul E. Peterson and David E. Campbell. Washington, DC: Brookings Institution Press.

———. 2002. The Young and the Realigning: A Test of the Socialization Theory of Realignment. *Public Opinion Quarterly* 66 (Summer):209–34.

Campbell, David E., Steven J. Yonish, and Robert D. Putnam. 1999. Tuning In, Tuning Out Revisited: A Closer Look at the Causal Links between Television and Social Capital. Paper read at the Annual Meeting of the American Political Science Association, Atlanta, GA.

Carmines, Edward G., and James A. Stimson. 1989. *Issue Evolution: Race and the Transformation of American Politics*. Princeton: Princeton University Press.

Carnegie Corporation of New York and Center for Information and Research on Civic Learning and Engagement. 2003. *The Civic Mission of Schools*. New York: Carnegie Corporation. Available at http://www.civicmissionofschools.org.

Cebula, Richard J., and Dennis R. Murphy. 1980. The Electoral College and Voter Participation Rates: An Exploratory Note. *Public Choice* 35:185–90.

Center for Information and Research on Civic Learning and Engagement. 2004. Turnout of Under-25 Voters Up Sharply, http://www.civicyouth.org/PopUps/Release_1824final.pdf.

Chambers, William N., and Philip C. Davis. 1978. Party Competition and Mass Participation: The Case of the Democratizing Party System, 1824–1852. In *The History of American Electoral Behavior*, edited by Joel H. Silbey, Allan G. Bogue, and William H. Flanigan. Princeton: Princeton University Press.

Citrin, Jack, Eric Schickler, and John Sides. 2003. What If Everyone Voted? Simulating the Impact of Increased Turnout in Senate Elections. *American Journal of Political Science* 47 (1):75–90.

Coleman, James S. 1988. Social Capital in the Creation of Human Capital. *American Journal of Sociology* 94 (Supplement):S95–S120.

———. 1990. *Foundations of Social Theory*. Cambridge, MA: Harvard University Press.

Coleman, James, and Thomas B. Hoffer. 1987. *Public and Private High Schools: The Impact of Communities*. New York: Basic Books.

Collins, Mary A., J. Michael Brick, Mary Jo Nolin, Nancy Vaden-Kiernan, Susan Gilmore, Kathryn Chandler, and Chris Chapman. 1997. *National Household Education Survey of 1996: Data File User's Manual, NCES 97–425*. Vol. 1. Washington, DC: U.S. Department of Education, National Center for Education Statistics.

Conover, Pamela Johnston, and Donald D. Searing. 2000. A Political Socialization Perspective. In *Rediscovering the Democratic Purposes of Education*, edited by Lorraine M. McDonnell, P. Michael Timpane, and Roger Benjamin. Lawrence: University Press of Kansas.

Converse, Philip E. 1964. The Nature of Belief Systems in Mass Publics. In *Ideology and Discontent*, edited by David Apter. Glencoe, IL: Macmillan.

Conway, M. Margaret. 1981. Political Participation in Midterm Congressional Elections: Attitudinal and Social Characteristics during the 1970s. *American Politics Quarterly* 9 (2):221–44.

Cook, Timothy E. 1985. The Bear Market in Political Socialization and the Costs of Misunderstood Psychological Theories. *American Political Science Review* 79 (4):1079–93.

Copeland, Gary W. 1983. Activating Voters in Congressional Elections. *Political Behavior* 5 (4):391–401.

Costa, Dora L., and Matthew E. Kahn. 2003a. Civic Engagement and Community Heterogeneity: An Economist's Perspective. *Perspectives on Politics* 1 (1):103–11.

———. 2003b. Understanding the American Decline in Social Capital, 1952–1998. *Kyklos* 56 (1):17–46.

Cox, Gary W. 1988. Closeness and Turnout: A Methodological Note. *Journal of Politics* 50 (3):768–75.

Cox, Gary W., and Michael C. Munger. 1989. Closeness, Expenditures, and Turnout in the 1982 House Elections. *American Journal of Political Science* 83 (1):217–31.

Crain, W. Mark, Donald R. Leavens, and Lynn Abbott. 1987. Voting and Not Voting at the Same Time. *Public Choice* 53:221–29.

Crenson, Matthew A., and Benjamin Ginsberg. 2002. *Downsizing Democracy: How America Sidelined Its Citizens and Privatized Its Public*. Baltimore: Johns Hopkins University Press.

Dahl, Robert A. 1961. *Who Governs? Democracy and Power in an American City*. New Haven: Yale University Press.

——. 2001. *How Democratic Is the American Constitution?* New Haven: Yale University Press.

Damon, William. 2001. To Not Fade Away: Restoring Civil Identity among the Young. In *Making Good Citizens: Education and Civil Society*, edited by Diane Ravitch and Joseph P. Viteritti. New Haven: Yale University Press.

Dawson, Richard E., and Kenneth Prewitt. 1969. *Political Socialization: An Analytic Study*. Boston: Little, Brown.

Downs, Anthony. 1957. *An Economic Theory of Democracy*. New York: Harper and Brothers.

Easton, David, and Jack Dennis. 1967. The Child's Acquisition of Regime Norms: Political Efficacy. *American Political Science Review* 61 (1):25–38.

——. 1969. *Children in the Political System: Origins of Political Legitimacy*. New York: McGraw-Hill.

Edwards, George C. 2004. *Why the Electoral College Is Bad for America*. New Haven: Yale University Press.

Ehrenhalt, Alan. 1995. *The Lost City: Discovering the Forgotten Virtues of Community in the Chicago of the 1950s*. New York: Basic Books.

Elam, Stanley M., Lowell C. Rose, and Alec M. Gallup. 1996. The 28th Annual Phi Delta Kappa/Gallup Poll of the Public's Attitudes toward the Public Schools. *Phi Delta Kappan*, September. Available at http://pdkintl.org/kappan/kappan.htm (accessed September 22, 2005).

Elazar, Daniel. 1972. *American Federalism: A View from the States*. 2nd ed. New York: Crowell.

Epps, Garrett. 2001. *To an Unknown God: Religious Freedom on Trial*. New York: St. Martin's Press.

Erikson, Erik H. 1968. *Identity: Youth and Crisis*. New York: W.W. Norton.

Erikson, Robert S., Michael B. MacKuen, and James A. Stimson. 2002. *The Macro Polity*. New York: Cambridge University Press.

Fenster, Mark J. 1994. The Impact of Allowing Day of Registration Voting on Turnout in U.S. Elections from 1960 to 1992. *American Politics Quarterly* 22 (1):74–87.

Ferejohn, John A., and Morris P. Fiorina. 1975. Closeness Counts Only in Horseshoes and Dancing. *American Political Science Review* 69 (3):920–25.

Filer, John E., and Lawrence W. Kenny. 1980. Voter Turnout and the Benefits of Voting. *Public Choice* 35:575–85.

Filer, John E., Lawrence W. Kenny, and Rebecca B. Morton. 1993. Redistribution, Income, and Voting. *American Journal of Political Science* 37 (1):63–87.

Finifter, Ada W. 1974. The Friendship Group as a Protective Environment for Political Deviants. *American Political Science Review* 68 (2):607–25.

Finn, Chester E., Bruno V. Manno, and Gregg Vanourek. 2000. *Charter Schools in Action: Renewing Public Education*. Princeton: Princeton University Press.

Fiore, Faye. 2000. Decision 2000. *Los Angeles Times*, November 8, 20.

Fiorina, Morris P. 1976. The Voting Decision: Instrumental and Expressive Aspects. *Journal of Politics* 38 (2):390–413.

Fiorina, Morris P., and Paul E. Peterson. 1998. *The New American Democracy*. Needham Heights, MA: Allyn and Bacon.

Fiorina, Morris P., with Samuel J. Abrams, and Jeremy C. Pope. 2005. *Culture War? The Myth of a Polarized America*. New York: Pearson Longman.

Foster, Carroll B. 1984. The Performance of Rational Voter Models in Recent Presidential Elections. *American Political Science Review* 78 (3):678–90.

Franklin, Daniel P., and Eric E. Grier. 1997. Effects of Motor Voter Legislation: Voter Turnout, Registration, and Partisan Advantage in the 1992 Presidential Election. *American Politics Quarterly* 25 (1):104–17.

Freeman, Richard B. 2001. What, Me Vote?: Paper for the Russell Sage Foundation Project on the Social Dimensions of Inequality.

Fukuyama, Francis. 1999. *The Great Disruption: Human Nature and the Reconstitution of Social Order*. New York: Free Press.

Galston, William A. 2001. Political Knowledge, Political Engagement, and Civic Education. *Annual Review of Political Science* 4:217–34.

Gelernter, David Hillel. 1995. *1939: The Lost World of the Fair*. New York: Free Press.

Giles, Michael, and Marilyn Dantico. 1982. Political Participation and Neighborhood Social Context Revisited. *American Journal of Political Science* 26 (1):144–50.

Gimpel, James G., J. Celeste Lay, and Jason E. Schuknecht. 2003. *Cultivating Democracy: Civic Environments and Political Socialization in America*. Washington, DC: Brookings Institution Press.

Glaeser, Edward L., David I. Laibson, Jose A. Scheinkman, and Andrei Shleifer. 2000. Measuring Trust. *Quarterly Journal of Economics* 115 (3):811–46.

Glenn, Charles. 1988. *The Myth of the Common School*. Amherst: University of Massachusetts Press.

Godwin, R. Kenneth, and Frank R. Kemerer. 2002. *School Choice Tradeoffs: Liberty, Equity, and Diversity*. Austin: University of Texas Press.

Gosnell, Harold F. 1927. *Getting Out the Vote: An Experiment in the Stimulation of Voting*. Chicago: University of Chicago Press.

Graham, John W., Gary Marks, and William B. Hansen. 1991. Social Influence Processes Affecting Adolescent Substance Abuse. *Journal of Applied Psychology* 76 (2):291–98.

Granovetter, Mark S. 1973. The Strength of Weak Ties. *American Journal of Sociology* 78 (6):1360–81.

Gray, Virginia. 1976. A Note on Competition and Turnout in the American States. *Journal of Politics* 38 (1):153–58.

Green, Donald P., and Alan S. Gerber. 2004. *Get Out the Vote! How to Increase Voter Turnout*. Washington, DC: Brookings Institution Press.

Green, Donald P., and Ian Shapiro. 1994. *Pathologies of Rational Choice Theory: A Critique of Applications in Political Science*. New Haven: Yale University Press.

Green, Donald P., Alan S. Gerber, and Ron Shachar. 2003. Voting May Be Habit Forming: Evidence from a Randomized Field Experiment. *American Journal of Political Science* 47 (3):540–50.

Green, Donald, Bradley Palmquist, and Eric Shickler. 2002. *Partisan Hearts and Minds: Political Parties and the Social Identities of Voters*. New Haven: Yale University Press.

Greene, Jay P. 1998. Civic Values in Public and Private Schools. In *Learning from School Choice*, edited by Paul E. Peterson and Bryan Hassel. Washington, DC: Brookings Institution Press.

———. 2000. Review of *Civic Education: What Makes Students Learn*, by Richard G. Niemi and Jane Junn. *Social Science Quarterly* 81:696–97.

Greenstein, Fred I. 1965. *Children and Politics*. New Haven: Yale University Press.

Gumbel, Andrew. 2000. Apathy Is the Loser as Crucial Race Bucks Trend of Falling Turnout. *The Independent*, November 8, 7.

Gutmann, Amy. 1999. *Democratic Education*. 2nd ed. Princeton: Princeton University Press.

———. 2000. Why Should Schools Care about Civic Education? In *Rediscovering the Democratic Purposes of Education*, edited by Lorraine M. McDonnell, P. Michael Timpane, and Roger Benjamin. Lawrence: University Press of Kansas.

Hadaway, C. Kirk, Penny Long Marler, and Mark Chaves. 1993. What the Polls Don't Show: A Closer Look at U.S. Church Attendance. *American Sociological Review* 58 (6):741–52.

Haines, Michael, and Sherilyn F. Spear. 1996. Changing the Perception of the Norm: A Strategy to Decrease Binge Drinking among College Students. *Journal of American College Health* 45:134–40.

Hajnal, Zoltan, and Jessica Trounstine. 2005. Where Turnout Matters: The Consequences of Uneven Turnout in City Politics. *Journal of Politics* 67 (2):515–32.

Hanks, Michael. 1981. Youth, Voluntary Associations, and Political Socialization. *Social Forces* 60 (1):211–23.

Hechter, Michael, and Karl-Dieter Opp. 2001. Introduction to *Social Norms*, edited by Michael Hechter and Karl-Dieter Opp. New York: Russell Sage Foundation.

Hess, Robert D., and Judith V. Torney. 1967. *The Development of Political Attitudes in Children*. Chicago: Aldine Publishing.

Highton, Benjamin. 1997. Easy Registration and Voter Turnout. *Journal of Politics* 59 (2):565–75.

Highton, Benjamin, and Raymond E. Wolfinger. 1998. Estimating the Effects on the National Voter Registration Act of 1993. *Political Behavior* 20 (2):79–104.

———. 2001. The First Seven Years of the Political Life Cycle. *American Journal of Political Science* 45 (1):202–9.

Himmelfarb, Gertrude. 1999. *One Nation, Two Cultures*. New York: Alfred A. Knopf.

Hodgkinson, Virginia A., and Murray S. Weitzman. 1997. Volunteering and Giving among Teenagers 12 to 17 Years of Age: Findings from a National Survey. Washington, DC: Independent Sector.

Hoffstetter, C. Richard. 1973. Inter-Party Competition and Electoral Turnout: The Case of Indiana. *American Journal of Political Science* 17 (2):351–66.

Huckfeldt, Robert. 1979. Political Participation and the Neighborhood Social Context. *American Journal of Political Science* 23 (3):579–92.

Huckfeldt, Robert, and John Sprague. 1993. Citizens, Contexts, and Politics. In *Political Science: The State of the Discipline II*, edited by Ada W. Finifter. Washington, DC: American Political Science Association.

———. 1995. *Citizens, Politics, and Social Communication: Information and Influence in an Election Campaign.* New York: Cambridge University Press.

Huckfeldt, Robert, Eric Plutzer, and John Sprague. 1993. Alternative Contexts of Political Behavior: Churches, Neighborhoods, and Individuals. *Journal of Politics* 55 (2):365–81.

Hyman, Herbert. 1959. *Political Socialization: A Study in the Psychology of Political Behavior.* Glencoe, IL: Free Press.

Institute of Politics. 2000. Attitudes toward Politics and Public Service: A National Survey of College Undergraduates. Cambridge, MA: John F. Kennedy School of Government, Harvard University.

International Association for the Evaluation of Educational Achievement. 1977. IEA Six Subject Study. Ann Arbor, MI: Inter-university Consortium for Political and Social Research.

Jaros, Dean, Herbert Hirsch, and Frederic J. Fleron. 1968. The Malevolent Leader: Political Socialization in an American Sub-Culture. *American Political Science Review* 62 (2):564–75.

Jenkins, Krista, Molly Andolina, Scott Keeter, and Cliff Zukin. 2003. Is Civic Behavior Political? Exploring the Multidimensional Nature of Political Participation. Paper presented at the Annual Conference of the Midwest Political Science Association, Chicago.

Jennings, M. Kent. 1971. The Division of Political Labor between Mothers and Fathers. *American Political Science Review* 65 (1):69–82.

———. 1979. Another Look at the Life Cycle and Political Participation. *American Journal of Political Science* 23 (4):755–71.

———. 1980. Comment on Richard Merelman's "Democratic Politics and the Culture of American Education." *American Political Science Review* 74 (2):333–37.

———. 1987. Residues of a Movement: The Aging of the American Protest Generation. *American Political Science Review* 81 (2):367–82.

———. 2000. Participation as Viewed through the Lens of the Political Socialization Project. Paper read at Political Participation: Building a Research Agenda, Center for the Study of Democratic Politics, Princeton University, October 12–14.

Jennings, M. Kent, and Gregory B. Markus. 1977. The Effect of Military Service on Political Attitudes: A Panel Study. *American Political Science Review* 71 (1):131–47.

———. 1984. Partisan Orientations over the Long Haul: Results from the Three-Wave Political Socialization Panel Study. *American Political Science Review* 78 (4):1000–1018.

———. 1988. Political Involvement in the Later Years: A Longitudinal Survey. *American Journal of Political Science* 32 (2):302–16.

Jennings, M. Kent, and Richard G. Niemi. 1968. The Transmission of Political Values from Parent to Child. *American Political Science Review* 62 (1):169–84.

———. 1974. *The Political Character of Adolescence: The Influence of Families and Schools*. Princeton: Princeton University Press.

———. 1975. Continuity and Change in Political Orientations: A Longitudinal Study of Two Generations. *American Political Science Review* 69 (4):1316–35.

———. 1981. *Generations and Politics: A Panel Study of Young Adults and Their Parents*. Princeton: Princeton University Press.

Jennings, M. Kent, and Laura Stoker. 2004. Social Trust and Civic Engagement across Time and Generations. *Acta Politica* 39(1): 342–79.

Jennings, M. Kent, Gregory B. Markus, and Richard G. Niemi. 1991. *Youth-Parent Socialization Panel Study, 1965–1982: Wave III Codebook*. Ann Arbor, MI: Inter-University Consortium for Political and Social Research.

Johnston, Lloyd D., Patrick M. O'Malley, and Jerald G. Bachman. 2001. *Monitoring the Future: National Survey Results on Drug Use, 1975–2000*. Bethesda, MD: University of Michigan, Institute for Social Research, and the National Institute on Drug Abuse.

Karp, Jeffrey A., and Susan A. Banducci. 2000. Going Postal: How All-Mail Elections Influence Turnout. *Political Behavior* 22 (3):223–39.

———. 2001. Absentee Voting, Mobilization, and Participation. *American Politics Research* 29 (2):183–95.

Kau, James B., and Paul H. Rubin. 1976. The Electoral College and the Rational Vote. *Public Choice* 27:101–7.

Keith, Bruce E., David B. Magleby, Candice J. Nelson, Elizabeth Orr, Mark C. Westlye, and Raymond E. Wolfinger. 1992. *The Myth of the Independent Voter*. Berkeley: University of California Press.

Kelly, Michael. 1996. Dangerous Minds. *The New Republic*, December 30, 6.

Key, V. O. 1949. *Southern Politics in State and Nation*. New York: Random House.

Kim, Jae-On, John R. Petrocik, and Stephen N. Enokson. 1975. Voter Turnout among the American States: Systemic and Individual Components. *American Political Science Review* 69 (1):107–23.

Kinder, Donald R., and Lynn M. Sanders. 1996. *Divided by Color: Racial Politics and Democratic Ideals*. Chicago: University of Chicago Press.

King, Gary. 1997. *A Solution to the Ecological Inference Problem: Reconstructing Individual Behavior from Aggregate Data*. Princeton: Princeton University Press.

Kleiner, Brian, and Chris Chapman. 1999. Youth Service-Learning and Community Service among 6th through 12th Grade Students in the United States: 1996 and 1999. Washington, DC: U.S. Department of Education, National Center for Education Statistics.

Klinkner, Philip A. 2004a. Counter Response from Klinkner to Bishop and Cushing. *The Forum* 2 (2):1–3. Article 9, available at http://www.bepress.com/forum (accessed September 22, 2005).

———. 2004b. Red and Blue Scare: The Continuing Diversity of the American Electoral Landscape. *The Forum* 2 (2):1–10. Article 2, available at http://www.bepress.com/forum (accessed September 22, 2005).

Knack, Stephen. 1992. Civic Norms, Social Sanctions, and Voter Turnout. *Rationality and Society* 4 (2):133–56.

———. 1994. Does Rain Help the Republicans? Theory and Evidence on Turnout and the Vote. *Public Choice* 79:187–209.

———. 1995. Does "Motor Voter" Work? Evidence from State-Level Data. *Journal of Politics* 57 (3):796–811.

———. 1997. The Reappearing American Voter: Why Did Turnout Rise in '92. *Electoral Studies* 16 (1):17–32.

———. 2001. Election-Day Registration: The Second Wave. *American Politics Research* 29 (1):65–78.

Knack, Stephen, and Philip Keefer. 1997. Does Social Capital Have an Economic Payoff? A Cross-Country Investigation. *Quarterly Journal of Economics* 112:1251–88.

Knack, Stephen, and Martha E. Kropf. 1998. For Shame! The Effect of Community Cooperative Context on the Probability of Voting. *Political Psychology* 19 (3):585–99.

Knack, Stephen, and James White. 1998. Did States' Motor Voter Programs Help the Democrats? *American Politics Quarterly* 26 (3):344–65.

———. 2000. Election Day Registration and Turnout Inequality. *Political Behavior* 22 (1):29–44.

Knoke, David. 1990. *Political Networks: The Structural Perspective.* New York: Cambridge University Press.

Kowalczyk, Liz. 2001. Patriotic Purchasing. Americans Are Being Urged to Spend, But Analysts Doubt the Strategy Will Have an Impact in the Long Run. *Boston Globe,* September 28, C1.

Kramer, Gerald H. 1970. The Effects of Precinct-Level Canvassing on Voter Behavior. *Public Opinion Quarterly* 34 (4):560–72.

Lake, Ronald La Due, and Robert Huckfeldt. 1998. Social Capital, Social Networks, and Political Participation. *Political Psychology* 19 (3):567–85.

Langton, Kenneth P., and M. Kent Jennings. 1968. Political Socialization and the High School Civics Curriculum in the United States. *American Political Science Review* 62 (3):852–67.

Layman, Geoffrey. 2001. *The Great Divide: Religious and Cultural Conflict in American Party Politics.* New York: Columbia University Press.

Lazarsfeld, Paul F., Bernard Berelson, and Hazel Gaudet. 1948. *The People's Choice: How the Voter Makes Up His Mind in a Presidential Campaign.* 2nd ed. New York: Columbia University Press.

Leighley, Jan E., and Jonathan Nagler. 1992. Individual and Systemic Influences on Turnout: Who Votes? 1984. *Journal of Politics* 54 (3):718–40.

Leon and Sylvia Panetta Institute for Public Policy. 2000. Panetta Institute Poll Shows College Students Turned off by Politics, Turned on by Other Public Service. Seaside, CA: Panetta Institute.

Levine, Peter, and Mark Hugo Lopez. 2002. Youth Voting Has Declined, by Any Measure. College Park, MD: Center for Information and Research on Civic Learning and Engagement.

Macedo, Stephen. 2000. *Diversity and Distrust: Civic Education in a Multicultural Democracy.* Cambridge, MA: Harvard University Press.

Madison, James. 1961. Federalist Ten. In *The Federalist Papers*, edited by Clinton Rossiter. New York: Mentor (Penguin). Original edition, 1787.

Magleby, David B. 1987. Participation in Mail Ballot Elections. *Western Political Quarterly* 40 (1):79–91.

Mann, Sheilah, and John J. Patrick, eds. 2000. *Education for Civic Engagement in Democracy: Service Learning and Other Promising Practices*. Bloomington, IN: Educational Resources Information Center.

Mansbridge, Jane J. 1980. *Beyond Adversary Democracy*. New York: Basic Books.

Marks, Gary, John W. Graham, and William B. Hansen. 1992. Social Projection and Social Conformity in Adolsecent Alcohol Use: A Longitudinal Analysis. *Personality and Social Psychology Bulletin* 18 (1):96–101.

Martinez, Michael D., and David Hill. 1999. Did Motor Voter Work? *American Politics Quarterly* 27 (3):296–315.

Matsusaka, John G. 1993. Election Closeness and Voter Turnout: Evidence from California Ballot Propositions. *Public Choice* 76:313–34.

Matthews, Donald R., and James W. Prothro. 1966. *Negroes and the New Southern Politics*. New York: Harcourt, Brace, and World.

McAdams, Richard H. 1997. The Origin, Development, and Regulation of Norms. *Michigan Law Review* 96 (November):338–433.

McDonald, Michael P., and Samuel L. Popkin. 2001. The Myth of the Vanishing Voter. *American Political Science Review* 95 (4):963–74.

McDonnell, Lorraine M., P. Michael Timpane, and Roger Benjamin. 2002. *Rediscovering the Democratic Purposes of Education*. Lawrence: University Press of Kansas.

Merelman, Richard M. 1969. The Development of Political Ideology: A Framework for the Analysis of Political Socialization. *American Political Science Review* 63 (3):750–67.

———. 1971. The Development of Policy Thinking in Adolescence. *American Political Science Review* 65 (4):1033–47.

———. 1973. The Structure of Policy Thinking in Adolescence: A Research Note. *American Political Science Review* 67 (1):161–66.

———. 1980a. Democratic Politics and the Culture of American Education. *American Political Science Review* 74 (2):319–32.

———. 1980b. A Reply to Jennings. *American Political Science Review* 74 (2):338–41.

Merriam, Charles. 1934. *Civic Education in the United States*. New York: Scribner's Sons.

Milbrath, Lester W. 1971. Individuals and Government. In *Politics in the American States: A Comparative Analysis*, edited by Herbert Jacob and Kenneth N. Vines. Boston: Little, Brown.

Miller, Warren E., and J. Merrill Shanks. 1996. *The New American Voter*. Cambridge, MA: Harvard University Press.

Mitchell, Glenn E., and Christopher Wlezien. 1995. The Impact of Legal Constraints on Voter Registration, Turnout, and the Composition of the American Electorate. *Political Behavior* 17 (2):179–202.

Moe, Terry M. 2000. The Two Democratic Purposes of Education. In *Rediscovering the Democratic Purposes of Education*, edited by Lorraine M. McDonnell,

P. Michael Timpane, and Roger Benjamin. Lawrence: University Press of Kansas.

Mooney, Brian C. 1989. Voter Flocks to the Polls—and Casts Precinct's Only Ballot. *Boston Globe*, September 28, 31.

Morone, James A. 1990. *The Democratic Wish: Popular Participation and the Limits of American Government*. New York: Basic Books.

Mutz, Diana C. 2002a. The Consequences of Cross-Cutting Networks for Political Participation. *American Journal of Political Science* 46 (4):838–55.

———. 2002b. Cross-Cutting Social Networks: Testing Democratic Theory in Practice. *American Political Science Review* 96 (1):111–26.

Nagler, Jonathan, and Jan Leighley. 1992. Presidential Campaign Expenditures: Evidence on Allocations and Effects. *Public Choice* 73:319–33.

National Association of Secretaries of State. 1999. New Millennium Project: A Nationwide Study of 15–24 Year Old Youth. Washington, DC: NASS.

National Commission on Civic Renewal. 1998. A Nation of Spectators: How Civic Disengagement Weakens America and What We Can Do about It. College Park, MD: Institute for Philosophy and Public Policy, University of Maryland.

Niemi, Richard G., and Jane Junn. 1998. *Civic Education: What Makes Students Learn*. New Haven: Yale University Press.

Niemi, Richard G., Mary A. Hepburn, and Chris Chapman. 2000. Community Service by High School Students: A Cure for Civic Ills? *Political Behavior* 22 (1):45–69.

Nolin, Mary Jo, Bradford Chaney, Chris Chapman, and Kathryn Chandler. 1997. Student Participation in Community Service Activity, NCES 97–331. Washington, DC: U.S. Department of Education, National Center for Education Statistics.

Oliver, J. Eric. 1996. The Effects of Eligibility Restrictions and Party Activity on Absentee Voting and Overall Turnout. *American Journal of Political Science* 40 (2):498–513.

———. 1997. Civil Society in Suburbia: The Effects of Metropolitan Social Contexts on Participation in Voluntary Organizations. Ph.D. diss., Political Science, University of California at Berkeley.

———. 2001. *Democracy in Suburbia*. Princeton: Princeton University Press.

Page, Benjamin I., and Robert Y. Shapiro. 1992. *The Rational Public: Fifty Years of Trends in Americans' Policy Preferences*. Chicago: University of Chicago Press.

Patterson, Samuel C., and Gregory A. Caldeira. 1983. Getting Out the Vote: Participation in Gubernatorial Elections. *American Political Science Review* 77 (3):675–89.

———. 1984. The Etiology of Party Competition. *American Political Science Review* 78 (3):691–707.

Patterson, Thomas E. 2002. *The Vanishing Voter: Public Involvement in an Age of Uncertainty*. New York: Alfred A. Knopf.

Perkins, H. Wesley, ed. 2003. *The Social Norms Approach to Preventing School and College Age Substance Abuse: A Handbook for Educators, Counselors, and Clinicians*. San Francisco: Jossey-Bass.

Perkins, H. Wesley, and Alan D. Berkowitz. 1986. Perceiving the Community Norms of Alcohol Use among Students: Some Research Implications for Campus Alcohol Education Programming. *International Journal of the Addictions* 21 (9 and 10):961–76.

Perkins, H. Wesley, and Henry Wechsler. 1996. Variation in Perceived College Drinking Norms and Its Impact on Alcohol Abuse: A Nationwide Study. *Journal of Drug Issues* 26 (4):961–74.

Perlmutter, Rosanne, and Ester R. Shapiro. 1987. Morals and Values in Adolescence. In *Handbook of Adolescent Psychology*, edited by Vincent B. Van Hasselt and Michael Hersen. New York: Pergamon Press.

Plutzer, Eric. 2002. Becoming a Habitual Voter: Inertia, Resources and Growth in Young Adulthood. *American Political Science Review* 96 (1):41–56.

Portes, Alejandro. 1998. Social Capital: Its Origins and Applications in Modern Sociology. *Annual Review of Sociology* 24:1–24.

Powell, Arthur G., Eleanor Farrar, and David K. Cohen. 1985. *The Shopping Mall High School: Winners and Losers in the Educational Marketplace*. Boston: Houghton Mifflin.

Powell, G. Bingham, Jr. 1986. American Voter Turnout in Comparative Perspective. *American Political Science Review* 80 (1):17–43.

Prentice, Deborah A., and Dale T. Miller. 1993. Pluralistic Ignorance and Alcohol Use on Campus: Some Consequences of Misperceiving the Social Norm. *Journal of Personality and Social Psychology* 64 (2):243–56.

Putnam, Robert D. 1966. Political Attitudes and the Local Community. *American Political Science Review* 60:640–54.

———. 1993. *Making Democracy Work: Civic Traditions in Modern Italy*. Princeton: Princeton University Press.

———. 1995. Tuning In, Tuning Out: The Strange Disappearance of Social Capital in America. *PS: Political Science and Politics* 27 (4):664–67.

———. 2000. *Bowling Alone: The Collapse and Revival of American Community*. New York: Simon and Schuster.

———. 2002. Bowling Together. *The American Prospect*, February 11. Available at http://www.prospect.org (accessed September 22, 2005).

Rahn, Wendy, and Thomas J. Rudolph. 2001. Spatial Variation in Trust in Local Government: The Roles of Institutions, Culture, and Community Heterogeneity. Paper presented at the Conference on Political Trust, Princeton University's Center for the Study of Democratic Politics.

Rahn, Wendy, and John Transue. 1998. Social Trust and Value Change: The Decline of Social Capital in American Youth, 1976–1995. *Political Psychology* 19: 545–65.

Raudenbush, Stephen W., and Anthony S. Bryk. 2002. *Hierarchical Linear Models: Applications and Data Analysis Methods*. 2nd ed. Thousand Oaks, CA: Sage.

Raudenbush, Stephen W., Anthony S. Bryk, Yuk Fai Cheong, and Richard T. Congdon, Jr. 2001. *HLM 5: Hierarchical Linear and Nonlinear Modeling*. Lincolnwood, IL: Scientific Software International.

Rhine, Staci L. 1995. Registration Reform and Turnout Change in the American States. *American Politics Quarterly* 23 (4):409–26.

———. 1996. An Analysis of the Impact of Registration Factors on Turnout in 1992. *Political Behavior* 18 (2):171–85.

Rice, Tom W., and Jan L. Feldman. 1997. Civic Culture and Democracy from Europe to America. *Journal of Politics* 59 (4):1143–72.

Riker, William, and Peter C. Ordeshook. 1968. A Theory of the Calculus of Voting. *American Political Science Review* 62:25–42.

Robinson, James A., and William H. Standing. 1960. Some Correlates of Voter Participation: The Case of Indiana. *Journal of Politics* 22 (1):96–111.

Robinson, William S. 1950. Ecological Correlations and the Behavior of Individuals. *American Sociological Review* 15:351–57.

Rosenberg, Gerald N. 1991. *The Hollow Hope: Can Courts Bring about Social Change?* Chicago: University of Chicago Press.

Rosenstone, Steven J., and John Mark Hansen. 1993. *Mobilization, Participation, and Democracy in America.* New York: Macmillan.

Rosenstone, Steven J., Roy L. Behr, and Edward H. Lazarus. 1996. *Third Parties in America.* 2nd. ed. Princeton: Princeton University Press.

Sapiro, Virginia, Steven J. Rosenstone, and National Election Studies. 2002. American National Election Studies Cumulative Data File, 1948–2000. Ann Arbor, MI: Inter-university Consortium for Political and Social Research.

Schattschneider, E. E. 1960. *The Semi-Sovereign People: A Realist's View of Democracy in America.* New York: Holt, Rinehart, and Winston.

Schlozman, Kay Lehman, Sidney Verba, and Henry E. Brady. 1995. Participation's Not a Paradox: The View from American Activists. *British Journal of Political Science* 25 (1):1–36.

Schneider, Mark, Paul Teske, Melissa Marschall, Michael Mintrom, and Christine Roch. 1997. Institutional Arrangements and the Creation of Social Capital: The Effects of School Choice. *American Political Science Review* 91 (March):82–93.

Schuck, Peter H. 2003. *Diversity in America: Keeping Government at a Safe Distance.* Cambridge, MA: Belknap Press of Harvard University Press.

Schudson, Michael. 1998. *The Good Citizen: A History of American Civic Life.* New York: Free Press.

———. 2001. The Emergence of the Objectivity Norm in American Journalism. In *Social Norms*, edited by Michael Hechter and Karl-Dieter Opp. New York: Russell Sage Foundation.

Sears, David O., and Nicholas A. Valentino. 1997. Politics Matters: Political Events as Catalysts for Preadult Socialization. *American Political Science Review* 91 (1):45–65.

Settle, Russell F., and Buron A. Abrams. 1976. The Determinants of Voter Participation: A More General Model. *Public Choice* 27:81–89.

Shachar, Ron, and Barry Nalebuff. 1999. Follow the Leader: Theory and Evidence on Political Participation. *American Economic Review* 89 (3):525–47.

Sharansky, Ira. 1969. The Utility of Elazar's Political Culture. *Polity* 2:66–83.

Silberman, Jonathan, and Garey Durden. 1975. The Rational Behavior Theory of Voter Participation: The Evidence from Congressional Elections. *Public Choice* 23:101–8.

Silver, Brian D., Barbara Anderson, and Paul Abramson. 1986. Who Overreports Voting? *American Political Science Review* 80 (2):613–24.

Skocpol, Theda. 2003. *Diminished Democracy: From Membership to Management in American Civic Life.* Norman: University of Oklahoma Press.

Skocpol, Theda, and Morris P. Fiorina. 1999. Making Sense of the Civic Engagement Debate. In *Civic Engagement in American Democracy*, edited by Theda Skocpol and Morris P. Fiorina. Washington, DC: Brookings Institution/Russell Sage Foundation.

Smith, Elizabeth S. 1999. The Effects of Investments in the Social Capital of Youth on Political and Civic Behavior in Young Adulthood: A Longitudinal Analysis. *Political Psychology* 20 (3):553–80.

Sprague, John. 1982. Is There a Micro Theory Consistent with Contextual Analysis? In *Strategies of Political Inquiry*, edited by Elinor Ostrom. Beverly Hills, CA: Sage.

Squire, Peverill, Raymond E. Wolfinger, and David P. Glass. 1987. Residential Mobility and Voter Turnout. *American Political Science Review* 81 (1):45–66.

Stein, Robert M. 1998. Early Voting. *Public Opinion Quarterly* 62:57–69.

Stein, Robert M., and Patricia A. Garcia-Monet. 1997. Voting Early but Not Often. *Social Science Quarterly* 78 (3):657–71.

Stepp, Diane R. 2000. Georgians Scurry Up and Wait to Cast Their Ballots. *Atlanta Constitution*, November 8, 1A.

Stolle, Dietlind, and Thomas R. Rochon. 1998. Are All Associations Alike? Member Diversity, Associational Type, and the Creation of Social Capital. *American Behavioral Scientist* 42 (1):47–65.

Sullivan, John L., James Piereson, and George E. Marcus. 1982. *Political Tolerance and American Democracy.* Chicago: University of Chicago Press.

Tate, Katherine. 1994. *From Protest to Politics: The New Black Voters in American Elections.* Cambridge, MA: Harvard University Press.

Teixeira, Ruy A. 1992. *The Disappearing American Voter.* Washington, DC: Brookings Institution Press.

Thombs, Dennis L., Bette Jean Wolcott, and Lauren G. E. Farkash. 1997. Social Context, Perceived Norms and Drinking Behavior in Young People. *Journal of Substance Abuse* 9:257–67.

Tingsten, Herbert. 1963. *Political Behavior: Studies in Election Statistics.* Translated by Vilgot Hammarling. Totowa, NJ: Bedminster. Original edition, 1937.

Tocqueville, Alexis de. 1988. *Democracy in America.* Translated by George Lawrence. Edited by J. P. Mayer. New York: Harper and Row. Original edition, 1966.

Torney-Purta, Judith, Rainer Lehmann, Hans Oswald, and Wolfram Schulz. 2001. Citizenship and Education in Twenty-Eight Countries: Civic Knowledge and Engagement at Age Fourteen. Amsterdam: International Association for the Evaluation of Educational Achievement.

Tullock, Gordon. 1967. *Toward a Mathematics of Politics.* Ann Arbor, MI: University of Michigan Press.

U.S. Department of Commerce, Bureau of the Census, and U.S. Department of Education, National Center for Education Statistics. 2000. Dropout Rates in the United States, unpublished tabulations. Available at http://nces.ed.gov/pubs2001/digest/tables/PDF/table106.pdf.

U.S. Department of Commerce. Census Bureau. 2002. Current Population Reports: Voting and Registration in the Election of November 2000. Washington, DC: U.S. Census Bureau.

Uslaner, Eric M. 2000. Producing and Consuming Trust. Political Science Quarterly 115 (4):569–90.

———. 2002. The Moral Foundations of Trust. New York: Cambridge University Press.

Verba, Sidney, and Norman H. Nie. 1972. Participation in America: Political Democracy and Social Equality. Chicago: University of Chicago Press.

Verba, Sidney, Kay Lehman Schlozman, and Henry E. Brady. 1995. Voice and Equality: Civic Voluntarism in American Politics. Cambridge, MA: Harvard University Press.

Vigdor, Jacob. 2001. Community Composition and Collective Action: Analyzing Initial Mail Response to the 2000 Census. Duke University.

Voss, Thomas. 2001. Game-Theoretical Perspectives on the Emergence of Social Norms. In Social Norms, edited by Michael Hechter and Karl-Dieter Opp. New York: Russell Sage Foundation.

Wald, Kenneth D., Dennis E. Owen, and Samuel S. Hill. 1988. Churches as Political Communities. American Political Science Review 82 (2):531–48.

Walker, Tobi. 2002. Service as a Pathway to Political Participation: What Research Tells Us. Applied Developmental Science 6 (4):183–88.

Wattenberg, Martin P. 2002. Where Have All the Voters Gone? Cambridge, MA: Harvard University Press.

White, John Kenneth. 2003. The Values Divide: American Politics and Culture in Transition. New York: Chatham House.

Wielhouwer, Peter W., and Brad Lockerbie. 1994. Party Contacting and Political Participation, 1952–90. American Journal of Political Science 38 (1):211–29.

Wolf, Patrick J., Jay P. Greene, Brett Kleitz, and Kristina Thalhammer. 2001. Private Schooling and Political Tolerance. In Charters, Vouchers, and Public Education, edited by Paul E. Peterson and David E. Campbell. Washington, DC: Brookings Institution Press.

Wolfinger, Raymond E., and Steven J. Rosenstone. 1980. Who Votes? New Haven: Yale University Press.

Wright, Gerald C. 1976. Community Structure and Voting in the South. Public Opinion Quarterly 40 (2):201–15.

———. 1977. Contextual Models of Electoral Behavior: The Southern Wallace Vote. American Political Science Review 71 (2):497–508.

Wuthnow, Robert. 1999. The Role of Trust in Civic Renewal. In Civil Society, Democracy, and Civic Renewal, edited by Robert K. Fullinwider. Lanham, MD: Rowman and Littlefield.

Youniss, James, and Miranda Yates. 1997. Community Service and Social Responsibility in Youth. Chicago: University of Chicago Press.

Youniss, James, Jeffrey A. McLellan, and Miranda Yates. 1997. What We Know about Engendering Civic Identity. American Behavioral Scientist 40 (5):620–31.

Zaller, John R. 1992. *The Nature and Origins of Mass Opinion.* New York: Cambridge University Press.

Zukin, Cliff, Scott Keeter, Molly Andolina, Krista Jenkins, and Michael Delli Carpini. 2006 *A New Engagement? Political Participation, Civic Life, and the Changing American Citizen.* New York: Oxford University Press.

Index

Achen, Christopher, 232n.22
adolescent-adult behavior: data regarding, 135–36; extracurricular activities as a youth and political participation, linkage of, 132–33; hypothesis regarding, 135; question of, 131; voluntarism in high school and as adults, linkage of, 136–38; the volunteering-voting linkage, 132–35, 138–43. *See also* civic motivation model
adolescents: adult public engagement and experiences as (*see* adolescent-adult behavior); dual motivations theory applied to, 101–5; high school as a community for (*see* high school); level of partisan heterogeneity in a community, impact on, 119; order and discipline, political heterogeneity and, 112–16, 218; place and civically motivated behavior of, 7; political efficacy, community political heterogeneity and feelings of, 119–22, 221; political heterogeneity and anticipated public engagement by, 102–5; political socialization of, communities and, 100–101; political tolerance of, community political heterogeneity and, 123–24, 221; public engagement, laments about low, 134; reasons for focusing on, 96–97; voice, political heterogeneity and fostering of, 116–19, 219–20; voluntarism by, political heterogeneity and, 106–12. *See also* socialization
Alesina, Alberto, 27–28
Almond, Gabriel, 97, 191
American Economic Review, 14
America Votes, 9
Archimedes, 194
Atlanta Constitution, 20

Barber, Benjamin, 107
Beck, Paul, 152
behavioral research, 18
Berelson, Bernard, 231n.6
Bishop, Bill, 182–83
Blais, Andre, 190

Brady, Henry, 14, 133, 190, 227n.6, 229n.19, 241n.10
Brehm, John, 80
Brown v. Board of Education, 151, 159
Bryk, Anthony, 112–13
Burnham, Walter Dean, 186
Bush, George W., 22, 36–37, 196

calculus of voting (COV), 15, 187–91
Campbell, Angus, 15, 191
Carnegie Corporation, 154
Catholic schools, communities in, 98, 112–13
Center for Information and Research on Civic Learning and Engagement, 154, 185
CES. *See* Civic Education Study
Citizen Participation Study, 9, 52, 55, 62–63, 201
civic climate: anticipated participation and, 161–62; impact on voter turnout, civic *vs.* political norms regarding, 170–72; measurement of, 156–57; political heterogeneity and, 158–61; the sleeper effect and, 172–73; voter turnout and high school, 166–70
civic duty/obligation: civic participation and, 54–62; decline in perception of importance among young people, 192; increasing voter turnout through appeal to, consequences of, 193–94; nonvoting collective action and motivations for voting, relationship of, 54–64; political participation as motivated by, 2–3, 14–16, 190–91; political science research regarding, 191; self-reported significance of for voters, 52–54; social network homogeneity and voter turnout, relation to, 86–87; social norms and (*see* social norms); voter turnout in homogeneous communities due to, 35, 51–52
civic education, 150–54
Civic Education Study (CES), 9, 102–5, 192, 202